GERMAN
GRAMMAR MADE EASY

A Comprehensive Workbook To Learn
German Grammar For Beginners
(Audio Included)

Lingo Mastery

ISBN: 978-1-951949-80-8

CONTENTS

PREFACE

Welcome to "German Grammar Made Easy"! Since you are reading this, you must be at least somewhat interested in learning more about German grammar. This is quite commendable, considering that the thought of memorizing verb conjugations, declension charts, and other grammar rules fills many of us with a sense of foreboding. However, you have come to the right place. Throughout this grammar book we aim to present the most important German grammar concepts to you in an accessible, orderly, and stimulating way. You will find that each chapter teaches the topic at hand in easily digestible bits without leaving you overwhelmed.

While it is true that, in some contexts, rules are there to be broken, we must not forget that grammar rules are indeed something useful. They can be thought of as a toolbox that makes our lives easier as language learners. "How so?" you might ask. Well, to put it somewhat philosophically, they enable us to move from the particular to the general. For example, knowing that the English simple past form for a regular verb like "to live" requires the ending "-ed" ("lived") allows us to apply that rule to other regular verbs broadly ("played", "talked", "asked", etc.). Without rules like these we would be forced to memorize every word separately in all its different forms and applications, which certainly would not be much fun.

This book therefore sets out to familiarize you with German grammar rules in a concise and clear way that allows you to apply (or break!) them with confidence. We took levels A1+A2 within the CEFR framework as an approximate guideline for the included content. As such, it is especially suitable as a reference and exercise book to be used alongside other volumes in the German book series by Lingo Mastery, such as *German Made Easy, Level 1*. However, any student of German from beginner up until intermediate level will benefit from the wealth of exercises, as well as the clearly structured grammar explanations that this book contains.

Whatever your motivation might be for sinking your linguistic teeth into the intricacies of German grammar, we are confident that this workbook will be a reliable reference and a valuable learning tool on your way to German proficiency.

INTRODUCTION

Though German grammar has a reputation for being more complex than that of English, the two systems of grammar have many things in common, and perhaps most strikingly this: the formal codification of both systems is still a relatively young discipline. Although highly educated monks during the Middle Ages had already made isolated attempts at applying their knowledge of grammar, rhetoric, and dialectics to the vernacular of their time, it was not until the 18th century that the first comprehensive grammar books in both English and German were published. This is mostly due to the fact that Latin was the primary language in which scientists, the clergy and other educated people published their writings. There simply was no great necessity to set up a framework for the rules of speech that the common man employed. Once scholars became more interested in finding a grammar system for the language of the people, they simply repurposed various rules derived from Latin and Greek, whose grammar was very formalized (and complex). To this day, that is the system still in use to make sense of and explain the various language phenomena in both English and German.

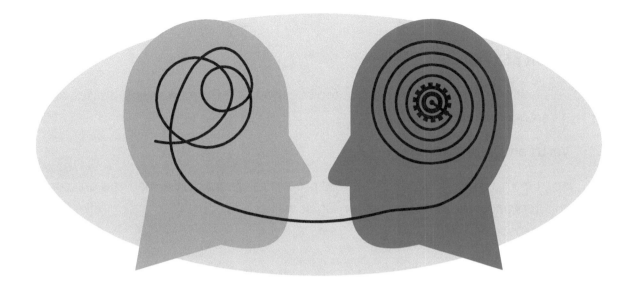

Broadly speaking, the word "grammar" therefore refers to the rules and conventions that govern human speech. In the preface we already hinted at the fact that in order to communicate effectively, we need to be able to rely on such rules and conventions. They are there to help the sender (writer, speaker) 'encode' their message, while the receiver (reader, listener) may use the same set of rules to 'decode' what is being said. Much like in English, the technicalities of German grammar are usually subdivided into *morphology* (i.e., the structure and construction of words, such as word roots, prefixes, and endings), *syntax* (i.e., the combination of words to form phrases and sentences), and *phonology* (i.e., the organization of sounds within a language).

Our aim in writing this book is to take these three branches of grammar into account, so as to equip you with a holistic overview of the basics of German grammar. The structure of the books reflects this, and the following paragraphs will give you an outline of what to expect and how to make the most of its content.

NOTES ON HOW TO USE THIS BOOK

This book is designed in a modular fashion. This means it can be viewed as a reference book for studying certain grammar topics alongside a coursebook, or you may work through individual chapters according to your interest.

The book starts out with an extensive pronunciation guide covering all the relevant sounds of standard High German. The example words used in this guide are included in the audio content, which allows you to practice your own pronunciation by listening to native speakers.

Following the pronunciation guide, the book is divided into six larger units, each containing several chapters:

- **Nouns and Pronouns:**

  This unit covers the most important topics concerning German nouns, articles, and the different types of pronouns.

- **Verbs and Verb Tenses:**

  Apart from a general introduction to the properties of verbs in German, this unit contains chapters about the different verb tenses, as well as additional chapters on reflexive verbs and transitivity.

- **Mood and Voice:**

  This unit covers how German verbs may be employed to form the imperative, as well as the two types of German subjunctive. Additionally, the formation of active and passive sentences in German is explained.

- **Cases, Clauses, and Word Order:**

  Apart from chapters about the rules governing German word order in declarative sentences, questions and subclauses, this unit also explains the function of the different elements in a sentence.

- **Modifiers:**

  This unit comprises chapters on the German adjectives, adverbs, their comparative forms, and on prepositions.

- **Other Features:**

  Different topics that do not conveniently fit into one of the other units are covered here. These include the German modal verbs, auxiliary verbs, separable and inseparable prefixes, as well as negations.

At the beginning of each chapter, you will find an introductory 'Checkbox', providing you with a high-level overview of the most important grammar terms and definitions concerning the respective chapter. This will enable you to better follow and understand the subsequent explanations in case any of the key grammatical terms and concepts are unfamiliar to you. Each chapter then continues with a discussion of the actual German grammar points. Where appropriate, we supplement the grammar sections with short, entertaining dialogues or texts to demonstrate the relevant grammar concepts. Since the scope of each chapter is rather focused, not all chapters lend themselves equally well to this format. However, every chapter contains a large selection of example words and/or phrases that go alongside the grammar explanations. Many of these example words, as well as the supplementary dialogues and texts, are included in the audio content.

Ch. 1, 2, 3 ...

 Whenever there is an overlap in content between chapters, or further reading on a particular topic may be helpful, we added a paperclip-symbol for cross-referencing the relevant chapter number.

 This headphone symbol next to a paragraph or dialogue indicates that audio content is available for the corresponding section.

 This headphone with a pencil next to an exercise means that you will need to refer to the corresponding audio content to complete the exercise.

⊘ CHECKBOX

Checkboxes at the beginning of each chapter contain succinct definitions of the key grammar terms and concepts covered in the subsequent chapter.

💬 DIALOGUE / TEXT

Dialogue or text boxes may appear in various chapters throughout the book.

LIST OF ABBREVIATIONS:

Acc.	→	accusative	*infml.*	→	informal
adj.	→	adjective	*interj.*	→	interjection
adv.	→	adverb	*jmdm.*	→	*jemandem* (= to someone; Dat.)
art.	→	article	*jmdn.*	→	*jemanden* (= someone; Acc.)
coll.	→	colloquialism	*lit.*	→	literally
conj.	→	conjunction	*n.*	→	noun
Dat.	→	dative	*part.*	→	particle
etw.	→	*etwas* (something)	*pl.*	→	plural
fml.	→	formal	*pron.*	→	pronoun
idiom	→	idiomatic expression	*v.*	→	verb

HOW TO GET THE AUDIO FILES

Some of the exercises throughout this book come with accompanying audio files.
You can download these audio files if you head over to:
www.lingomastery.com/german-gme-audio

If you're having trouble downloading the audio, contact us at
www.lingomastery.com/contact

PRONUNCIATION GUIDE

Since German pronunciation is mostly phonetic and regular, gaining an understanding of the basic sound and stress patterns of German will allow you to pronounce most words easily and correctly.

Although both German and English employ the same basic alphabet, there are still significant differences in the pronunciation of the individual German and English sounds represented by the standard letters. This pronunciation guide groups the various sound patterns according to consonants, vowels, and other letter combinations.

Sound approximations are given based on familiar English sounds as far as possible. Please note that these are not exact equivalents and that it is indispensable to listen to native speakers while trying to emulate the way they enunciate the German sounds. To this end, all the example words from the pronunciation guide have been recorded by German native speakers and are included in the audio content.

THE GERMAN ALPHABET

Just like in English, the German alphabet has 26 basic letters, ranging from A to Z. However, it also has four additional characters: *ä*, *ö*, *ü* (called "*Umlaute*"), and *ß* (called "*Eszett*"). The pronunciation of most of the consonant letters creates rather similar sounds in both German and English. The differences become a bit more striking with the pronunciation of each of the five vowels, as well as the Umlaute and some of the German consonant groups. The following sections group all of these individual sound categories and provide explanations to each of them, as well as example words and English sound approximations. A short guide to syllabification and pronunciation is included in section 8.

 ## 1. CONSONANTS (Find audio on page 7.)

The pronunciation of the consonants is very similar in both English and German, with only a few exceptions. There are, however, several letters that require special attention as their pronunciation changes, depending on their position in the word and/or the letters that precede or follow them. In particular, note the different possible pronunciations of the letters *c, d, g, r, s,* and *y*:

LETTER	IPA OF NAME	GERMAN EXAMPLE	APPROXIMATE ENGLISH SOUND
Bb	/beː/	*Bett* (bed) /bɛt/ *geben* (to give) /ˈɡeːbən/	'b' as in "big"
Cc	/t͡seː/	1) 'ts'-sound before e, i, ö, and ä: *Cäsar* /ˈt͡sɛːzaʁ/ 2) 'k'-sound elsewhere: *Computer* / kɔmˈpjuːtɐ/	1) 'ts' as in "hits" 2) 'c' as in "cat"
Dd	/deː/	1) 't'-sound at the end of a word or between a vowel and a consonant: *Land* (country) /lant/ 2) 'd'-sound elsewhere: *deutsch* (German) /dɔytʃ/	1) 't' as in "eat" 2) 'd' as in "do"
Ff	/ɛf/	*fragen* (to ask) /ˈfraːɡən/ *fünf* (five) /fʏnf/	Same as in English
Gg	/ɡeː/	1) *geben* (to give) /ˈɡeːbən/ 2) 'k'-sound at the end of a word: *weg* (away) /vɛk/ 3) when preceded by 'i' at the end of a word, the sound is similar to the 'g' in the English word 'huge': *richtig* (right, correct) /ˈrɪçtɪç/	1) 'g' as in "go" 2) 'ck' as in "tack" 3) 'g' as in "huge"

Hh	/ha:/	*hören* (to hear) /ˈhøːrən/ *wohin* (where ... to) /voˈhɪn/	Same as in English
Jj	/jɔt/; /je:/	*Jahr* (year) /jaːɐ/ *jetzt* (now) /jɛtst/	'y' as in "yes"
Kk	/ka:/	*kochen* (to cook) /ˈkɔxən/ *erklären* (to explain) /ɛɐˈklɛːrən/	'c' as in "cat"
Ll	/ɛl/	*lachen* (to laugh) /ˈlaxən/ *Liebe* (love) /ˈliːbə/	Same as in English
Mm	/ɛm/	*Mann* (man) /man/ *Baum* (tree) /baum/	Same as in English
Nn	/ɛn/	*Name* (name) /ˈnaːmə/ *anders* (differently) /ˈandɐs/	Same as in English
Pp	/pe:/	*Papier* (paper) /paˈpiːɐ/ *Ampel* (traffic light) /ˈampəl/	Same as in English
Qq	/ku:/	*Quark* (quark) /kvark/ *quälen* (to torment) /ˈkvɛːlən/	Like 'k' followed by 'v'
Rr	/ɛʁ/	1) *rot* (red) /roːt/ *Büro* (office) /byˈroː/ 2) *für* (for) /fyːɐ/ *Messer* (knife) /ˈmɛsɐ/	1) Generally rolled in the back of the mouth; think Scottish "loch" but make it vibrate 2) Soft, more like 'a'
Ss	/ɛs/	1) sharp 'z'-sound before or between vowels: *Sie* (formal You) /ziː/ 2) 'sh'-sound before p and t at the beginning of syllable: *spät* (late) /ʃpɛːt/ 3) regular 's'-sound elsewhere: *Obst* (fruits) /oːpst/	1) 'z' as in "zoo" 2) 'sh' as in "shut" 3) 's' as in "sit"

Tt	/te:/	*Tausend* (thousand) /ˈtauznt/ *tanzen* (dance) /ˈtantsn/	Same as in English
Vv	/faʊ̂/	*Vater* (father) /ˈfaːtɐ/ *Vogel* (bird) /ˈfoːɡl/	'f' as in "father"
Ww	/ve:/	*wie* (how) /viː/ *wahr* (true) /vaːɐ/	'v' as in "vice"
Xx	/ɪks/	*Xylophon* /ksyloˈfoːn/ *Xerxes* /kseːɛ̂ksəs/	Like 'k' followed by 's'
Yy	/ˈʏpsilɔn/	1) *Yeti* /ˈjeːti/ 2) *Sylt* /zʏlt/	1) 'y' as in "yellow" 2) Like German Umlaut 'ü'
Zz	/t͡sɛt/	*Zebra* /ˈtseːbra/ *zeigen* (to show) /ˈtsaign/	'ts' as in "hits"

 2. VOWELS (Find audio on page 7.)

Just like in English, there are five main vowels in German: **a, e, i, o,** and **u**. Their pronunciation, however, differs in that the German vowels produce a single, "pure" sound. Unlike in English, they do not glide into another sound towards the end, as would be the case with English "a" ("a-eeh") or "u" ("yoo").

Furthermore, German vowels each have a long and a short form. The **short** vowel sounds are "clipped", and thus pronounced shorter than their English equivalent. **Long** vowels retain the same "pure" vowel sound, only prolonged. As a rule of thumb, vowels are pronounced long when they are either **followed by the letter 'h'** ('*Bahn*', '*Uhr*') or by a **single consonant** ('*Lid*', '*tragisch*'), or if the vowel is **doubled** ('*Haar*', '*Beeren*'). Short vowels are mostly followed by two or more consonants ('*rennen*', '*lassen*').

When a German vowel follows a consonant, it is not usually joined up with the preceding consonant, as would be the case in English. "An enormous amount" would sound something like 'anneenormousamount' in English, whereas "*ein Apfel*" would be pronounced as two separate words.

The following list gives examples for the long and the short vowel forms each, along with some pointers as to the corresponding English sound approximations.

VOWEL	IPA OF NAME	GERMAN EXAMPLE LONG	GERMAN EXAMPLE SHORT	APPROXIMATE ENGLISH SOUND
Aa	/aː/	1) *lahm* (lame) /laːm/ 2) *Rad* (wheel) /raːt/ 3) *Saat* (seed(s)) /zaːt/	4) *Affe* (ape) /ˈafə/	1-3) 'a' as in "father" 4) 'u' as in "hut"
Ee	/eː/	1) *Lehre* (teaching(s)) / ˈleːrə/ 2) *beten* (to pray) /ˈbeːtn/ 3) *Beere* (berry) /ˈbeːrə/	4) *rennen* (to run) / ˈrɛnən/	1-3) 'ay' as in "day" but without gliding towards 'ee' at the end 4) 'e' as in "den"
Ii	/iː/	1) *ihre* (her) /ˈiːrə/ 2) *Titel* (title) /ˈtiːtl/ *There are no German words naturally containing a double 'i'. This is a combination that can only occur in compound words.*	3) *Bitte* (please) /ˈbɪtə/	1-2) 'ee' as in "seed" 3) 'i' as in "mitten"
Oo	/oː/	1) *Bohne* (bean) /ˈboːnə/ 2) *loben* (to praise) / ˈloːbn/ 3) *Moos* (moss) /moːs/	4) *Koffer* (suitcase) / ˈkɔfe/	1-3) 'o' as in "so" but without gliding at the end 4) 'o' as in British "hot"
Uu	/uː/	1) *Ruhm* (fame) /ruːm/ 2) *Ufer* (shore) /ˈuːfe/ *There are no German words naturally containing a double 'u'. This is a combination that can only occur in compound words.*	3) *Suppe* (soup) / ˈzʊpə/	1-2) 'oo' as in "pool" but with rounded lips and without gliding at the end. 3) 'oo' as in "foot"

3. UMLAUTE (Find audio on page 7.)

Umlaute are altered sounds of the German vowel sounds for **a, o**, and **u** and they present themselves with two dots on top: *ä, ö, ü*. They are not part of the regular 26-letter German alphabet.

Their pronunciation can most closely be approximated by pronouncing a German 'a', 'o', or 'u' sound, then locking the position your lips assume for each of them respectively and adding a German 'i'-sound ('ee' as in "seed") on to each of these three letters.

UMLAUT	IPA OF NAME	GERMAN EXAMPLE	APPROXIMATE ENGLISH SOUND
Ää	/ɛ:/	*Mädchen* (girl) /ˈmɛːtçən/ *Träne* (tear) /ˈtrɛːnə/ *säen* (to sow) /ˈzɛːən/	'ai' as in "air"
Öö	/ø:/	*schön* (beautiful) /ʃøːn/ *Löwe* (lion) /ˈløːvə/ *Friseur* (hairdresser/barber) /friˈzøːɐ̯/	'i' as in "girl" 'eu' as in French "bleu"
Üü	/y:/	*küssen* (to kiss) /ˈkʏsn/ *blühen* (to bloom) /ˈblyːən/ *Tür* (door) /tyːɐ̯/	*Does not exist in English.* 'u' as in French "tu"

4. THE *ESZETT SS* (Find audio on page 7.)

The German letter 'ß' (called 'Eszett', or 'sharp S') is not so much a letter that generates its own distinct sound, but more of a spelling convention that sometimes replaces a double 's'. It generally produces a 'hissing' s-sound, much like the double 's' in "boss" or "loss". You will notice that there are in fact many German words containing a double 's', instead of an Eszett, while producing exactly the same sound.

LETTER	IPA OF NAME	GERMAN EXAMPLE	APPROXIMATE ENGLISH SOUND
ß	/ɛsˈt͡sɛt/, /ˈʃaʁfəs ɛs/	*Straße* (street) /ˈʃtraːsə/ *groß* (tall) /groːs/ *weiß* (white) /vais/	'ss' as in "boss"

 5. DIPHTHONGS (Find audio on page 7.)

Diphthongs are vowel combinations occurring in one syllable. They start out as one vowel and glide towards another. The most common German diphthongs are listed below and can be imitated quite well using an English sound approximation.

DIPHTHONG	IPA	GERMAN EXAMPLE	APPROXIMATE ENGLISH SOUND
ai / ei	/ai/	*beide* (both) /ˈbaidə/ *laichen* (to spawn) /ˈlaiçn/	'y' as in "my"
au	/au/	*Bauer* (farmer) /ˈbaue/	'ow' as in "cow"
eu / äu	/ɔy/	*heute* (today) /ˈhɔytə/ *Käufer* (buyer) /ˈkɔyfe/	'oy' as in "boy"
ie	/iː/	*sieben* (seven) /ˈziːbn/	'ee' as in "seed"

6. CONSONANT GROUPS (Find audio on page 7.)

Consonant groups are frequently occurring consonant clusters with a consistent pronunciation. The following table lists a few frequently occurring consonant groups in German. Note that there is no English 'th'-sound in German and that the German consonant group **'th'** simply produces a **/t/** sound.

CONSONANT GROUP	IPA	GERMAN EXAMPLE	APPROXIMATE ENGLISH SOUND
ck	/k/	*Rock* (skirt) /rɔk/ *backen* (to bake) /ˈbakn/	hard 'k-sound 'ck' as in "luck'
pf	/pf/	*Apfel* (apple) /ˈapfl/ *Pferd* (horse) /pfeːɐt/	'pf' as in "stepfather" but pronounced as one explosive sound.
ph	/f/	*Alphabet* (alphabet) / alfaˈbeːt/ *Philosophie* (philosophy) / filozoˈfiː/	same as in English
sch	/ʃ/	*Schule* (school) /ˈʃuːlə/ *Asche* (ashes) /ˈaʃə/	'sh' as in "cash"
th	/t/	*Theater* (theater) /teˈaːtɐ/ *Athen* (Athens) /aˈteːn/	't' as in "take" *There is no English 'th'-sound in German*

 7. THE GERMAN 'CH'-SOUND (Find audio on page 7.)

The German grouped consonant 'ch' is quite notorious among non-native speakers due to its challenging pronunciation. There are at least five different ways that 'ch' can be pronounced in German, and most of these sounds do not exist in English. Here are some rules and tips for pronouncing the German 'ch'.

7.1 The 'ch' after dark vowels

CONTEXT	IPA	GERMAN EXAMPLE	APPROXIMATE ENGLISH SOUND
After 'a', 'o', 'u' and 'au'	/x/	*Sache* (thing) /ˈzaxə/ *kochen* (to cook) /ˈkɔxən/ *Buch* (book) /buːx/	'ch' as in Scottish "loch"

After '**a**', '**o**', '**u**' and '**au**' (called "dark vowels" in German), 'ch' is pronounced similarly to how you would pronounce it in "Loch Ness". It is articulated with the back of the tongue close to or touching the soft palate, generating a rather "throaty" sound.

7.2 The 'ch' after light vowels

CONTEXT	IPA	GERMAN EXAMPLE	APPROXIMATE ENGLISH SOUND
After 'i', 'e', 'ä', 'ö', 'ü', 'ei', 'ai', 'eu', and 'äu'	/ç/	*sicher* (safe) /ˈzɪçɐ/ *Beichte* (confession) /ˈbaiçtə/ *möchte* (would like) /ˈmœçtə/ *Fächer* (fan) /ˈfɛçɐ/ *euch* (you) /ɔyç/	'h' as in "huge"

After '**i**', '**e**', '**ä**', '**ö**', '**ü**', '**ei**', '**ai**', '**eu**', and '**äu**' (called "light vowels" in German), a different sound is required in pronouncing the 'ch'. It is articulated farther to the front of the mouth and can most closely be compared to the sound the 'h' produces in English words such as "huge" or "humane". This arguably is the most common 'ch'-sound you will encounter in German.

7.3 The 'ch' before 's'

CONTEXT	IPA	GERMAN EXAMPLE	APPROXIMATE ENGLISH SOUND
Before 's'	/ks/	*Lachs* (salmon) /laks/ *Achse* (axle) /ˈaksə/	'x' as in "oxen"

If 'ch' precedes an '**s**' it is pronounced like the letter 'x' in words such as "oxen" or "fox".

7.4 The 'ch' at the beginning of a word

CONTEXT	IPA	GERMAN EXAMPLE	APPROXIMATE ENGLISH SOUND
At the start of a word	/ç/, /k/	1) *Chemie* (chemistry) /çeˈmiː/ *China* (China) /ˈçiːna/ 2) *Cholera* (cholera) /ˈkoːlera/ *Christus* (Christ) /ˈkrɪstʊs/	1) 'h' as in "huge" 2) 'k' as in "kitten"

In cases where 'ch' marks the beginning of a word there are two possible pronunciations, each depending on the letter that follows:

- When 'ch' is followed by the letters '**e**' or '**i**', it is pronounced the same way you would pronounce it after a light vowel ('h' as in "huge").

- When 'ch' is followed by the letters '**r**', '**l**', '**a**', or '**o**', it is pronounced like the 'k' in "kitten".

7.5 The 'ch' in loanwords

There are various commonly used loanwords in German that have retained the pronunciation of their original language. As such they do not necessarily follow the above rules. Many of them have French roots ("*Champagner*" /ʃamˈpanjɐ/, "*Chauffeur*" /ʃɔˈføːɐ/). However, there is also a growing number of English loanwords containing the letter combination 'ch' whose pronunciation has been adopted from English: *Chat, Cheeseburger, checken, Sandwich, Trenchcoat*.

 8. SYLLABIFICATION AND PRONUNCIATION (Find audio on page 7.)

A syllable is the **smallest unit of a word**. It can be made up of **one or more sounds**. Several syllables taken together may form a word, or a word may consist of only one syllable.

In German, every syllable **must contain a vowel** (a, e, i, o, u), an **Umlaut** (ä, ö, ü), or a **diphthong** (au, ei, eu, etc.). These are joined by either a single consonant or consonant group to form a whole syllable:

WORDS WITH 1 SYLLABLE	WORDS WITH 2 SYLLABLES	WORDS WITH 3 OR MORE SYLLABLES
Hand (hand) *Buch* (book) *Brot* (bread)	*Gar-ten* (garden/backyard) *Freu-de* (joy) *Bie-ne* (bee)	*Ge-bäu-de* (building) *Scho-ko-la-de* (chocolate) *Ge-burts-tags-tor-te* (birthday cake)

Being able to identify German syllables allows you to correctly stress individual syllables within a word. As a general rule, German words are stressed on the **first** syllable, unless the first syllable is an **unstressed prefix**, e.g., an inseparable prefix such as *be-, ge-, ver-, zer-*, etc. (🎤 **Ch. 24**):

WORD STRESSED ON THE 1ST SYLLABLE	IPA	WORD WITH UNSTRESSED PREFIX	IPA
Abenteuer (adventure) **freund**lich (friendly) **Win**ter (winter) **lau**fen (to run)	/ˈaːbəntɔʏe/ /ˈfrɔʏntlɪç/ /ˈvɪnte/ /ˈlaufən/	ver**lie**ren (to lose) Ge**dan**ke (thought) be**glück**wünschen (to congratulate) zer**stö**ren (to destroy)	/fɛɐˈliːrən/ /gəˈdaŋkə/ /bəˈglʏkvʏnʃən/ /ʦɛɐˈʃtøːrən/

In the case of words that have been borrowed from foreign languages, these pronunciation rules are less predictable and do not necessarily apply. Such loanwords are often stressed according to the rules of their originating language. For instance:

der Py**ja**ma (pajama)	/pyˈdʒaːma/?	→	from Persian	*pīsch dschāma*
das Mono**pol** (monopoly)	/monoˈpoːl/	→	from Greek	*monopólion*
das Spek**ta**kel (spectacle)	/ʃpɛkˈtaːkəl/	→	from Latin	*spectāculum*

However, there are certain **suffixes** that entail more predictable stress patterns. These include:

SUFFIX	STRESS	EXAMPLES		IPA
-tät	last syllable	*Aktivi**tät*** *Elektrizi**tät*** *Sentimentali**tät***	(activity) (electricity) (sentimentality)	/aktiviˈtɛːt/ /elɛktʁitsiˈtɛːt/ /zɛntimɛntaliˈtɛːt/
-ik	last syllable	*Mu**sik*** *Poli**tik*** *Repub**lik***	(music) (politics) (republic)	/muˈziːk/ /poliˈtiːk/ /repuˈbliːk/

-ie	last syllable	*Poe**sie*** *Che**mie*** *Theo**rie***	(poetry) (chemistry) (theory)	/poeˈziː/ /çeˈmiː/ /teoˈriː/
-erei	last syllable	*Büche**rei*** *Sklave**rei*** *Zaube**rei***	(library) (slavery) (sorcery)	/byːçəˈrai/ /sklaːvəˈrai/ /ʦaubəˈrai/
-eum	next to last syllable	*Mu**se**um* *Mauso**le**um* *Kolos**se**um*	(museum) (mausoleum) (Colosseum)	/muˈzeːʊm/ /mauzoˈleːʊm/ /kolɔˈseːʊm/
-ieren	next to last syllable	*stu**die**ren* *argumen**tie**ren* *ser**vie**ren*	(to study) (to debate) (to serve)	/ʃtuˈdiːrən/ /argumenˈtiːrən/ /zɛrˈviːrən/

EXERCISES

 Ü P1) Listen to the list of words from the audio content for this exercise. The words you hear each contain one vowel sound (*a*, *e*, *i*, *o*, or *u*). Once you identify the vowel, decide whether it is pronounced as a long or short vowel and write the word down in the appropriate place in the table below: (Find audio on page 7.)

(rasch, tot, ihm, Stock, mehr, Nacht, gut, Stadt, Mund, Depp, knapp, mit, rot, Wurst, Lohn, Rahm, Fuß, Tag, Test, Tick, Los, Mist, Band, Lehm)

VOWEL	SHORT	LONG
a		
e		
i		
o		
u		

 Ü P2) In the following e-mail, the dots for the German *Umlaute* have been left out. Listen to the audio recording very carefully and decide which of the vowels should be *Umlaute*: (Find audio on page 7.)

Hallo Herr Muller,

Ich habe mich sehr uber unser Treffen letzte Woche gefreut. Ihre Ideen fur die anstehende Handelsmesse haben unserem Geschaftsfuhrer gefallen. Wir wurden allerdings vorschlagen, dass Sie auch Ihren Vorstand zur Messe mitbringen. Dann konnen wir die Optionen gemeinsam besprechen. Ich hoffe, Sie hatten noch ein paar schone Tage in Berlin. Wir sehen uns also nachste Woche!

Mit freundlichen Grußen
Peter Scholz

Ü P3) Read the following text out loud. Then mark each 'ch' according to whether it has a dark vowel pronunciation (d), a light vowel pronunciation (l), or a 'k'-pronunciation (k):

Gestern Na<u>ch</u>t wa<u>ch</u>te <u>Ch</u>ristian plötzli<u>ch</u> auf. Er su<u>ch</u>te na<u>ch</u> dem Li<u>ch</u>tschalter der

_____

Na<u>ch</u>ttischlampe, die re<u>ch</u>ts neben ihm stand. Es war eine teure Lampe aus <u>ch</u>inesischem

_____

Porzellan. Als er den Schalter zunä<u>ch</u>st ni<u>ch</u>t fand, hörte er etwas dur<u>ch</u> den Raum schlei<u>ch</u>en.

_____

Er hor<u>ch</u>te in die Dunkelheit hinein. Do<u>ch</u> es war still. Er da<u>ch</u>te si<u>ch</u>, dass er wohl wieder

_____

schlafen sollte. Er schlief glei<u>ch</u> wieder ein. Als er am nä<u>ch</u>sten Morgen die Augen öffnete,

_____

wurde ihm sofort klar, wer für die nä<u>ch</u>tli<u>ch</u>e Störung verantwortli<u>ch</u> gewesen war:

_____

Sein Kater <u>Ch</u>amillo schnurrte behagli<u>ch</u> neben ihm.

_____

Ü P4) Underline the stressed syllable in each word from the following list:

a. Abend	**f.** Fantasie	**k.** versprechen	**p.** terminieren
b. Leute	**g.** Suppe	**l.** Kuriosität	**q.** Abfall
c. Musik	**h.** Universität	**m.** Physik	**r.** Computer
d. sagen	**i.** bedauern	**n.** widerlegen	**s.** Malerei
e. Bäckerei	**j.** studieren	**o.** Gelehrter	**t.** Majestät

Unit 1

NOUNS AND PRONOUNS

This unit deals with the German nouns and pronouns, their declensions, as well as the definite and indefinite articles that can go with them.

Nouns and pronouns are an essential part of speech, and they help us name the persons, things, objects, or concepts that we want to talk about in a sentence.

Having a good grasp of the German nouns and pronouns, a solid understanding of the different genders they take, and the ability to decline them in relation to the verb of a sentence are essential skills for expressing yourself in a correct and natural way.

CHAPTER 1
NOUNS AND THEIR MAIN PROPERTIES

⊘ CHECKBOX – WHAT IS A NOUN?

A noun is a word that *names* a person, thing, object, or idea. It can describe **real** and **tangible** things, or it may also express a more **abstract** concept. In German, a noun is called *Substantiv* or *Hauptwort* ("main word").

Der <u>Fluss</u> ist sehr lang.
(The river is very long.)

Der <u>Rhein</u> fließt durch Deutschland.
(The Rhine flows through Germany.)

Common noun
(*"Fluss"* is a **common noun** and **refers to any river** in general sense.)

Proper noun
(*"Rhein"* is a **proper noun** and **refers to a specific river**, the Rhine.)

1.1 THE DIFFERENT TYPES OF GERMAN NOUNS

Unlike in English, all German nouns and words used as nouns are always **capitalized**, regardless of their position within a sentence. German is the only major language that uses this feature, which can be helpful in recognizing unknown words as nouns.

 The German umbrella term for noun is *"Substantiv"* or *"Hauptwort"*. Similarly to English, German nouns can be categorized into two groups: **proper nouns** (*"Eigennamen"* in German) and **common nouns** (*"Namenwörter"* in German). Each of these categories can be further subdivided, as the following table shows:

PROPER NOUNS	
Sub-category	**Examples**
Proper names of persons or animals	*Hans Müller, Albert Einstein, Mickey Mouse, Bambi ...*
Names of streets, cities, and countries	*Kölnstraße, Alexanderplatz, Düsseldorf, Rom, Österreich ...*
Geographical names (including names of rivers, lakes, oceans, mountains, nature reserves etc.)	*Rhein, Schwarzwald, Ostsee, Mount Everest, Rocky Mountains ...*
Names of buildings and organizations	*Kölner Dom, Olympiastadion, Bundestag, Vereinte Nationen ...*

COMMON NOUNS	
Sub-category	**Examples**
Things that we can perceive with our senses, also called **concrete nouns** (seeing, hearing, feeling, smelling, tasting).	*Haus* (house), *Baum* (tree), *Eisen* (iron), *Tisch* (table), *Fisch* (fish), *Arzt* (physician), *Lehrer* (teacher), *Auto* (car), *Brot* (bread), *Buch* (book), *Klavier* (piano), *Fahrrad* (bicycle) ...
Things that we cannot perceive with our senses, also called **abstract nouns** (abstract concepts or ideas).	*Glück* (luck/happiness), *Liebe* (love), *Freundschaft* (friendship), *Intelligenz* (intelligence), *Stunde* (hour), *Ewigkeit* (eternity), *Spaß* (fun) ...

1.2 GERMAN NOUNS AND GENDER

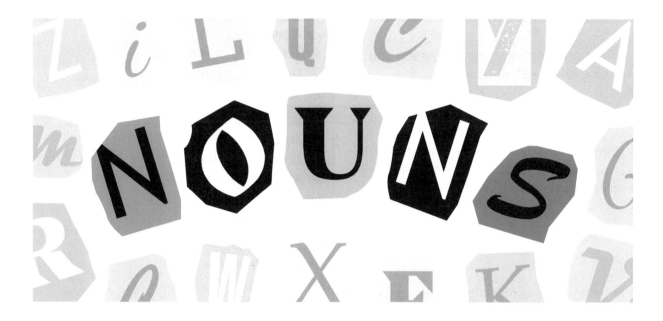

German nouns always take one of three possible genders: **masculine**, **feminine**, or **neuter**. It is important to remember that "gender" is a grammatical term and does not necessarily refer to biological gender in this context. For instance, the words "*Kind*" or "*Baby*" are neuter in German and could each refer to either a male or a female person. On the other hand, the noun "*Mädchen*" always refers to a female person, although it is grammatically neuter.

 There are no watertight rules as to which gender a noun takes in German. Sometimes, such gender allocations can seem quite arbitrary, and we generally recommend that you always memorize the relevant definite article ("***der***" for masculine, "***die***" for feminine, and "***das***" for neuter ⬳ **Ch. 3**) together with the noun. There are, however, some general hints that can help determine the gender of a given noun with a reasonable level of reliability:

MASCULINE (ARTICLE: *DER*)	
Noun ending or category	**Examples**
All nouns referring to a male person and ending in **-er**, **-ist**, **-ling**, **-ent**	*der Arbeiter* (worker) *der Kommunist* (communist) *der Lehrling* (apprentice) *der Student* (student)
Names of seasons, months, days, times of day (except *die Nacht*), geographical direction, weather phenomena	*der Sommer* (summer) *der Juli* (July) *der Donnerstag* (Thursday) *der Abend* (evening) *der Westen* (west) *der Nebel* (fog)
Most nouns ending in **-ig**, **-or**, **-ismus**, **-pf**, **-f**, **-ast**, **-ich**	*der Honig* (honey) *der Tenor* (tenor) *der Idealismus* (idealism) *der Kopf* (head) *der Senf* (mustard) *der Fantast* (daydreamer) *der Strich* (line, dash)

FEMININE (ARTICLE: *DIE*)	
Noun ending or category	**Examples**
Most two-syllable nouns that end in **-e** Some common exceptions include *der Name* (name), *der Käse* (cheese), *das Auge* (eye)	*die Liebe* (love) *die Ratte* (rat) *die Ferse* (heel) *die Frage* (question)
All nouns referring to female persons ending in **-in**	*die Studentin* (female student) *die Lehrerin* (female teacher)
All nouns ending in **-ei**, **-ie**, **-heit**, **-keit**, **-schaft**, **-ung**, **-ion**, **-tät**, **-ur**, **-ik**, **-a**	*die Polizei* (police) *die Ironie* (irony) *die Vergangenheit* (past) *die Freundlichkeit* (friendliness) *die Freundschaft* (friendship) *die Lieferung* (delivery) *die Version* (version) *die Universität* (university) *die Korrektur* (correction) *die Republik* (republic) *die Pizza* (pizza)

NEUTER (ARTICLE: *DAS*)	
Noun ending or category	Examples
All nouns ending in **-lein** or **-chen**	*das Mädchen* (young woman) *das Männlein* (small man)
All nouns ending in **-um**, **-ium**, **-tum**	*das Datum* (date) *das Gymnasium* (secondary school) *das Christentum* (christianity)
Most nouns beginning with **Ge-**	*das Gefühl* (feeling, sensation) *das Gesicht* (face) *das Gespräch* (conversation)

Note that masculine nouns used for male persons and animals can often be changed into their female counterpart by adding the ending *-in*:

Masculine   **Feminine**

(der) Lehrer (male teacher)   →   *(die) Lehrerin* (female teacher)

(der) Freund (male friend/boyfriend) →   *(die) Freundin* (female friend/girlfriend)

(der) Besitzer (male owner)   →   *(die) Besitzerin* (female owner)

In many instances, the female form additionally requires an Umlaut shift if the male form contains the vowels **a**, **o**, or **u**:

Masculine   **Feminine**

(der) Arzt (male physician)   →   *(die) Ärztin* (female physician)

(der) Franzose (male French person) →   *(die) Französin* (female French person)

(der) Hund (male dog)   →   *(die) Hündin* (female dog)

Note that some names for occupations use the suffix **-mann** for male persons. Changing those into the female form requires the suffix **-frau**:

Feuerwehrmann   →   Feuerwehr**frau**
(male firefighter)   (female firefighter)

1.3 PLURAL FORMS OF GERMAN NOUNS

A noun can appear in either its **singular** or in its **plural** form. In English, this distinction is fairly straightforward since almost all English nouns form their plurals by adding -s or -es to the singular forms.

father   →   father**s**

name   →   name**s**

volcano   →   volcano**es**

There are only a few exceptions to this rule in English, including the irregular plural forms for words like mouse (*mice*), ox (*oxen*), or child (*children*), which are remnants of past noun declensions that resembled the present-day German declensions.

Things are a bit more complicated in German and nouns rarely form their plural forms by adding **-s**. Some German nouns change their vowels to an **Umlaut**, others add **-e**, some add **-er** or **-en**, other nouns use a mix of Umlaut shifts and these endings, and there also are nouns that remain completely unchanged in the plural. Although there are no definitive rules, it is possible to structure the formation of the plural noun forms into five distinct groups. Also note that the definite article for the nominative plural form is always **die**, regardless of the noun's gender (⬐ **Ch. 3**). The abbreviations given in the second column are what you will often see in dictionary entries after a noun. They are a short way of indicating how a noun's plural is formed.

GROUP	ABBREVIATION	DESCRIPTION	EXAMPLES	
			Singular	Plural
Group Ia Group Ib	- ··	No change in plural Plural adds Umlaut	*das Fenster* (window) *der Koffer* (suitcase) *der Vater* (father) *der Mantel* (coat)	**die Fenster** (windows) **die Koffer** (suitcases) **die Väter** (fathers) **die Mäntel** (coats)

Group IIa Group IIb	-e ¨e	Plural adds -e Plural adds -e and Umlaut	*das Tier* (animal) *der König* (king) *der Arzt* (doctor) *die Kraft* (force)	***die Tiere*** (animals) ***die Könige*** (kings) ***die Ärzte*** (doctors) ***die Kräfte*** (forces)
Group IIIa Group IIIb	-er ¨er	Plural adds -er Plural adds -er and Umlaut	*das Kind* (child) *das Lied* (song) *das Buch* (book) *das Haus* (house)	***die Kinder*** (children) ***die Lieder*** (songs) ***die Bücher*** (books) ***die Häuser*** (houses)
Group IVa Group IVb Group IVc	-n -en -nen	Plural adds -n Plural adds -en Plural adds -nen	*die Lampe* (lamp) *der Junge* (boy) *die Datei* (file) *der Staat* (state) *die Chefin* (female boss) *die Lehrerin* (female teacher)	***die Lampen*** (lamps) ***die Jungen*** (boys) ***die Dateien*** (files) ***die Staaten*** (states) ***die Chefinnen*** (female bosses) ***die Lehrerinnen*** (female teachers)
Group V	-s	Plural adds -s	*das Auto* (car) *die Party* (party)	***die Autos*** (cars) ***die Partys*** (parties)

Below, we offer some further explanations regarding each group, along with additional example words.

Group I:

 Nouns in this group form the plural either by umlauting the vowel of the singular form or they remain unchanged. Masculine and neuter nouns are most commonly found in this group, although two frequently used feminine nouns also belong to it. Examples include:

MASCULINE		NEUTER		FEMININE	
Singular	Plural	Singular	Plural	Singular	Plural
der Bruder (brother) der Finger (finger) der Schüler (pupil/student) der Apfel (apple) der Löffel (spoon)	die Brüder die Finger die Schüler die Äpfel die Löffel	das Messer (knife) das Zimmer (room) das Theater (theater) das Rätsel (puzzle/riddle) das Kissen (pillow)	die Messer die Zimmer die Theater die Rätsel die Kissen	die Mutter (mother) die Tochter (daughter)	die Mütter die Töchter

Group II:

 These nouns add **-e** to the singular to form the plural. Some nouns also add an Umlaut. Masculine, feminine, and neuter nouns may all fall into this category. Many of these nouns have only one syllable. Examples include:

MASCULINE		NEUTER		FEMININE	
Singular	Plural	Singular	Plural	Singular	Plural
der Hund (dog) *der Monat* (month) *der Sohn* (son) *der Schuh* (shoe) *der Zug* (train)	***die Hunde die Monate die Söhne die Schuhe die Züge***	*das Brot* (bread) *das Gedicht* (poem) *das Heft* (notebook) *das Jahr* (year) *das Boot* (boat)	***die Brote die Gedichte die Hefte die Jahre die Boote***	*die Frucht* (fruit) *die Hand* (hand) *die Nacht* (night) *die Stadt* (city/town) *die Wurst* (sausage)	***die Früchte die Hände die Nächte die Städte die Würste***

Group III:

 These nouns add **-er** to the singular in order to form the plural. All nouns containing **a**, **o**, **u**, and **au** in the singular show an Umlaut shift in the plural. Nouns of this group are primarily neuter, though a few masculine nouns also belong to it. There are no feminine nouns in this group. Examples include:

MASCULINE		NEUTER		FEMININE	
Singular	Plural	Singular	Plural	Singular	Plural
der Geist (spirit/ghost) *der Gott* (god) *der Irrtum* (mistake/fallacy) *der Mann* (man) *der Wald* (forest)	***die Geister die Götter die Irrtümer die Männer die Wälder***	*das Ei* (egg) *das Kleid* (dress) *das Land* (country) *das Blatt* (leaf) *das Volk* (people)	***die Eier die Kleider die Länder die Blätter die Völker***		

Group IV:

 Nouns of this group add **-n** or **-en** to the singular and never show an Umlaut shift in the plural. Most of these nouns are feminine. Feminine nouns ending in **-in** add **-nen** in the plural (Group IVc). Examples include:

MASCULINE		NEUTER		FEMININE	
Singular	Plural	Singular	Plural	Singular	Plural
der Hase (rabbit) der Name (name) der Mensch (human being)	die Hasen die Namen die Menschen	das Auge (eye) das Herz (heart) das Ohr (ear)	die Augen die Herzen die Ohren	die Blume (flower) die Katze (cat) die Stunde (hour) die Anwältin (female lawyer) die Tür (door)	die Blumen die Katzen die Stunden die Anwältinnen die Türen

Group V:

 These nouns add **-s** to the singular. This group consists mainly of loanwords that originated in foreign languages. However, German words that end in a vowel are also included in this group (especially those that are abbreviated forms of German words or terms of endearment). Examples include:

MASCULINE		NEUTER		FEMININE	
Singular	Plural	Singular	Plural	Singular	Plural
der Job (job) der Park (park) der Vati (Daddy) der VW (VW/Volkswagen)	die Jobs die Parks die Vatis die VWs	das Baby (baby) das Foto (photo) das Hobby (hobby) das Radio (radio) das Sofa (sofa)	die Babys die Fotos die Hobbys die Radios die Sofas	die Kamera (camera) die Mama (Mommy) die Bar (bar) die CD (CD) die Uni (university)	die Kameras die Mamas die Bars die CDs die Unis

Note that the plural ending **-s** can also be applied to family names to mean all the individual members of a particular family:

Familie Müller (the Müller family)	→	**die Müllers** (all members of the Müller family)
Familie Meier (the Meier family)	→	**die Meiers** (all members of the Meier family)

✏️ EXERCISES

Ü 1.1) Have a look at the following list of nouns. Decide whether each of them is a proper noun (name of person, city, street, geographical feature, etc.) or a common noun (concrete or abstract). You may use a dictionary if you are unsure about any of the meanings. Use the abbreviations "PN", "CNC", "CNA":

a. Jupiter _____

b. Hunger _____

c. Oktoberfest _____

d. Stuhl _____

e. Konrad Adenauer _____

f. Hass _____

g. Europäische Zentralbank _____

h. Ferien _____

i. Königsstraße _____

j. Lassie _____

k. Hitze _____

l. Matterhorn _____

m. Bleistift _____

n. Hamburg _____

o. Petersdom _____

p. Familie _____

q. Donau _____

r. Frank Sinatra _____

s. Taj Mahal _____

t. Wasser _____

Ü 1.2) Depending on each noun's gender, supply the correct definite article (*der*, *die*, or *das*) to complete the following short sentences. The noun endings should help you in making your decision:

a. _____ Lehrer kommt.

b. _____ Rose ist schön.

c. _____ Universität ist groß.

d. _____ Honig ist süß.

e. _____ Wohnung ist sauber.

f. _____ Köchin kocht das Essen.

g. _____ Pianist spielt Klavier.

h. _____ Instrument ist teuer.

i. _____ Datum steht hier.

j. _____ Regen hört nicht auf.

k. _____ Judentum ist eine Religion.

l. _____ Krankheit ist tödlich.

m. _____ Rektor leitet die Schule.

n. _____ Flagge flattert im Wind.

o. _____ Auge ist gerötet.

p. _____ Familie ist zu Hause.

q. _____ Morgen graut.

r. _____ Vöglein singt.

s. _____ Zucker ist weiß.

t. _____ Käse kommt aus Frankreich.

Ü 1.3) Change the following masculine nouns for persons or animals into their feminine counterparts:

Example

der Politiker   →   **die Politikerin**

a. der Verkäufer   _____

b. der Astronaut   _____

c. der Bär   _____

d. der Dirigent   _____

e. der Bauer   _____

f. der Bischof   _____

g. der Kollege   _____

h. der Ehemann (!)   _____

Ü 1.4) Find the correct plural forms for the nouns in the list below. You may use a dictionary if you are unsure. Put them in the appropriate column of the table, according to the group they belong to:

der Beruf / das Hotel / die Kultur / das Bad / die Friseurin / der Fuß / der Ball / die Blume / der Tag / der Wald / das Mädchen / die Tasche / der PC / das Radio / der Spiegel / die Hand / der Schuh / der Ton / das Bild / das Telefon / die Stadt / die Bäckerei / das Dorf / das Regal / das Handy

GROUP I (Plural:– / ¨)	GROUP II (Plural: -e / ¨e)	GROUP III (Plural: -er / ¨er)	GROUP IV (Plural: -n / -en / -nen)	GROUP V (Plural: -s)

CHAPTER 2
THE FOUR GERMAN CASES

⊘ CHECKBOX – WHAT IS A CASE?

A **case** (in German *Kasus* or *Fall*) denotes the **grammatical function** (subject, possessive, indirect object, or direct object) of a noun within a sentence. Sometimes, this necessitates changing the noun endings, as well as those of articles (🔗 **Ch. 3),** modifying adjectives (🔗 **Ch. 18**) and pronouns (🔗 **Ch. 4&5**) that might accompany the noun. The process of applying these changes is called **declension**.

There are **four** cases in German: **nominative**, **genitive**, **dative**, and **accusative**.

(The father of the boy is telling his son a story.)
Der Vater des Jungen erzählt seinem Sohn eine Geschichte.

Nominative	Genitive	Dative	Accusative
(subject)	(possessive)	(indirect object)	(direct object)

🎧 ⟲ TEXT – JULIA STELLT SICH VOR

(In this text, somebody called Julia introduces herself while telling you a bit about her family. The highlighted words are nouns, articles, and pronouns appearing in different cases.)

*Mein Name ist **Julia** und ich komme aus **Österreich**. **Ich** bin 22 **Jahre** alt und studiere **Chemie** in **Wien**. **Ich** habe **zwei Brüder**, die noch bei **meinen Eltern** in **Graz** leben. **Wir** haben auch **einen Hund**, **zwei Katzen** und im **Garten einen Teich** mit **Goldfischen**. **Das Haus meiner Eltern** ist sehr groß. **Ich** besuche **jedes Wochenende meine Familie**. **Ich** bringe für **jeden** immer etwas mit. **Ich** bringe **meiner Mutter** immer **Blumen** mit. **Meinen Brüdern** schmeckt **Schokolade** besonders gut. **Weine** sind **die Leidenschaft meines Vaters**. Deshalb schenke **ich ihm** oft **eine Flasche** des **neuesten Jahrgangs**.*

VOCABULARY LIST—JULIA INTRODUCES HERSELF			
aus ... kommen [*prep.*] [*v.*]	(to) be/come from	(die) Blume [*n.*] (-n)	flower
(das) Jahr [*n.*] (-e)	year	jmdm. schmecken [*v.*]	(to) be to sb's liking
studieren [*v.*]	(to) study	(der) Wein [*n.*] (-e)	wine
(der) Bruder [*n.*] (¨)	brother	(die) Leidenschaft [*n.*] (-en)	passion
(die) Eltern [*pl.*]	parents	deshalb [*adv.*]	therefore
(der) Teich [*n.*] (-e)	pond	(die) Flasche [*n.*] (-n)	bottle
(der) Goldfisch [*n.*] (-e)	goldfish	schenken [*v.*]	(to) give/gift
besuchen [*v.*]	(to) visit	(der) Jahrgang [*n.*] (¨e)	vintage
immer [*adv.*]	always		

2.1 WHAT IS THE PURPOSE OF A GRAMMATICAL CASE?

For English speakers, the concept of grammatical cases can sometimes be challenging, simply because the case system has almost completely disappeared from the English language. This is in contrast to many Indo-European languages (including German), as well as languages from the Slavic and Baltic regions, where grammatical cases still play a vital role. Yet, even in contemporary English there are remnants of its former case system, especially when we look at English pronouns. Read the following sentence and see if you can make sense of it:

"He praised the book without giving I credit, although he
had based it protagonist on an idea of I."

Even though, after a bit of creative thinking, you can probably figure out what this sentence is supposed to convey, immediate comprehension is much more difficult as none of the personal pronouns have been put in the appropriate case. In other words, the way the pronouns are used in the above sentence is not suited to the function they are supposed to serve in this particular context. We only end up with a correct sentence once we put the pronouns into a case that matches their function:

"He praised **his** (function: *possessive*) book without giving **me** (function:
indirect object) credit, although he had based **its** (function: *possessive*)
protagonist on an idea of **mine** (function: *possessive*)."

This same principle of putting nouns, pronouns, articles, and adjectives into different cases to make them suitable for their function within a sentence also applies in German. The only difference to English is that the rules are a bit more complex due to a greater variety of inflections that need to be added in different scenarios. The mechanics of declension, however, are not as difficult as they are said to be, and with the aid of a few rules you can master them easily.

2.2 THE FOUR CASES IN GERMAN

There are four cases in German: **nominative**, **genitive**, **dative**, and **accusative**. The following table lists the most important usage scenarios for each of them, along with examples from the introductory text at the beginning of this chapter.

CASE	EXPLANATIONS AND EXAMPLES
Nominative Answers the question *Who or what is performing the action?*	• The most important role of the nominative case is to mark **who or what is carrying out the action** expressed through the verb of a sentence (i.e., to mark the **subject** of the sentence). "**Das Haus** *meiner Eltern ist sehr groß.*" → Verb: "*ist*" → Who or what is very big? Answer: "*Das Haus*" → "*Das Haus*" is in the nominative case. • The nominative is also used after the verbs *sein*, *werden*, *bleiben*, and *heißen*. Nouns that come after these verbs are called **predicate nouns**. "*Mein Name ist* **Julia**." → "*Julia*" is a predicate noun following the verb "*ist*" (3rd person singular form of "*sein*"). Consequently, it is in the nominative case.

Genitive Answers the question *Whose?*	• The most important role of the genitive is to indicate **possession** or **close relation** between two nouns. In English this is expressed by the preposition *of* or *'s*. *"Weine sind die Leidenschaft **meines Vaters.**"* → Whose passion are wines? Answer: That of my father. → *"Meines Vaters"* is in the genitive case. • The genitive usually follows the noun on which it depends. → "eine Flasche <u>des neuesten Jahrgangs</u>" The genitive follows *"eine Flasche"*, on which it depends.
Dative Answers the question *"To whom/what, or for whom/ what is the action done?"*	• The main syntactic role of the dative is to mark **for whom/ what** or **to whom/what the action of the verb is being done** (i.e., to mark the **indirect object** of a sentence). *"Ich bringe **meiner Mutter** immer Blumen mit."* → The action of bringing flowers is done for the mother. → Consequently, *"meiner Mutter"* is in the dative case.

Accusative Answers the question *"Who or what is affected by the action?"*	• The main syntactic role of the accusative is to mark **who or what is being affected by the action** expressed through the verb of a sentence (i.e., to mark the **direct object** of a sentence). *"Wir haben auch **einen Hund**, **zwei Katzen** und im Garten **einen Teich** mit Goldfischen."* → Who is affected by the verb *"haben"*? Answer: *"einen Hund, zwei Katzen, und [...] einen Teich"* → Consequently, *"einen Hund"*, *"zwei Katzen"*, and *"einen Teich"* are in the accusative case. • The accusative is also used with expressions of **definite time** and **duration of time**. *"Ich besuche **jedes Wochenende** meine Familie"* → The time indication *"jedes Wochenende"* is in the accusative case. → Other common time expressions used in this way include:

jeden Tag	-	every day
einen Moment	-	one moment
jedes Jahr	-	every year
letzten Montag, etc.	-	last Monday, etc.
diesen Monat	-	this month

The accusative form of *der* is used when dating a letter:

*Berlin, **den** 10. 9. 2022*

2.3 THE FOUR CASES AS APPLIED TO GERMAN NOUNS

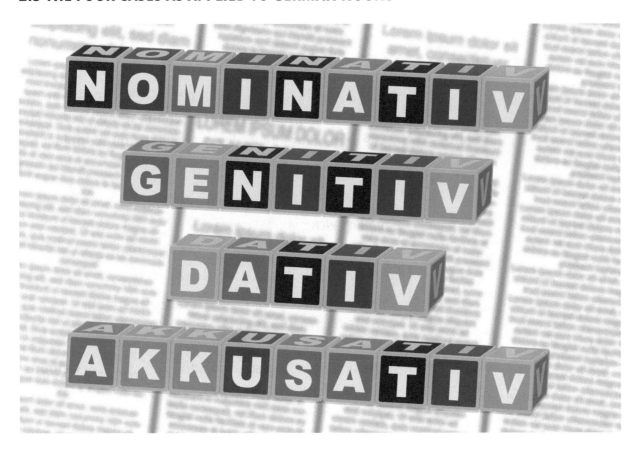

As we have already seen in the above paragraphs, different cases can be applied not only to nouns but also to any accompanying articles, adjectives, and pronouns. Since the declension of articles, pronouns, and adjectives requires the use of a greater number of inflections than the declension of nouns does, the following section will only consider the declension of **nouns** in the different cases. The declension of articles (📎 **Ch. 3**), pronouns (📎 **Ch. 4&5**), and adjectives (📎 **Ch. 18**) is covered in separate chapters.

The following rules for noun declension hold true for the vast majority of German nouns. The few exceptions to these rules can be learned individually. For better context, we have added the definite article for each noun and case, but the focus here is on the nouns themselves.

Declension of the singular forms

Feminine nouns never add an ending to their singular form. **Masculine** and **neuter** nouns require only **one ending** in the singular, namely *-(e)s* for the genitive.

	MASCULINE	**FEMININE**	**NEUTER**
Singular noun	*der **Vater** (the father)*	*die **Frau** (the woman)*	*das **Buch** (the book)*
Nominative	*der Vater*	*die Frau*	*das Buch*
Genitive	*des Vater**s***	*der Frau*	*des Buch**es***
Dative	*dem Vater*	*der Frau*	*dem Buch*
Accusative	*den Vater*	*die Frau*	*das Buch*

Note that sometimes (but rarely) the ending *-e* is added to the singular dative case. You will mostly come across this inflection in fixed expressions such as *in diesem Sinne* (in this sense), *im Grunde genommen* (basically/after all), or *im Laufe der Zeit* (in the course of time).

Declension of the plural forms

The key to the declension of the German plural nouns is each noun's **nominative plural form**, as outlined in 📎 **Ch. 1**. All the other plural forms are exactly like the respective noun's nominative plural, **except** that the **dative plural** must always end in *-(e)n*. If the nominative plural ends in *-n*, no additional *n* is required for the dative case.

	MASCULINE	**FEMININE**	**NEUTER**
Plural noun	*die **Väter** (the fathers)*	*die **Frauen** (the women)*	*die **Bücher** (the books)*
Nominative	*die Väter*	*die Frauen*	*die Bücher*
Genitive	*der Väter*	*der Frauen*	*der Bücher*
Dative	*den Väter**n***	*den Frauen*	*den Büche**rn***
Accusative	*die Väter*	*die Frauen*	*die Bücher*

2.4 ADDITIONAL FACTORS THAT DETERMINE GERMAN CASES

There are **three factors** that determine the case of a noun, pronoun, adjective or article in German. In the above paragraphs we already outlined the first one of these factors, namely the **function** of the respective noun, pronoun, etc. within a sentence (i.e., subject, direct object, indirect object, possessive). The two other factors that determine which case must be used are **the verb** and the **prepositions** in a sentence.

A more in-depth discussion of these last two factors can be found in 🔗 **Ch. 10&11** (verbs) and 🔗 **Ch. 21** (prepositions). However, in the following section we offer a few examples of how verbs and prepositions can determine which case is necessary in a particular context. Where possible, we have used examples from this chapter's introductory text.

Verbs

The verb generally determines which case is used for the object (either direct or indirect) within a sentence.

- Most German verbs require the **accusative**.

   *"Ich besuche jedes Wochenende **meine Familie.**"*

   → The verb *"besuchen"* requires the accusative case.
   → *"meine Familie"* is in the accusative.

- Certain verbs always require the **dative**, such as *helfen* (to help), *gehören* (to belong), or *jmdm. schmecken* (to be to sb's liking).

   *"**Meinen Brüdern** schmeckt Schokolade besonders gut."*

   The verb *"jmdm. schmecken"* requires the dative case.

   "Meinen Brüdern" is in the dative.

- A small number of verbs require the genitive, including *sich besinnen* (to think of/ remember), *sich erfreuen* (to enjoy), or *gedenken* (to commemorate).

   *"Wir gedenken **der Opfer**."*

   → The verb *"gedenken"* requires the genitive case.
   → *"Der Opfer"* is in the genitive.

<u>Prepositions</u>

German prepositions (words such as *mit* (with), *auf* (on), *neben* (next to) or *bei* (at)) always require a certain case.

- Some prepositions take the **accusative**, including, for instance, *durch* (through) or *für* (for).

  *"Ich bringe für **jeden** immer etwas mit."*

  → The preposition *"für"* requires the accusative case.
  → *"Jeden"* is in the accusative.

- Other prepositions take the **dative**, such as *mit* (with) or *von* (from).

  *"Wir haben einen Teich mit **Goldfischen**."*

  → The preposition *"mit"* requires the dative case.
  → *"Goldfischen"* is in the dative.

- A small number of prepositions take the **genitive**. These include *statt* (instead of) and *trotz* (despite).

  *"Trotz **des schlechten Wetters** gehen wir wandern."*

  The preposition *"trotz"* requires the genitive case.

  "Des schlechten Wetters" is in the genitive.

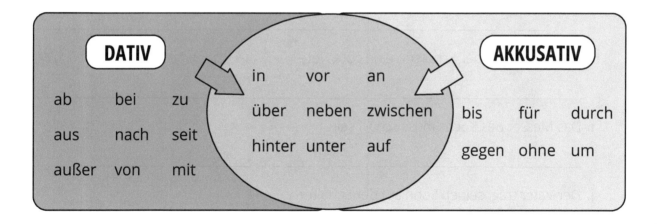

📝 EXERCISES

Ü 2.1) The following sentences contain nouns in the nominative, genitive, dative and accusative. Underline all nouns and determine the case in which they appear in the respective sentence. Use the abbreviations N, G, D, A:

    a. Die Frau gibt dem Mann den Autoschlüssel.

_____

    b. Die Lehrer erzählen Geschichten für die Kinder.

_____

    c. Die Frau des Bürgermeisters hat ein Auto gekauft.

_____

    d. Hier ist ein Foto unseres Hauses.

_____

    e. Zum Geburtstag bekam er ein Buch.

_____

    f. Karl versprach seiner Tochter ein Eis.

_____

    g. Der Koch bereitet die Speisen vor.

_____

    h. Der Lehrer gibt der Schülerin eine gute Note.

_____

    i. Das Messer des Kochs muss scharf sein.

_____

    j. Der Vater trägt seinen Sohn auf der Schulter.

_____

Ü 2.2) The following table provides you with one noun for each gender. Complete the declension table of each noun through all the cases in the singular and plural, both for the noun and its accompanying definite article:

NOUN	DER BERG (-E)		DIE STUNDE (-N)		DAS FENSTER (-)	
	Singular					
	article	noun	article	noun	article	noun
Nominative						
Genitive						
Dative						
Accusative						
	Plural					
Nominative						
Genitive						
Dative						
Accusative						

Ü 2.3) Supply the correct noun endings for the nouns in the following sentences. All cases in both singular and plural may be applicable but keep in mind that not all cases require the noun to take a particular ending:

Familie(____) Müller macht heute einen Ausflug(____) in den Zoo(____). Die Kinder(____) wollen die exotischen Tier(____) sehen. Gleich am Eingang(____) sehen sie zwei Papagei(____). Sie geben den bunten Vögel(____) einen Keks(____). Als Nächstes sehen sie sich die Affe(____) an. Die lustigen Schrei(____) der Primat(____) gefallen den Kinder(____). Am Löwengehege(____) staunen sie über die Mähne(____) des Löwe(____). Auch die Elefant(____) gefallen den Kinder(____). Am liebsten würden sie den Elefant(____) Erdnüss(____) in den Rüssel(____) stecken. Am Ende(____) des Ausflug(____) bekommen die Kinder(____) noch ein Eis(____). Am Ausgang(____) winkt Familie(____) Müller den Papagei(____) wieder zu.

CHAPTER 3
DEFINITE AND INDEFINITE ARTICLES

⊘ CHECKBOX – WHAT IS AN ARTICLE?

Articles (*Artikel* or *Begleiter* in German) are words that always appear together with a noun. There are **definite** and **indefinite** articles. In English, the definite article is always "the", while the indefinite article is "a" or "an".

In German, both definite (***der***, ***die***, ***das***) and indefinite articles (***ein***, ***eine***, ***ein***) are declined together with the noun they belong to and thus help determine the **gender**, **number** and **case** of the accompanying noun. This also means that they frequently change form, depending on the factors that govern the choice of the correct case, as explained in **Ch. 2**.

(My parents' dog is old.)
Der Hund meiner Eltern ist alt. ⟷

(My parents have a dog.)
Meine Eltern haben **einen Hund**.

↓

Definite article accompanying the noun "*Hund*" (masc., sing., Nom.)

↓

Indefinite article, accompanying the noun "*Hund*" (masc., sing., Acc.)

⊙ TEXT – DER WEIHNACHTSBAUM

(In this text, we are reading about the Christmas tree of the Kaufmann family. Both definite and indefinite articles have been used in different cases and are highlighted throughout the text.)

*Familie Kaufmann hat heute **einen** Weihnachtsbaum gekauft. **Der** Baum ist **eine** Tanne und **die** Farbe **der** Nadeln ist dunkelgrün. Familie Kaufmann schmückt **den** Weihnachtsbaum für **das** Fest. Am Heiligabend brennt für jedes Familienmitglied **eine** Kerze am Weichnachtsbaum. **Die** Geschenke liegen auf **einem** Tisch neben **dem** Weihnachtsbaum. Am Heiligabend singt Familie Kaufmann gemeinsam **das** Lied "O Tannenbaum". **Das** ist **ein** bekanntes Weihnachtslied.*

VOCABULARY LIST – DER WEIHNACHTSBAUM			
(der) Weihnachtsbaum [*n.*] (¨e)	Christmas tree	(der) Heiligabend [*n.*] (-e)	Christmas Eve
(der) Baum [*n.*] (¨e)	tree	brennen [*v.*]	(to) burn
kaufen [*v.*]	(to) buy	(die) Kerze [*n.*] (-n)	candle
(die) Tanne [*n.*] (-n)	fir tree	(das) Geschenk [*n.*] (-e)	present
(die) Farbe [*n.*] (-n)	color	liegen [*v.*]	(to) lie / lay
(die) Nadel [*n.*] (-n)	needle	(der) Tisch [*n.*] (-e)	table
dunkelgrün [*adj.*]	dark green	singen [*v.*]	(to) sing
schmücken [*v.*]	(to) decorate	gemeinsam [*adv.*]	together / jointly
(das) Fest [*n.*] (-e)	celebration / holiday	(das) Lied [*n.*] (-er)	song
		bekannt [*adj.*]	famous

3.1 ARTICLES AND THEIR RELATION TO NOUNS

Articles are not considered a separate part of speech since they never appear on their own but always in conjunction with a noun. They play an important role in German as they help indicate whether a noun is **masculine**, **feminine** or **neuter** and if the noun is in the **singular** or **plural** form (⬗ **Ch. 1**). Furthermore, articles signal the grammatical function of a noun in a sentence (such as subject, direct object, etc.) (⬗ **Ch. 2**). Thus, they assume a vital role in determining the appropriate case to be used. Conversely, this means that they frequently change their form, depending on context. The following example aims to illustrate how the definite article can change when accompanying the same noun in different cases.

Der Sänger singt bekannte Lieder. (The singer sings famous songs.)

⎣————→ (masc., sing., subject → **nominative**)

*Kennst du **den** Sänger?* (Do you know the singer?)

⎣————→ (masc., sing., direct object → **accusative**)

***Dem** Sänger wurde ein Plattenvertrag angeboten.* (A recording contract was offered to the singer.)

⎣————→ (masc., sing., indirect object → **dative**)

3.2 THE DEFINITE ARTICLE IN GERMAN

As a basic rule, the definite article is used **if the person or thing in question is known** or **has already been mentioned**. If the definite article refers to a generally well-known person, thing, or idea we use the definite article as well. The declension of the definite article for all three genders, through all the cases and in both the singular and plural is outlined in the following table.

SINGULAR			
	Masculine	Feminine	Neuter
Nominative	*der* Baum	*die* Nadel	*das* Lied
Genitive	*des* Baums	*der* Nadel	*des* Lieds
Dative	*dem* Baum	*der* Nadel	*dem* Lied
Accusative	*den* Baum	*die* Nadel	*das* Lied

PLURAL	
The plural forms of the definite articles are the same for all three genders.	
Nominative	*die* Bäume, *die* Nadeln, *die* Lieder
Genitive	*der* Bäume, *der* Nadeln, *der* Lieder
Dative	*den* Bäumen, *den* Nadeln, *den* Liedern
Accusative	*die* Bäume, *die* Nadeln, *die* Lieder

GERMAN ARTICLE DICE

It is important to memorize these forms since the definite articles are among the most commonly used words in German. Their different endings are also used to form independent adjectives (📎 **Ch. 18**), as well as certain pronouns (📎 **Ch. 5**).

There are a few patterns in the declension of the definite articles which are worth noting:

- The nominative and accusative forms of the feminine article are identical, as are the respective forms of the neuter article.

- In the genitive and dative cases singular, the masculine and neuter forms are identical.

- Feminine singular forms are the same in the genitive and dative.

- All genders share the same forms in the plural.

3.3 THE INDEFINITE ARTICLE IN GERMAN

The German indefinite articles *ein*, *eine*, *ein* refer to an **unspecified person**, **thing**, or **idea**. They correspond to the English words "a" or "an" and, much like the definite articles, they agree in case and gender with the noun they accompany. Their forms are:

	MASCULINE	**FEMININE**	**NEUTER**
Nominative	*ein* Baum	*eine* Nadel	*ein* Lied
Genitive	*eines* Baums	*einer* Nadel	*eines* Lieds
Dative	*einem* Baum	*einer* Nadel	*einem* Lied
Accusative	*einen* Baum	*eine* Nadel	*ein* Lied

There is **no plural form** for the indefinite article as it always refers to a single thing. If an otherwise unspecified noun that would take the indefinite article in the singular is to be put in the plural, the indefinite article is dropped:

*Am Heiligabend brennt für jedes Familienmitglied **eine Kerze** am Weihnachtsbaum.*

↓

*Am Heiligabend brennen für die Familienmitglieder **Kerzen** am Weihnachtsbaum.*

3.4. THE NEGATIVE FORM *KEIN*

The German word *kein* is essentially the negation of the indefinite article and it is normally linked to a noun. Its English counterpart would be "no" or "not any". *Kein* behaves exactly like the indefinite article and consequently has to agree with the noun in **gender** (masculine, feminine, neuter), **number** (singular, plural) and **case** (nominative, genitive, dative, accusative). The only difference is that *kein* <u>does</u> have plural forms for negating nouns in the plural:

*Er hat **einen** Weihnachtsbaum gekauft.*　　　　*Er hat **keinen** Weihnachtsbaum gekauft.*
*Am Weihnachtsbaum brennen **Kerzen**.*　→　*Am Weihnachtsbaum brennen **keine Kerzen**.*

Here is an overview of the declension for *kein*. Take note of the plural forms, which are identical with the plural forms for the possessive pronouns, such as *mein* (📎 **Ch. 4**).

	SINGULAR			PLURAL
	Masculine	Feminine	Neuter	
Nominative	**kein** Baum	**keine** Nadel	**kein** Lied	**keine** Bäume/Nadeln/Lieder
Genitive	**keines** Baums	**keiner** Nadel	**keines** Lieds	**keiner** Bäume/Nadeln/Lieder
Dative	**keinem** Baum	**keiner** Nadel	**keinem** Lied	**keinen** Bäumen/Nadeln/Liedern
Accusative	**keinen** Baum	**keine** Nadel	**kein** Lied	**keine** Bäume/Nadeln/Lieder

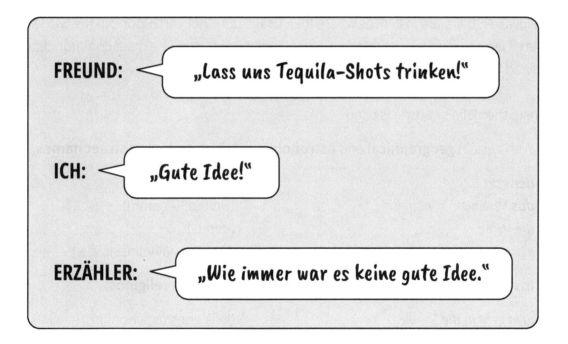

FREUND: „Lass uns Tequila-Shots trinken!"

ICH: „Gute Idee!"

ERZÄHLER: „Wie immer war es keine gute Idee."

If you compare this table to the declension chart for the indefinite articles, you will realize that adding the letter **k-** to the indefinite articles will give you the corresponding negation word in the singular.

It is also important to note that you can only negate nouns with *kein* if the respective noun is either used **without articles** (e.g., in the plural form) or **with an indefinite article**:

Without article

   *Auf dem Tisch liegen **Geschenke**.*   ⟷   *Auf dem Tisch liegen **keine Geschenke**.*

With indefinite article

   *Das ist **ein** bekanntes Weihnachtslied.*   ⟷   *Das ist **kein** bekanntes Weihnachtslied.*

The use of the negation word *kein*, along with other ways of constructing negative sentences, is explained in more detail in (📎 **Ch. 25**).

3.5 ADDITIONAL POINTS ABOUT DEFINITE ARTICLES

In most situations, German and English agree in the use of definite, indefinite or no article with nouns. However, there are instances where their usage does not correspond in the two languages and where German uses a definite article when English does not. The most common differences are outlined below.

In German, the definite article is used:

- With certain **geographical** and **astronomical** names, as well as **street names**.

***der** Iran*	(Iran)
***das** Vereinigte Königreich*	(United Kingdom)
***die** Venus*	(Venus)
*Ich wohne in **der** Wilhelmsstraße.*	(I live on Wilhelmsstraße.)

- **Institutions, movements in history** or **philosophy and religions:**

*Julia geht in **die** Schule.*	(Julia goes to school.)
*Er schrieb eine Arbeit über **den** Marxismus.*	(He wrote a paper on Marxism.)
***Der** Islam ist eine Weltreligion.*	(Islam is a world religion.)

- Names of **months** and **seasons**, as well as **meals**. Many names of **diseases** and **substances** also take an article if referred to as a general concept:

***Der** Sommer ist die schönste Jahreszeit.*	(Summer is the most beautiful season.)

Der Dezember wird kalt.	(December is going to be cold.)
*Wir trafen uns nach **dem** Abendessen.*	(We met up after dinner.)
*Sie ist an **den** Masern erkrankt.*	(She is ill with measels.)
***Die** Butter kostet hier zwei Euro.*	(Butter costs two Euros here.)

- Several abstract nouns that often lack an article in English:

***Das** Leben ist schön.*	(Life is beautiful.)
***Die** Medizin hat Fortschritte gemacht.*	(Medicine has made progress.)
*Sie liebte **die** Musik.*	(She loved music.)

3.6 CONTRACTIONS WITH PREPOSITIONS

Some prepositions form contractions with the definite article to become one word. This topic is discussed in more detail in 🔖 **Ch. 21**, but here are a few examples frequently found in both written and spoken German:

Preposition + dem (Dat. sing. m. and. n): *am, beim, im, vom, zum*

*Er lief **vom** (= von dem) Haus **zum** (= zu dem) Bahnhof.*
(He ran from the house to the train station.)

Preposition + der (Dat. sing. f.): *zur*

*Vom Bahnhof lief er **zur** (= zu der) Kirche.*
(From the train station he ran to the church.)

Preposition + das (acc. sing. n.): *ans, ins*

*Der Polizist kam nah **ans** (= an das) Auto heran und leuchtete mit seiner Taschenlampe **ins** (= in das) Innere des Wagens.*
(The policeman came close to the car and shone his flashlight into the interior of the vehicle.)

 **EXERCISES**

Ü 3.1) Complete the following sentences with *der*, *die*, or *das*:

a. _____ Universität ist alt.

b. _____ Mann schreibt.

c. Ist _____ Mädchen krank?

d. _____ Junge studiert.

e. _____ Wohnung ist kalt.

f. _____ Wetter ist schön.

g. Warum schreit _____ Kind?

h. _____ Frau ist hübsch.

i. _____ Lehrer ist jung.

j. _____ Vogel singt.

Ü 3.2) Supply the definite article using the correct case in each of the following sentences. Be mindful of the different noun genders:

a. Ich gehe in _____ Schule.

b. Ich fahre zu _____ Arzt.

c. Das ist das Spielzeug _____ Kindes.

d. Ich bin in _____ Büro.

e. Ich gehe zu _____ Apotheke.

f. Ich gehe in _____ Büro.

g. Der Chef dankte _____ Mitarbeitern.

h. Ich muss _____ E-Mails beantworten.

i. Welcher Polizist untersucht _____ Fall?

Ü 3.3) Complete the following sentences with *ein*, *eine*, or *ein*:

a. Dort ist _____ Junge.

b. _____ Gabel ist aus Silber.

c. Das ist _____ Käfer.

d. _____ Mädchen kommt.

e. Dort steht _____ Museum.

f. Ist das _____ Lilie?

g. Dort liegt _____ Pille.

h. _____ Wohnung ist teuer.

i. Das ist _____ Cent.

j. Dort hängt _____ Apfel.

Ü 3.4) Give a negative response to all questions by using the correct form of *kein*:

Example: Ist das ein BMW?   →   Nein, das ist kein BMW.

a. Ist das ein Museum?   _____

b. Ist das eine Bushaltestelle?   _____

c. Hat Dieter ein Auto?   _____

d. Möchtest du einen Kaffee?   _____

e. Hat Peter einen Bruder?   _____

f. Hat Mareike ein neues Haustier? _____

g. Hat das Hotel eine Bar?   _____

h. Brauchst du eine neue Kamera?   _____

i. Hat Augsburg eine U-Bahn?   _____

Ü 3.5) One of the two nouns in each of the following sentences is used with an article and one without any article. Indicate the noun without an article with an X and fill in the other gap with an article from the box below:

der	das	der	dem	das	der	eine	der

Example: Ergün kommt aus _____ Türkei und spielt gern _____ Klavier.
    →   Ergün kommt aus der Türkei und spielt gern X Klavier.

a. Frau Bäcker ist _____ Bankkauffrau und wohnt in _____ Ottomannstraße.

b. Ich finde _____ Leben als _____ Journalist ziemlich gut.

c. Er ist _____ Österreicher, aber sie ist _____ gebürtige Französin.

d. Karin ist in _____ Schweiz geboren und ist _____ Ärztin.

e. Nach _____ Abendessen werden sie _____ Gitarre spielen.

f. In _____ Schule lernen wir viel über _____ Großbritannien.

g. Obwohl _____ Christentum hier weit verbreitet ist, ist er _____ Buddhist.

CHAPTER 4
PERSONAL PRONOUNS AND POSSESSIVE PRONOUNS

⊘ CHECKBOX – WHAT IS A PRONOUN?

Pronouns (*Pronomen* in German) are words that "stand in" for a noun. This means they can be **used instead of a noun**, especially in instances where the noun in question has already been mentioned or the reference is clear from the context. Just like nouns, pronouns undergo declension according to **gender**, **number**, and **case**.

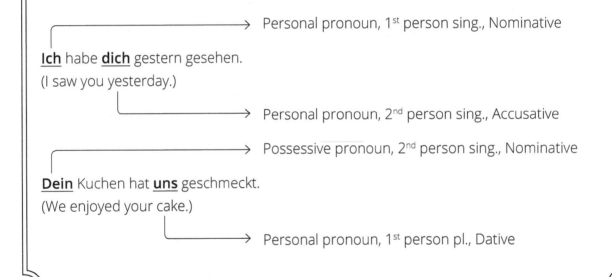

→ Personal pronoun, 1st person sing., Nominative

Ich habe **dich** gestern gesehen.
(I saw you yesterday.)

→ Personal pronoun, 2nd person sing., Accusative

→ Possessive pronoun, 2nd person sing., Nominative

Dein Kuchen hat **uns** geschmeckt.
(We enjoyed your cake.)

→ Personal pronoun, 1st person pl., Dative

○ **DIALOGUE – IN DER KNEIPE**

(Two friends named Ralf and Bernd are sharing their news over a beer at the pub. During their conversation, they are using several personal and possessive pronouns, which are highlighted.)

Ralf: Na, Bernd, wie geht **es dir**? Wie geht es **deiner** Familie? **Ich** denke oft an **euch**.

Bernd: Alles gut. **Meine** Tochter geht jetzt aufs Gymnasium. **Sie** ist sehr fleißig. **Unserem** Hund geht es nicht so gut. **Sein** Bein ist gebrochen.

Ralf: Was ist **ihm** passiert?

Bernd: **Sein** Bein blieb beim Aussteigen in der Autotür stecken. **Wir** haben **es** nicht bemerkt und die Tür zugeschlagen.

Ralf: O nein! Habt **ihr ihn** gleich zu **eurer** Tierärztin gebracht?

Bernd: Natürlich. **Unsere** Tierärztin hat sich gut um **ihn** gekümmert.

VOCABULARY LIST – IN DER KNEIPE			
Na, ... [*interj.*] [*coll.*]	So, ...	jmdm. passieren [*v.*]	(to) happen to sb.
Wie geht es ...? [*idiom*]	How is/are ...?	steckenbleiben [*v.*]	(to) get stuck
jetzt [*adv.*]	now	bemerken [*v.*]	(to) notice/realize
(das) Gymnasium [*n.*] (-ien)	*a type of secondary school*	zuschlagen [*v.*]	(to) slam shut
fleißig [*adj.*]	hard-working	(der/die) Tierarzt/-ärztin	vet
(der) Hund [*n.*] (-e)	dog	natürlich [*adv.*]	naturally
		sich um jmdn. kümmern [*v.*]	(to) look after sb.

4.1 PERSONAL PRONOUNS IN GERMAN

Personal Pronouns replace nouns that have already been mentioned. They are therefore used to avoid repeating a noun over and over. It is probably (at least in part) due to this useful feature that pronouns are one of the few English grammar items where cases and syntactic function still have a bearing on your word choice. While most other parts of speech do not undergo any or very few morphological changes in English, it is important to distinguish, for instance, between subject pronouns (I, you, he/she/it, we, they) and object pronouns (me, you, him, her, it, us, them). So as not to get into too much detail about these distinctions as regards English grammar, suffice it to say that it essentially comes down to the difference between *I love her* and *She loves me*, which could be significant.

In German grammar, personal pronouns are declined depending on **gender**, **number** and the **case** they are in. We use personal pronouns to talk about ourselves and to address other people. To this end, we also have to be mindful of the **grammatical person** that needs to be put in the relevant case. A more comprehensive introduction to the concept of grammatical person is provided in 🔖 **Ch. 6** but the following overview shall serve as a quick reference to aid comprehension:

Grammatical person is a concept that is used for referring to either oneself or to other people. There are three grammatical persons each for the singular and for the plural.

1ˢᵗ Person: → Used to refer to oneself (*"ich"* – "I") in the singular, or to a group of people to which the speaker belongs (*"wir"* – "we") in the plural.

Ich gehe in die Schule ⟷ *Wir gehen in die Schule.*
(I go to school.) (We go to school.)

2ⁿᵈ Person: → Used to refer to one person that the speaker is addressing (*"du"* – "you") in the singular, or to a group of people that the speaker is addressing (*"ihr"* – "you") in the plural.

Lebst du in Frankfurt? ⟷ *Lebt ihr in Frankfurt?*
(Do you live in Frankfurt?) (Do you [pl.] live in Frankfurt?)

3ʳᵈ Person: → Used to refer to any other, "3ʳᵈ-party" person or object in the singular (*"er/sie/es"* – "he/she/it"), or group of people or objects in the plural (*"sie"* – "they").

Er redet gern. ⟷ *Sie reden gern.*
(He likes to talk.) (They like to talk.)

With that, we are able to compile a declension chart of all the personal pronouns as they may appear throughout the cases and through all the grammatical persons in both singular and plural:

SINGULAR					
	1ˢᵗ Person	**2ⁿᵈ Person**	**3ʳᵈ Person**		
			Masculine	**Feminine**	**Neuter**
Nominative	*ich*	*du*	*er*	*sie*	*es*
Genitive	*meiner*	*deiner*	*seiner*	*ihrer*	*seiner*
Dative	*mir*	*dir*	*ihm*	*ihr*	*ihm*
Accusative	*mich*	*dich*	*ihn*	*sie*	*es*

PLURAL				
	1st Person	2nd Person	3rd Person	
Nominative	*wir*	*ihr*	*sie*	There is only one 3rd person plural pronoun for all three genders.
Genitive	*unser*	*euer*	*ihrer*	
Dative	*uns*	*euch*	*ihnen*	
Accusative	*uns*	*euch*	*sie*	

4.2 PERSONAL PRONOUNS AND CASES

The following section mostly uses sentences and examples from the dialogue at the beginning of this chapter to illustrate the use of personal pronouns through the different cases. An overview of the different cases and their functions is given in 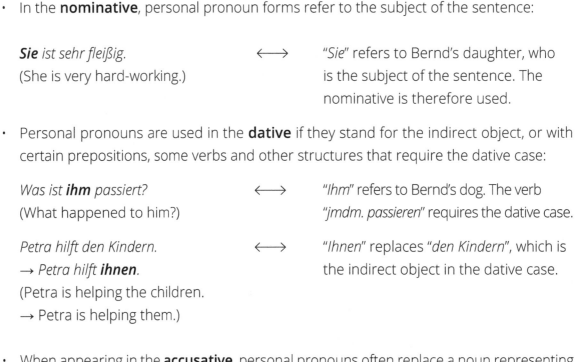 **Ch. 2**

- In the **nominative**, personal pronoun forms refer to the subject of the sentence:

Sie *ist sehr fleißig.* (She is very hard-working.)	⟷	*"Sie"* refers to Bernd's daughter, who is the subject of the sentence. The nominative is therefore used.

- Personal pronouns are used in the **dative** if they stand for the indirect object, or with certain prepositions, some verbs and other structures that require the dative case:

Was ist ***ihm*** *passiert?* (What happened to him?)	⟷	*"Ihm"* refers to Bernd's dog. The verb *"jmdm. passieren"* requires the dative case.
Petra hilft den Kindern. → *Petra hilft* ***ihnen***. (Petra is helping the children. → Petra is helping them.)	⟷	*"Ihnen"* replaces *"den Kindern"*, which is the indirect object in the dative case.

- When appearing in the **accusative**, personal pronouns often replace a noun representing the direct object or they follow a preposition that requires the accusative:

Ich denke oft an ***euch***. (I often think of you guys.)	⟷	*"Euch"* refers to Bernd and his family. The verb *"an jmdn. denken"* requires the accusative case because of the preposition *"an"*.
Ich liebe ***dich***. (I love you.)	⟷	*"Dich"* is the direct object and therefore in the accusative case.

- Personal pronouns in the **genitive** have fallen out of use in contemporary German. They sometimes still appear in literary texts, fixed phrases or religious prayers:

*Wir gedenken **seiner**.*
(We commemorate him.)

$\longleftrightarrow$

"*Seiner*" is the genitive of the personal pronoun "*er*". It is used because of the somewhat dated verb construction with "*gedenken*", which requires the genitive.

*Herr, erbarme dich **unser**!*
(Lord, have mercy on us!)

$\longleftrightarrow$

"*Unser*" is the genitive of the personal pronoun "*wir*". It is used because of the verb construction with "*erbarmen*", which requires the genitive.

4.3. SPECIAL USE OF THE PRONOUN *ES*

PRONOMEN "ES"

Es regnet.   **Es riecht hier gut.**   **Es ist 3 Uhr.**

The personal pronoun "*es*" deserves special attention since it has a broader range of uses than the other personal pronouns. As we have seen in the preceding sections, "*es*" is the neuter personal pronoun in the nominative and accusative of the 3rd person singular:

Nominative: *Das ist mein Haus. Es ist sehr groß.*
                      (This is my house. It is very big.)

Accusative: *Das ist mein Haus. Ich habe es gerade gekauft.*
                      (This is my house. I have just bought it.)

However, the following uses also apply to the German personal pronoun "es":

- Some **verbs** are frequently used together with "es". This is especially true of verbs relating to **time** or the **weather**. Several **fixed expressions** also require "es":

regnen (to rain)	*Heute regnet **es**.* (It is raining today.)
schneien (to snow)	*Morgen schneit **es**.* (It's going to snow tomorrow.)
Es ist _ Uhr (It is … o'clock)	***Es** ist 12 Uhr.* (It is 12 o'clock.)
es heißt (people say …)	***Es** heißt, er sei im Gefängnis.* (People say he's in prison.)
es geht (How is/are …)	*Wie geht **es** dir?* (How are you?)

- "*Es*" can **replace a noun** in the nominative if the subject carrying out the action is **unknown** or **not important**:

Der Postbote klingelt an der Tür.   →   ***Es** klingelt an der Tür.*
(The mailman is ringing the doorbell.)   (The doorbell is ringing.)

- If an **active** sentence consists of only an **impersonal nominative** ("*man*") and a **verb**, then "*es*" **replaces the nominative in a passive construction**. For more information about active and passive constructions see 📎 **Ch. 12**.

Active: *Man arbeitet.*   →   Passive: ***Es** wird gearbeitet.*
            (People are working.)   (Work is being done,)

- "*Es*" can refer to an entire preceding sentence:

*Ich war auf Bali im Urlaub. **Es** war wunderbar!*   →   "*Es*" refers to the whole
(I have been on vacation in Bali. It was wonderful!)   vacation.

4.4 POSSESSIVE PRONOUNS IN GERMAN

The possessive pronouns indicate **ownership** of a thing, and they specify to whom a person or thing belongs. The term "pronoun" is actually a bit of a misnomer since possessives can be used in two ways: they may **accompany a noun,** or they **can replace a noun** and stand on their own. In cases where they accompany a noun they may more aptly be called "possessive articles" as they indeed share many of the characteristics of the **indefinite articles** *ein-eine-ein*, including their declension endings in the singular ⬙ **Ch. 3**. It is this type of possessive pronoun that this section outlines. An overview of the possessives in the "true" pronominal sense (i.e., where they replace a noun) is given in section 4.5.

The German possessive articles correspond to the English possessive adjectives "my, your, his, her, its, our, their". Here is a list of them for each grammatical person:

	SINGULAR	PLURAL
1ˢᵗ Person	*mein*	*unser*
2ⁿᵈ Person	*dein*	*euer*
3ʳᵈ Person	*sein / ihr / sein*	*ihr*

Possessive articles may accompany a noun and are therefore declined according to **gender**, **number**, and **case**. The declension through all the cases is the same for each of the possessive articles in the above table (i.e., for each grammatical person). We therefore use "*mein*" as an example in the declension chart below. However, "*mein*" could be swapped out for "*dein*", "*sein*", etc. and be given the same endings.

	SINGULAR		
	before masculine nouns	before feminine nouns	before neuter nouns
Nominative	*mein* *Hund*	*meine* *Tochter*	*mein* *Bein*
Genitive	*meines* *Hundes*	*meiner* *Tochter*	*meines* *Beines*
Dative	*meinem* *Hund*	*meiner* *Tochter*	*meinem* *Bein*
Accusative	*meinen* *Hund*	*meine* *Tochter*	*mein* *Bein*
	PLURAL		
	Before plural nouns the possessive articles take the same endings for all three genders.		
Nominative	*meine*	*Hunde / Töchter / Beine*	
Genitive	*meiner*	*Hunde / Töchter / Beine*	
Dative	*meinen*	*Hunden / Töchtern / Beinen*	
Accusative	*meine*	*Hunde / Töchter / Beine*	

The choice of which possessive article to use in a given situation is determined by who or what possesses the noun in question. Take a look at this sentence from the dialogue at the beginning of the chapter:

Meine *Tochter geht jetzt aufs Gymnasium.*

        → The ending "*-e*" for the possessive article *mein* is **feminine, singular, nominative** because the word *Tochter*, as used in this sentence, is feminine, singular, nominative.

However, possessive articles do not only refer to the noun that is "owned" (i.e., *Tochter* in the above sentence) but also to the "owner" (i.e., *meine*, which is the speaker, which is Bernd). This two-way dependence becomes clear when speaking about people in the **3**rd **person singular**: the **gender of the owner** determines whether **sein** or **ihr** must be used. The **gender, number and case of the "owned" noun** determine which **ending** must be added to the possessive article:

Bernd = masculine, therefore *sein-*

*Bernd hat sein**en** Hund zur Tierärztin gebracht.* (Bernd took his dog to the vet.)

Hund is a masculine noun and is used in the accusative singular
→ possessive article requires the ending "*-en*"

Finally, note that the possessive article **euer** is normally contracted to "**eur-**" when an ending is added (i.e., the second *e* is dropped):

*Habt ihr ihn gleich zu **eurer** Tierärztin gebracht?*

4.5 POSSESSIVES USED AS PRONOUNS

As mentioned in 4.4, possessives can be used to replace a noun entirely. This means that a possessive only becomes a "true" pronoun if it is **not followed by a dependent noun**. This distinction is important, not least because the endings for 'possessive articles' and 'possessive pronouns' differ for the nominative and accusative.

Nevertheless, a possessive pronoun needs to agree in gender, number, and case with the noun that it is replacing as that is its point of reference:

Ist das sein Haus?	→	*Ja, das ist **seines***	→	"*seines*" refers to "*Haus*"
(Is that his house?)		(Yes, that is his.)		(neuter noun, singular)
Du hast einen braven Hund. **Meiner** *hört nie auf mich.*			→	"*meiner*" refers to "*Hund*"
(You have a well-behaved dog. Mine never listens to me.)				(masculine noun, singular)

The following declension chart uses the pronoun *mein-* as an example but the same endings are added to the basic forms of all the other possessives *dein-, sein-, ihr-, sein-, unser-,* and *eu(e)r-*.

	MASCULINE	FEMININE	NEUTER	PLURAL (same for all genders)
Nominative	*mein**er***	*mein**e***	*mein**es***	*mein**e***
Genitive	*mein**es***	*mein**er***	*mein**es***	*mein**er***
Dative	*mein**em***	*mein**er***	*mein**em***	*mein**en***
Accusative	*mein**en***	*mein**e***	*mein**es***	*mein**e***

There are other types of pronouns, which are discussed in different chapters. Demonstrative pronouns are explained in ⋃ **Ch. 5**, reflexive pronouns in ⋃ **Ch. 10**, and a discussion of relative pronouns can be found in ⋃ **Ch. 17**.

✏️ EXERCISES

Ü 4.1) Complete the following sentences by filling in the correct personal pronoun in the nominative:

Example: Der Computer kostet sehr viel, aber _____ ist der beste.

→ Der Computer kostet sehr viel, aber **er** ist der beste.

a. Unser Auto ist nicht hier, weil _____ in der Garage steht.

b. Du hast doch einen Garten. Ist _____ groß?

c. Wir möchten bitte diese Suppe, aber _____ muss heiß sein!

d. Ich mag mein Haus, nur ist _____ leider zu klein.

e. Die Schuhe passen gut und außerdem waren _____ billig.

f. Wie viel hat der Laptop gekostet und wird _____ noch verkauft?

Ü 4.2) Replace the nouns in italics with the appropriate personal pronoun in the following text. Either the nominative, the dative or the accusative could be required:

Ein Junge fand im Garten eine Rose. *Die Rose* (_____) duftete wunderbar. Das gefiel *dem Jungen* (_____) sehr. *Der Junge* (_____) meinte: „Aus *der Rose* (_____) kommt ein so herrlicher Duft, sicher kann man *die Rose* (_____) auch essen. *Die Rose* (_____) schmeckt sicher so köstlich, wie *die Rose* (_____) duftet." Neugierig nahm *der Junge* (_____) einige Blütenblätter in den Mund. Ihr bitterer Geschmack überraschte *den Jungen* (_____). *Der Junge* (_____) verzog das Gesicht. „Betrügerin!", schrie *der Junge* (_____) und warf *die Rose* (_____) auf die Erde. „Mit deinem Duft hast du mich getäuscht!" Die Rose erwiderte *dem Jungen* (_____): „Wer mehr als Duft von mir erwartet, täuscht sich selbst."

Ü 4.3) Fill in the possessive articles with their correct endings. You may consult a dictionary if you are unsure about any of the vocabulary used. The required gender and case have been provided in brackets:

Wie wir unsere Nachbarn kennenlernten

a. _____ Postbote (m, Nom.) ist schon seit vielen Jahren in _____ Stadtviertel (n, Dat.) tätig.

b. _____ Lächeln (n, Akk.), _____ Freundlichkeit (f, Akk.) und _____ Fröhlichkeit (f, Akk.) mögen wir sehr.

c. _____ Job (m, Akk.) erledigt er immer sehr pünktlich.

d. Jeden Morgen um 10 Uhr wirft er die Post in _____ Briefkästen (Pl., Akk.).

e. Aber manchmal finde ich Briefe für _____ neuen Nachbarn (Pl., Akk.) in _____ Postkasten (m, Dat.).

f. Sie dagegen finden in _____ (m, Dat.) Kasten Briefe an _____ Adresse (f, Akk.).

g. Das ist nicht schlimm, wir geben ihnen einfach _____ Postsendungen (Pl, Akk.) und bekommen _____ Briefe (Pl., Akk.) von ihnen.

h. Auf diese Weise haben wir _____ neuen Nachbarn (Pl., Akk.) kennengelernt.

i. Jetzt laden wir sie gern zum Grillen in _____ Garten (m, Akk.) ein, und sie bitten uns zu Partys in _____ Haus (n, Akk.).

j. Wir freuen uns über _____ neue Freundschaft (f, Akk) und lieben deshalb _____ Postboten (m, Akk.) noch mehr.

Ü 4.4) Replace the noun with the appropriate form of the possessive pronoun:

Example:

Das ist das Fahrrad von Martin.	→	Das ist _____ .
Das ist das Fahrrad von Martin.	→	Das ist **seines**.

a. Wir nehmen das Auto von mir. → Wir nehmen _____ .

b. Ist das Bettinas Tasche? → Ja, das ist _____ .

c. Ist das Arnolds Mantel? → Ja, das ist _____ .

d. Das ist der Computer von Steffi. → Das ist _____ .

e. Sind das die Bücher von dir? → Ja, das sind _____ .

f. Das sind Susis und Margrets Bücher. → Das sind _____ .

CHAPTER 5
DEMONSTRATIVE PRONOUNS

⊘ CHECKBOX – WHAT IS A DEMONSTRATIVE PRONOUN?

Demonstrative pronouns (*Demonstrativpronomen* or *hinweisende Fürwörter* in German) are words like **dieser** ('this one'), **jener** ('that one'), **solcher** ('such'), and others, which are used for emphazising and "pointing out" a person or thing in context. They may either **accompany** a noun for emphasis or they can be **used in place of** a previously mentioned noun. Their pronunciation also carries a certain vocal stress and they are often positioned at the beginning of a sentence.

(This evening has been wonderful. We should have such evenings more often.)
*<u>**Dieser**</u> Abend war wunderbar. <u>**Solche**</u> Abende sollten wir öfter haben.*

Demonstrative pronouns accompanying "*Abend*" and "*Abende*"

(He didn't buy the expensive ring, but that cheap one.)
*Er kaufte nicht den teuren Ring, sondern <u>**jenen**</u> billigen.*

Demonstrative pronoun replacing "Ring" in the subclause

○ **DIALOGUE – BEGEGNUNG AM BAHNHOF**

(This dialogue features two friends, Ute and Lea, having a chance encounter at the train station. They get talking about one of their mutual friends. The demonstrative pronouns are highlighted.)

Lea: *Hallo Ute! Hast du etwa auch* **diesen** *Zug genommen?*

Ute: *Ja! Das ist ja witzig. Dann waren wir in* **demselben** *Zug. Was machst du so?*

Lea: **Das** *möchtest du wohl gern wissen? Mal* **dieses**, *mal* **jenes**. *Du kennst mich ja. Hast du eigentlich mal wieder was von Jörg gehört?*

Ute: *Nein, ich weiß nicht, wie es* **dem** *geht.*

Lea: *Hm, Okay. Ich glaube, ich habe ihn neulich mit* **dieser** *Karin gesehen. Kennst du die?*

Ute: *Vielleicht. Ist das* **dieselbe** *Karin, die bei dir in der WG gewohnt hat?*

Lea: *Ja, genau. Schon komisch, dass sich Jörg mit* **der** *blicken lässt. Ich glaube, die sind jetzt zusammen.*

Ute: **Solche** *Neuigkeiten erfahre ich auch immer nur durch dich …*

VOCABULARY LIST – BEGEGNUNG AM BAHNHOF			
(die) Begegnung [n.] (-en)	encounter	neulich [adv.]	recently, lately
(der) Zug [n.] (ꞏe)	train	vielleicht [adv.]	maybe, perhaps
witzig [adj.]	funny	(die) Wohngemeinschaft [n.] (-en) (short: WG)	group sharing a house/flat
kennen [v.]	(to) know (i.e., to be familiar with a person/ situation)	komisch [adj.]	strange, odd
		(sich) blicken lassen [v.]	(to) show one's face
		zusammen sein [v.]	(to) be together
wissen [v.]	(to) know (i.e., to have knowledge of sth.)	(die) Neuigkeit [n.] (-en)	news
glauben [v.]	(to) believe / think	erfahren [v.]	(to) find out

5.1 THE DEMONSTRATIVE PRONOUNS IN GERMAN

Demonstrative pronouns are words that serve to **emphasize** or more closely **identify** a person or thing within the context of a sentence. In spoken German, they are stressed more than, for example, the definite article and they are often placed at the beginning of a sentence. Demonstrative pronouns can either appear **in place of the noun** they are referring to (i.e., in a true pronominal sense) or they can serve as an article by **accompanying a noun**. A more detailed overview of the function and characteristics of pronouns is included in 📎 **Ch. 4**.

There are different German words which fall under the category of demonstrative pronouns, including the words *der*, *die*, *das*. Do not confuse these with the <u>definite articles</u> (📎 **Ch. 3**) since their declension differs in some instances. The **most important demonstrative pronouns** are:

- *der / die / das*

  *Von welcher Wurst möchten Sie einen Aufschnitt? – Von **der** da ("that one over there"), bitte.*
  (Which cold cut would you like? – This one, please.)

  In German, "da" can act as a spatial reference, so in this case the meaning becomes "that one over there.

- *dieser / diese / dieses*; *jener / jene / jenes*

  *Hast du **diesen** Film schon gesehen? – Nein, **diesen** noch nicht, aber **jenen**.*
  (Have you seen this movie yet? – No, not this one, but that one.)

- *derjenige / diejenige / dasjenige*

  Derjenige, *der das gesagt hat, soll bitte hervortreten.*
  (May the one who said that please step forward.)

- *derselbe / dieselbe / dasselbe*

  Er gab mir **dieselbe** *Antwort.*
  (He gave me the same answer.)

- *solcher / solche / solches*

  Ein **solches** *Haus können sich nicht viele leisten.*
  (Not many can afford such a house.)

5.2 THE DEMONSTRATIVE PRONOUNS *DER, DIE, DAS*

The demonstrative pronouns **der**, **die**, and **das** are used in order to avoid repeating a noun. They can refer to and replace a person, a thing, or even a whole clause or sub-clause. These demonstrative pronouns **must not be confused** with the definite articles (📎 **Ch. 3**), which have the same basic forms (*der, die, das*) but whose declension is somewhat different:

THE DECLENSION OF THE DEMONSTRATIVE PRONOUNS *DER, DIE, DAS*			
Singular			Plural
Masculine	Feminine	Neuter	same for all genders
Nominative der	die	das	die
Genitive dessen	deren	dessen	deren / derer
Dative dem	der	dem	denen
Accusative den	die	das	die

These demonstrative pronouns are often used for emphasizing or pointing out a particular person or thing (as opposed to the personal pronouns (📎 **Ch. 4**), which do not carry any emphasis). Such "stressed" pronouns frequently take the first position within a German sentence.

Was machst du so?	→	***Das** möchtest du wohl gern wissen.*
What do you keep yourself busy with?		I bet you'd like to know that.
Wie findest du die Schuhe?	→	***Die** finde ich sehr schick, aber ziemlich teuer.*
How do you like the shoes?		I think they are very fashionable, but rather expensive.
Was hältst du von Jörg und Karin?	→	*Mit **denen** will ich nichts mehr zu tun haben.*
What do you think of Jörg and Karin?		I no longer want to have anything to do with them.

When the demonstrative pronoun "*das*" is used in conjunction with the verb "*sein*", the resulting construction often points to a person, thing, or object. The adverbs "*hier*", "*da*", or "*dort*" can be added to such a construction.

*Papa, was ist **das** hier?*	→	***Das** ist ein Dosenöffner, mein Sohn.*
Daddy, what's that here?		That's a can opener, son.
Wer ist der Mann dort?	→	***Das** ist Herr Schulz, unser Nachbar.*
Who is that man over there?		That's Mr. Schulz, our neighbor.
Wem gehören die Stiefel dort?	→	***Das** sind meine.*
Whose boots are those over there?		Those are mine.

"*Das*" can also refer to an entire preceding sentence and may function as the nominative or the accusative.

Unser Hund ist gestern gestorben	→	***Das** ist sehr traurig.*	("Das" = **nominative**)
Our dog died yesterday		That is very sad.	
Jörg und Karin sind jetzt zusammen	→	***Das** habe ich auch gehört.*	("Das" = **accusative**)
Jörg and Karin are together now		I've heard that, too.	

The two genitive forms in the plural ("*deren*" and "*derer*") have different meanings. "*Deren*" points back at something that has already been mentioned. "*Derer*" points towards something that will be mentioned, often in a subsequent relative clause (📎 **Ch. 17**).

Meine Brüder und **deren** *Kinder besuchen uns nächstes Wochenende.*
(My brothers and their children are visiting us next weekend.)

→ *"Deren"* refers to the previously mentioned brothers.

Die Zahl **derer***, die sich scheiden lassen, hat zugenommen.*
(The number of people getting a divorce has increased.)

→ *"Derer"* refers to 'the people getting a divorce' in the subsequent relative clause.

5.3 THE DEMONSTRATIVE PRONOUNS *DIESER, DIESE, DIESES* AND *JENER, JENE, JENES*

Just like many other pronouns, the demonstrative pronouns "**dieser, diese, dieses**" and "**jener, jene, jenes**" can either stand **in place of a noun**, or they may **accompany a noun**. "*Dies-*" is used if a person or thing is **closer in space or time**, relative to the speaker. "*Jen-*" is used if a person or thing is more **distant** from the speaker in either space or time. As such, they correspond to English 'this' and 'that'. Both of these pronouns can be used within the same sentence in order to draw a distinction or comparison between two people or things.

Both pronouns have identical declensions, and the endings are the same as for the definite articles (📎 **Ch. 3**). The following table therefore shows the declension for "*dies-*", which can be switched out for "*jen-*" while adding the same endings.

THE DECLENSION OF THE DEMONSTRATIVE PRONOUNS *DIESER, DIESE, DIESES*			
	Singular		Plural
	Masculine	Feminine	Neuter	same for all genders
Nominative	dies**er**	dies**e**	dies**es**	dies**e**
Genitive	dies**es**	dies**er**	dies**es**	dies**er**
Dative	dies**em**	dies**er**	dies**em**	dies**en**
Accusative	dies**en**	dies**e**	dies**es**	dies**e**

"*Dies-*" is sometimes shortened to just "*dies*", without any endings. This is especially true when it does not refer to any particular noun, but to an **entire sentence** and the facts conveyed in that sentence.

> *Es regnete während unseres Campingausflugs.* **Dies** *war für uns eine Überraschung.*
> (It rained during our camping trip. This came as a surprise to us.)

5.4 THE DEMONSTRATIVE PRONOUNS *DERJENIGE, DIEJENIGE, DASJENIGE*

The demonstrative pronouns "***derjenige, diejenige***" and "***dasjenige***" consist of two words. The first part is comprised of the definite articles (*der, die, das*) and is correspondingly declined like the definite articles (◊ **Ch. 3**). The second part "*-jenig-*" follows the weak declension for adjectives (◊ **Ch. 18**). The demonstrative pronouns "*derjenige, diejenige, dasjenige*" refer to **a person or thing defined in a subsequent relative clause** (◊ **Ch. 17**), where more information about the person or thing is given. It corresponds to the English 'that (one), which/who'.

THE DECLENSION OF THE DEMONSTRATIVE PRONOUNS *DERJENIGE, DIEJENIGE, DASJENIGE*			
Singular			Plural
	Masculine	Feminine	Neuter	same for all genders
Nominative	der*jenige*	die*jenige*	das*jenige*	die*jenigen*
Genitive	des*jenigen*	der*jenigen*	des*jenigen*	der*jenigen*
Dative	dem*jenigen*	der*jenigen*	dem*jenigen*	den*jenigen*
Accusative	den*jenigen*	die*jenige*	das*jenige*	die*jenigen*

Ich möchte **denjenigen** *kennenlernen,* der *dieses Buch geschrieben hat.*
(I would like to meet the person who wrote this book.)

→ "*Denjenigen*" refers to "the person who wrote this book". This information is given in a relative clause introduced by the relative pronoun "*der*".

Diejenigen, die *zu viel rauchen, schaden sich selbst.*
(Those who smoke too much harm themselves.)

→ "*Diejenigen*" refers to "those who smoke too much". This information is given in a relative clause introduced by the relative pronoun "*die*".

5.5 THE DEMONSTRATIVE PRONOUNS *DERSELBE, DIESELBE, DASSELBE*

Just like *"derjenige, diejenige, dasjenige"*, the demonstrative pronouns *"**derselbe, dieselbe, dasselbe**"* consist of two words. The first part is comprised of the definite articles (*der, die, das*) and is therefore declined like the definite articles (📎 **Ch. 3**). The second part *"-selb-"* follows the weak declension for adjectives (📎 **Ch. 18**). The demonstrative pronouns *"derselbe, dieselbe, dasselbe"* refer to **a person or thing identical to one another**. They may also be connected to a relative clause (📎 **Ch. 17**), where more information about the person or thing is provided. They correspond to English 'the same (who)'.

THE DECLENSION OF THE DEMONSTRATIVE PRONOUNS *DERSELBE, DIESELBE, DASSELBE*			
Singular			Plural
	Masculine	Feminine	Neuter	same for all genders
Nominative	derselbe	dieselbe	dasselbe	dieselben
Genitive	desselben	derselben	desselben	derselben
Dative	demselben	derselben	demselben	denselben
Accusative	denselben	dieselbe	dasselbe	dieselben

*Dann waren wir in **demselben** Zug.*
(So, we were on the same train.)

→ *"Demselben"* indicates Ute's observation that she and Lea took the same train (cf. chapter dialogue). The dative is used since the preposition *"in"* requires it in this instance.

*Ist das **dieselbe** Karin, die bei dir in der WG gewohnt hat?*
(Is that the same Karin who used to share a flat with you?)

→ *"Dieselbe"* indicates that Ute is asking about the same person that Lea used to share a flat with (cf. chapter dialogue). This information is given in the relative clause starting with *'die'*.

5.6 THE DEMONSTRATIVE PRONOUNS *SOLCHER, SOLCHE, SOLCHES*

The demonstrative pronouns *"**solcher**, **solche**, **solches**"* are used for pointing out and referring to **people or things of a certain category**. They correspond to the English 'such (a)'. The declension of *solcher, solche, solches* is the same as for *dieser, diese, dieses*, except for the genitive singular masculine and neuter, which has the ending -**en**, not -es (as was once the norm).

THE DECLENSION OF THE DEMONSTRATIVE PRONOUNS *SOLCHER, SOLCHE, SOLCHES*				
	Singular			Plural
	Masculine	Feminine	Neuter	same for all genders
Nominative	solcher	solche	solches	solche
Genitive	solchen	solcher	solchen	solcher
Dative	solchem	solcher	solchem	solchen
Accusative	solchen	solche	solches	solche

Solche Neuigkeiten erfahre ich auch immer nur durch dich.
(I only ever hear of such news from you.)

→ "*Solche*" indicates that it is a particular kind of news that the speaker always learns from the person spoken to.

Einen **solchen** Wagen würde ich nie kaufen.
(I would never buy a car like that.)

→ "*Solchen*" indicates a particular kind of car that the speaker would never buy.

"*Solch*" can also be used without an ending, usually followed by an indefinite article (📎 **Ch. 3**). When used in this way, the speaker often conveys a sense of either indignation or praise.

Solch ein Unsinn!
(Such nonsense!)

Solch eine Meisterleistung!
(What a masterpiece!)

However, in colloquial speech, '*solch* + indefinite article' is often replaced by '*so* + indefinite article'. In the plural, simple *so* may be used, too, but this is not something usually found in written German.

Solch ein Unsinn!   So eine Meisterleistung!   Das sind so Probleme!

 **EXERCISES**

Ü 5.1) Each of the following sentences or sentence pairs contain either one or two demonstrative pronouns. Underline all the demonstrative pronouns you can find:

a. Hast du von Klaus gehört? Den habe ich schon lang nicht mehr gesehen.

b. Ich finde diesen Hut nicht schön, aber jener Hut gefällt mir gut.

c. Sie ist diejenige, die gestern einen Autounfall hatte.

d. Schön, dass du hier bist. Das ist eine solche Überraschung!

e. Dasselbe habe ich dir gestern schon am Telefon gesagt.

f. Dieses Foto habe ich gemacht, aber jenes Foto hat meine Frau gemacht.

g. Karin trifft ihre Schwester und deren Mann.

h. Das sind alles Laptops derselben Marke.

i. Kennst du diesen Mann? Der kommt mir bekannt vor.

j. Tanja und Anke? Mit denen habe ich erst gestern Kaffee getrunken.

Ü 5.2) Supply the correct endings for the demonstrative pronouns *dieser/diese/dieses* and *jener/jene/jenes* in the following sentences. Make sure to apply the correct ending according to number, gender, and case.

a. Dies_____ Pullover gefällt mir nicht, aber jen_____ sieht schön aus.

b. Ich habe dies_____ Frau hier schon einmal gesehen, aber jen_____ noch nicht.

c. Dies_____ Gläser sind sauber, aber jen_____ müssen in die Spülmaschine.

d. Ich bin mit dies_____ Fluggesellschaft schon oft geflogen, aber von jen_____ habe ich noch nie gehört.

e. Mit dies_____ Dingen kenne ich mich nicht aus, aber ich bin ein Experte

für jen_____ *Dinge.*

Ü 5.3) The following sentences all require either a form of *derjenige/diejenige/dasjenige* or *derselbe/dieselbe/dasselbe*. Fill in the gaps.

    a. Das ist _____ Mann, den ich gestern im Supermarkt getroffen habe.

    b. Das sind alles Produkte _____ Unternehmens.

    c. _____, die mit der Arbeit fertig sind, dürfen in die Pause gehen.

    d. Ich habe _____ Fehler zwei Mal gemacht.

    e. Ich werde in_____ Hotel übernachten, das am günstigsten ist.

    f. Sie geht mit _____ Jürgen aus, der mit dir in die Schule gegangen ist.

Ü 5.4) Match the sentences from the left column to the appropriate responses from the right column. Fill in the gaps with the correct demonstrative pronoun. Any demonstrative pronoun you are familiar with may be needed:

    1. Seit wann kennst du Klaus?

    2. Welches Kind hat sich verletzt?

    3. Welches ist dein Auto?

    4. Wem gehört der Laptop?

    5. Sollen wir uns einen Horrorfilm ansehen?

    6. Das Lied kommt mir bekannt vor.

    7. Wer bekommt einen Preis?

    8. Fährst du mit Karin nach Berlin?

    9. In jenem Winter vor 10 Jahren hat es viel geschneit.

    10. Mein Chef hat mich gefeuert.

    a. _____ dort drüben, auf dem Parkplatz.

    b. Ja, es ist _____ Lied, das auf der Party gespielt wurde.

    c. Nein, mit _____ fahre ich nirgends mehr hin.

    d. _____ eine Frechheit!

    e. Ja, aber in _____ Winter hat es noch kaum geschneit.

    f. _____ kenne ich seit einem Monat.

    g. _____, das mit dem Ball gespielt hat.

    h. Nein, _____ Filme mag ich nicht.

    i. Er gehört _____, der vorher nach dem Wifi-Passwort gefragt hat.

    j. Einen Preis bekommen _____, die alle Fragen richtig beantworten.

1)	2)	3)	4)	5)	6)	7)	8)	9)	10)

VERBS & VERB TENSES

Verbs are one of the most important parts of a language, and German verbs are no exception. They are used to indicate action and states of being, and they are instrumental in forming the tenses of a sentence, which tell us when something happened or is happening.

German and English verbs have some similarities. For example, both languages make use of auxiliary verbs to form certain tenses, and both use verb conjugation to indicate the person, number, mood, and tense of a verb. However, there are some significant differences between the two languages, such as the greater number of verb forms used in German.

This unit looks at German verbs in more detail, including how to conjugate them, how to form the different tenses, as well as the function of reflexive and intransitive verbs. Studying the different chapters of this unit should equip you with a solid understanding of German verbs, such that you will be able to use them confidently in your everyday conversations.

CHAPTER 6
VERBS AND THEIR MAIN PROPERTIES

⊘ CHECKBOX – WHAT IS A VERB?

Verbs are words that express an **action**, **state**, or **process**. They are the most important part of a sentence and are used to convey something that a person, animal, object, or force of nature does. Verbs can be used in different tenses, such as **present**, **past**, and **future**, to indicate when the action is taking place. Verbs can also be used to express a command, a wish, or a possibility. In German, a verb is called *Verb* or *Tätigkeitswort* ("action word").

Peter <u>spielt</u> Gitarre.	Anna <u>ist</u> müde.	Er <u>öffnete</u> das Fenster.
(Peter <u>is playing</u> the guitar.)	(Anna <u>is</u> tired.)	(He <u>opened</u> the window.)
↓	↓	↓
Verb	**Verb**	**Verb**
describing an activity	describing a state of being	describing a process in the past

---

🎧 💬 TEXT – BEISPIELSÄTZE

(All the verbs – both finite and non-finite – are highlighted in the following compilation of example sentences.)

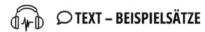

Franks Wecker **klingelt** jeden Tag um 6:30 Uhr.

Die Kundenanfragen **häufen** sich.

Das Abendessen **steht** auf dem Tisch.

Ich **lerne** Deutsch. / Wir **lernen** Deutsch.

Was **machst** du? / Was **macht** ihr?

Er **geht** / Sie **gehen** um 8 Uhr zur Arbeit.

Kaffee **trinkend liest** er oft die Zeitung.

Peter **ist** ein **liebender** Sohn.

Im Konzert **wurde** ein Stück von Bach **gespielt**.

Wir **haben** lange im Stau **gestanden**.

VOCABULARY LIST – BEISPIELSÄTZE			
(der) Wecker [*n.*] (-)	alarm clock	gehen [*v.*]	(to) walk, (to) go
klingeln [*v.*]	(to) ring	(die) Arbeit [*n.*] (-en)	work
(die) Kundenanfrage [*n.*] (-n)	customer query	trinken [*v.*]	(to) drink
(sich) häufen [*v.*]	(to) pile up	lesen [*v.*]	(to) read
(der) Tisch [*n.*] (-e)	table	(die) Zeitung [*n.*] (-en)	newspaper
lernen [*v.*]	(to) learn, (to) study	(das) Stück [*n.*] (-e)	piece
machen [*v.*]	(to) do, (to) make	(der) Stau [*n.*] (-s)	traffic jam

6.1. VERBS AND THEIR MOST IMPORTANT CHARACTERISTICS

In a general sense, verbs are the most important **link** between other **parts of a sentence**, and they establish relationships between them. For example, the sentence *"Ich ein Haus"* (I a house) is incomplete and does not make much sense. A verb is therefore required to complete the sentence:

Ich baue / kaufe / verkaufe / möchte ... ein Haus
(I am building / buying / selling / would like ... a house).

Verbs can describe **actions**, **processes**, or **states** and they indicate what somebody or something 'does' within a sentence. In German, verbs always start with a lowercase letter.

- **Actions**

  Franks Wecker <u>klingelt</u> *jeden Tag um 6:30 Uhr.*

  This sentence is governed by the verb '*klingelt*' and it refers to the subject '*Wecker*'. The alarm clock <u>rings</u>, which is an activity. Other verbs that express an activity include *spielen* (to play), *erzählen* (to tell), *laufen* (to run), *lernen* (to learn), and many more.

- **Processes**

  Die Kundenanfragen <u>häufen sich</u>.

In this sentence, the verb '*sich häufen*' describes a process since the increase in customer inquiries is not the result of any specific action but a cumulative development. Other verbs describing processes include *abnehmen* (to decrease), *altern* (to age), *verändern* (to change), or *wachsen* (to grow).

- **States**

Das Abendessen <u>steht</u> *auf dem Tisch.*

This sentence describes a state of being or a state of affairs (i.e., dinner being on the table). This means, the subject ('dinner') is not affected by any activity and the current situation is therefore not changing. Some other verbs describing states include *wohnen* (to live), *sich befinden* (to be situated in), or *schlafen* (to sleep).

6.1.1 Transitive and Intransitive Verbs

Just like in English, German verbs are divided into two basic categories: **transitive verbs** and **intransitive verbs.** A transitive verb is a verb that requires a **direct object**, such as, for example, 'to deny'. 'She denies' would be an incomplete sentence, since we are missing information about what is being denied. 'She denies any involvement', however, gives us the information that the verb 'to deny' requires.

An intransitive verb, on the other hand, **does not require a direct object**. An example would be the verb 'to sleep'. Saying 'I sleep' is considered a complete sentence that can stand alone. Some verbs can belong to both categories, such as 'to call'. It is possible to say 'He called', meaning that somebody placed a phone call, or one might say 'He called his name', expressing that somebody called somebody else's name.

Transitive and intransitive verbs are covered more closely in (📎 **Ch. 11**).

6.1.2 Personal Endings

In contrast to most English verb forms, German verbs normally take **personal endings**. These indicate both the person and the number of the dependent subject, since a verb must agree with its subject in **number** and **person**.

Verbs, like nouns, have **two numbers (singular and plural)** and **three persons (first, second and third)**. The singular number denotes a single person or thing. The plural number denotes more than one person or thing.

Since verbs thus interact with the subject of a sentence, it is important to know about the German **personal pronouns** (📎 **Ch. 4**). They often function as placeholders for other nouns in conjugation tables but can also appear as the actual subject within a sentence. The German personal pronouns are:

	SINGULAR	PLURAL
1st **person**	ich	wir
2nd **person**	du	ihr
3rd **person**	er / sie / es	sie / Sie

The **first** person denotes **the speaker**.

Ich *lerne Deutsch. /* Wir *lernen Deutsch.*   →   I / we learn German.

The **second** person denotes **the person spoken to**.

Was machst du? / Was macht ihr?   →   What are you doing? (sing.) /
                                         What are you doing? (pl.)

The **third** person denotes **the person or thing spoken of**.

Er geht / Sie gehen um 8 Uhr zur Arbeit.   →   He goes / They go to work at 8am.

6.1.3 Tenses

In German, as in other languages, verbs can appear in different **tenses**. This means that the verb can take on different forms to indicate the time when the action of the verb takes place, i.e., **present**, **past**, or **future** tense. Tense can be indicated by adding certain endings to the verb, as well as by the choice of the **auxiliary verb** (⚓ **Ch. 23**) used to form the compound tenses. The correct application of the auxiliary verbs *haben* and *sein* is especially important in this context.

6.1.4 Strong and Weak Verbs

When we change the form of a verb, as described in the previous paragraphs, we call this **conjugating** a verb. To conjugate a verb, it is important to distinguish between **weak verbs** (also known as *regular verbs*) and **strong verbs** (also referred to as *irregular verbs*). Conjugations for irregular verbs often differ from those of verbs with a weak conjugation, especially throughout the different tenses. Another important factor in the correct conjugation of verbs is the distinction between verbs with a **separable prefix** and those with an **inseparable prefix** (⚓ **Ch. 24**).

6.2. INFINITE VERBEN (NON-FINITE VERBS)

Non-finite verbs are verb forms that remain unchanged, since they are <u>not conjugated</u>. However, this also means that they cannot indicate a grammatical number or person on their own.

In German (as in English), there are three different non-finite verb forms: the ***Infinitiv*** (infinitive), the ***Partizip Präsens*** (present participle), and the ***Partizip Perfekt*** (past participle).

6.2.1 Infinitive

The **infinitive** is the basic form of the verb as you would find it in a dictionary. In English, this form is often listed together with the particle "to", as in '(to) eat' or '(to) live'. In German, the vast majority of verbs form the infinitive by adding the endings '-*en*' or '-*n*' to the **stem** of the verb:

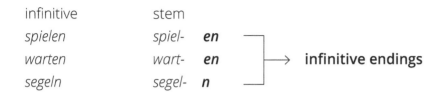

6.2.2 Present Participle

The **present participle** ('*Partizip Präsens*' or '*Partizip I*' in German) is sometimes also referred to as '*Mittelwort der Gegenwart*' (middle word of the present) because it is not quite a verb and not quite an adjective, as it were. One striking feature of the present participle is its usage in describing ongoing activities. In English, the present participle is easily recognized by its '-ing' ending ('playing', 'standing') and often used as the main verb in compound tenses ('I am playing') or as an adjective ('Peter is a loving son').

The German present participle is always formed by adding **-d** to the infinitive form of the verb:

*Kaffee trinken**d** liest er oft die Zeitung.*
(He often reads the newspaper while drinking coffee.)

Although this example uses the present participle in an adverbial way (it describes the way in which the main verb 'lesen' is carried out), it is more common to see it used as an adjective in German. In that case, the present participle will also take the **adjective endings**, as grammatically required for each scenario:

Peter ist ein zunehmendes Problem.
(Peter is an increasing/growing problem.)

However, getting into the different grammar rules for adjective endings is beyond the scope of this chapter. Further information on the adjective endings can be found in 🔗 **Ch. 18**.

6.2.3 Past Participle

The **past participle** is called *'Partizip Perfekt'* or *'Partizip II'* in German. Analogously to the *Partizip Präsens*, it is also referred to as *'Mittelwort der Vergangenheit'* (middle word of the past). In English, it can be recognized by its ending **-ed**, as in 'play**ed**' or 'liv**ed**'. There are irregular past participle forms as well, such as 'spok**en**' or 'do**ne**'.

The German past participle takes different forms, depending on whether a verb is **weak** or **strong**. While most regular verbs form their past participles in a predictable way, the past participles of irregular verbs must be memorized. Just like in English, the German past participle is used to form the **perfect tense** (◐ **Ch. 8**) and the **passive** (◐ **Ch. 12**), together with one of the auxiliary verbs **haben**, **sein** (perfect) or **werden** (passive) (◐ **Ch. 23**).

To form the past participle, German **weak verbs** add the prefix **ge-** and the ending **-t** to the stem of the infinitive verb:

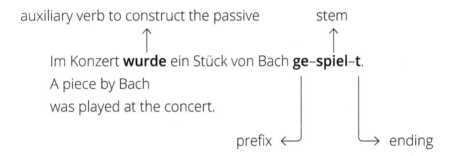

German **strong verbs** often undergo a change to their stem vowel, and occasionally to some of their consonants, when forming the past participle. The prefix **ge-** and the ending **-en** or **-n** are usually added to the stem:

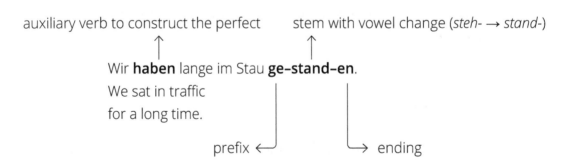

Further details about the past participle are discussed in the respective chapters about the passive, the perfect tense, and the auxiliary verbs (◐ **Ch. 8, 12, 23**).

📝 EXERCISES

Ü 6.1) Have a look at the following German verbs and decide if they indicate an action, a process, or a state of being. Put them in the appropriate column. You may consult a dictionary if you are unsure about any of the meanings.

gehen, einschlafen, leben, schlafen, bevorzugen, schreiben, essen, sitzen, verhungern, staunen, erfrieren, fragen, altern, drücken, sterben, kehren, bauen, glauben, wachsen, aufwachen, lieben

ACTION	PROCESS	STATE OF BEING

Ü 6.2) Decide if the underlined verbs in the following sentences indicate the 1st, 2nd, or 3rd grammatical person. Also determine if they are singular or plural.

Example: Irene und Mark <u>gehen</u> heute zum Einkaufen.   →   3rd person plural

    a. Er <u>sieht</u> am Abend oft fern.   _____

    b. Am Wochenende <u>besuche</u> ich meinen Freund.   _____

    c. Bei schönem Wetter <u>gehen</u> wir heute Abend noch joggen. _____

    d. Danke, dass du mir <u>hilfst</u>.   _____

    e. Kurt und Alex <u>spielen</u> gern gemeinsam Tennis.   _____

    f. Warum <u>sagt</u> ihr eurem Chef nichts davon?   _____

Ü 6.3) Have a look at the following German non-finite verb forms. Decide which of them are in the infinitive, the present participle, or the past participle and put them in the correct column.

warten, sprechend, gesungen, hören, gesagt, winkend, gelebt, lügen, gefüllt, essend, gebracht, gesucht, schreiben, lachend, zunehmen, gekommen, schlafend, grüßen

INFINITIVE	PRESENT PARTICIPLE	PAST PARTICIPLE

CHAPTER 7
THE GERMAN PRESENT TENSE

⊘ **CHECKBOX – WHAT IS THE PRESENT TENSE?**

The present tense (*Präsens* or *Gegenwart* in German) is a verb tense that is used for actions that are **currently happening**, for **habitual actions**, and **general truths**. In German, it can also be used to describe the future, as well as ongoing actions that started in the past. It is one of the so-called "simple tenses" as its formation does not require an *auxiliary verb* (📎 **Ch. 23**).

Ich esse gerade ein Stück Kuchen.
(I'm eating a piece of cake at the moment.)

→ Present tense form of "essen", to describe a current activity.

Sie ist seit Jahren arbeitslos.
(She has been unemployed for years.)

→ Present tense form of "sein", to describe ongoing activity that started in the past.

Wir fahren nächstes Jahr nach Spanien.
(We are going to Spain next year.)

→ Present tense form of "fahren", to describe future activity.

⏅ 🗩 **DIALOGUE – IM SUPERMARKT**

(Anna and Uli are having a chance encounter at the supermarket. They exchange a few words before continuing with their shopping. The verbs in the present tense are highlighted.)

Anna: Hallo Uli! **Kaufst** du auch gerade ein? Was **macht** ihr heute zum Abendessen?

Uli: Wir **kochen** mittwochs immer ein Nudelgericht. Kohlenhydrate **sind** auch wichtig. Außerdem **ist** meine Frau seit Jahren Vegetarierin.

Anna: Ach so! Mein Mann **ernährt** sich auch gesund. Aber ich **nasche** oft.

Uli: Na ja, man **muss** sich auch mal etwas **gönnen**. Wir **fahren** am Wochenende in die Berge.

Anna: Wie schön! Wir **planen** schon seit Monaten eine Urlaubsreise. Wahrscheinlich **fliegen** wir im Winter nach Thailand.

Uli: Das **klingt** gut! Also, viel Spaß noch beim Einkaufen!

VOCABULARY LIST – IM SUPERMARKT			
einkaufen [*v.*]	(to) shop/go shopping	(sich) etw. gönnen [*v.*]	(to) treat oneself
gerade [*adv.*]	at the moment	(der) Berg [*n.*] (-e)	mountain
kochen [*v.*]	(to) cook	seit [*prep.*]	since
(das) Nudelgericht [*n.*] (-e)	pasta dish	fliegen [*v.*]	(to) fly
wichtig [*adj.*]	important	klingen [*v.*]	(to) sound
(sich) gesund ernähren [*v.*]	(to) eat a healthy diet	viel Spaß! [*coll.*]	Have fun!

7.1 CONSTRUCTING THE GERMAN PRESENT TENSE

German is one of those languages that feature **weak** (also known as 'regular') and **strong** ('irregular') verbs (🔖 **Ch. 6**). While this distinction is especially important in forming the *Perfekt* and the *Präteritum* tenses, it also has an impact on the way we form the *Präsens* in German. Let us first have a look at the way regular verbs form the *Präsens*.

7.1.1 Regular Verbs

As you know, the infinitive ending for all German verbs is either '-en' or '-n'. In order to conjugate a verb, we need to separate the infinitive ending from the verb stem and replace it with the appropriate **personal ending**. The required ending is determined by the **subject** of the sentence, i.e., by the person, animal, thing, concept, etc. that carries out the action of the verb (also called the 'grammatical person'). There are three grammatical persons each for the singular and plural. Thus, the following table shows the German present-tense endings, using the regular verb '*leben*' as an example:

	ENDING	EXAMPLE		ENGLISH	
1st person (sing.)	**-e**	*ich*	*lebe*	I	live
2nd person (sing.)	**-st**	*du*	*lebst*	you	live
3rd person (sing.)	**-t**	*er/sie/es*	*lebt*	he/she/it	lives
1st person (pl.)	**-en**	*wir*	*leben*	we	live
2nd person (pl.)	**-t**	*ihr*	*lebt*	you	live
3rd person (pl.)	**-en**	*sie*	*leben*	they	live
Formal (sing. & pl.)	**-en**	*Sie*	*leben*	you	live

Note that the **formal address** '*Sie*' (with a capitalized 's') is the same for both singular and plural and that it takes the same ending as the 3rd person plural. In German, this is the way in which adults who are unfamiliar to the speaker, or people of authority, are formally addressed. Thus, instead of saying "*Herr Müller, wo lebst du?*" you would ask "*Herr Müller, wo leb**en Sie?***".

7.1.2 Strong Verbs

German **strong verbs** show one peculiarity in the present tense: They undergo a <u>stem vowel change.</u> This applies to those irregular verbs whose stem contains one of the following vowels or diphthongs:

a	becomes	*ä*
e	becomes	*i* or *ie*
au	becomes	*äu*
o	becomes	*ö*

These changes happen in the **2nd** ('*du*') and **3rd** ('*er/sie/es*') **person singular** only and they do **not affect the personal endings**. Take a look at the following table, which lists an example word for each vowel change:

STEM	ICH	DU	ER/SIE/ES
schlafen (to sleep)	*schlafe*	*schläfst*	*schläft*
helfen (to help)	*helfe*	*hilfst*	*hilft*
laufen (to run)	*laufe*	*läufst*	*läuft*
sehen (to see)	*sehe*	*siehst*	*sieht*
stoßen (to push)	*stoße*	*stößt*	*stößt*

There is no hard and fast rule as to whether a verb has a vowel change in the present tense and irregularities of this type must be learned by heart. However, as you gain more exposure to German through reading and listening to native speakers, you will develop a feel for the correct usage.

Further, it is advisable to commit the following irregular present-tense verb forms to memory, since all of these verbs are frequently used in German:

	KÖNNEN (to be able to)	WISSEN (to) know	SEHEN (to see)	TUN (to do)	SEIN (to be)	HABEN (to have)	WERDEN (to become)
ich	*kann*	*weiß*	*sehe*	*tue*	*bin*	*habe*	*werde*
du	*kannst*	*weißt*	*siehst*	*tust*	*bist*	*hast*	*wirst*
er/sie/es	*kann*	*weiß*	*sieht*	*tut*	*ist*	*hat*	*wird*
wir	*können*	*wissen*	*sehen*	*tun*	*sind*	*haben*	*werden*
ihr	*könnt*	*wisst*	*seht*	*tut*	*seid*	*habt*	*werdet*
sie/Sie	*können*	*wissen*	*sehen*	*tun*	*sind*	*haben*	*werden*

7.2 THE USAGE OF THE GERMAN PRESENT TENSE

The German *Präsens* is one of the most frequently used tenses due to its versatility. In fact, there are scenarios where it can be used not only to describe current actions and events, but also to express things with a connection to the past, as well as to the future. We will now have a look at those usage scenarios in some more detail. Thus, we use the *Präsens* in the following instances:

· **To express an ongoing activity or state:**

Kaufst du auch gerade ein?   (Are you also doing your shopping right now?)
Peter ist krank.   (Peter is ill.)

→ The activity is taking place at the moment. Note that, unlike in English, there is **no present progressive form** in German (e.g., '**doing** the shopping'). If the ongoing nature of an activity needs to be emphasized, we may include an adverbial time expression such as *gerade* (right now), *momentan* (currently), or *im Augenblick* (at the moment).

· **For habitual or recurring actions:**

Wir kochen mittwochs immer ein Nudelgericht.   (We always cook a pasta dish on Wednesdays.)
Der Zug fährt um 13:30 Uhr ab.   (The train departs at 1:30pm.)

→ The activity takes place regularly or according to schedule. Common signal words to indicate regularity include *immer* (always), *oft* (often), *häufig* (frequently), *selten* (rarely), *nie* (never).

- **To express something that is always true:**

*Kohlenhydrate **sind** auch wichtig.*   (Carbs are important, too.)
*Die Sonne **geht** im Osten **auf**.*   (The sun rises in the east.)

→ General truth.

- **For actions that started in the past and are still ongoing:**

*Meine Frau **ist** seit Jahren Vegetarierin.*   (My wife has been a vegetarian for years.)
*Ich **arbeite** hier seit 2005.*   (I have worked here since 2005.)

→ Action started at some point in the past and is still taking place. Note that these scenarios would usually require the present perfect (progressive) tense in English (e.g., 'I **have worked**'). The preposition **seit** is used to indicate both the point at which the action started ('*seit 2005*') as well as the time span during which the action has been going on ('*seit Jahren*').

- **For future actions that are planned or have been agreed to:**

*Wir **fahren** am Wochenende in die Berge.*   (We're taking a trip to the mountains at the weekend.)
*Wir **fliegen** im Winter nach Thailand.*   (We're going to Thailand this winter.)

→ There is a definite plan or intention to carry out the action. This usage is similar to how the present progressive can be used in English to express a future plan ('We're **going** to Thailand'). If the *Präsens* is used to indicate a future action it needs to be clear from either the context or by adding an adverbial time expression that we are talking about the future.

7.3 EXCEPTIONS

There are certain situations where exceptions to the above conjugation rules apply. Those exceptions are mostly due to facilitating easier pronunciation and/or spelling of the conjugated verbs.

- If the infinitive **stem of a verb ends in '-d'** or **'-t'**, an '**-e-**' is added before the present tense endings '-st' or '-t'.

  Example:

  warten (to wait) – *du wart**e**st, er wart**e**t, ihr wart**e**t*

- However, this rule does <u>not</u> apply if the verb in question undergoes a **vowel change**. Verbs undergoing a vowel change <u>and</u> with a **stem ending in '-t'** even drop the personal ending '-t' in the 3rd person singular.

  Example:

  laden (to load) – *du l**ä**dst, er l**ä**dt, ihr ladet* (vowel change a → ä)
  gelten (to apply) – *du g**i**ltst, er g**i**lt, ihr geltet* (vowel change e → i)

- If the **verb stem ends in s/ß/x/z**, the personal ending -s (2nd person sing.) is dropped.

  Example:

  tanzen (to dance) – *du tan**zt*** (not: ~~tanzst~~)
  küssen (to kiss) – *du küs**st*** (not: ~~küssst~~)

- If the **verb stem ends in -ie**, the -e- in personal endings is dropped.

  Example:

  knien (to kneel) – *ich kn**ie**, wir kn**ien**, sie kn**ien*** (not: ~~kniee~~, ~~knieen~~)

- If the infinitive ends in **-eln/-ern**, the -e in personal endings is dropped. Furthermore, the -e- contained in the stem of verbs ending in -eln can be dropped in the 1st person singular.

  Example:

  lächeln (to smile) – *ich läch**(e)le**, wir läch**eln**, sie läch**eln***
  wandern (to hike) – *ich wander**e**, wir wand**ern**, sie wand**ern***

 **EXERCISES**

Ü 7.1) Fill in the correct present tense verb forms:

    a. Hallo, wie ＿＿＿＿＿＿ (heißen) du?

    b. Alexander ＿＿＿＿＿＿ (wohnen) in Berlin.

    c. Er ＿＿＿＿＿＿ (gehen) jeden Tag joggen.

    d. Carmen ＿＿＿＿＿＿ (sprechen) Spanisch, Chinesisch und Deutsch.

    e. Worauf ＿＿＿＿＿＿ (warten) du?

    f. Wir ＿＿＿＿＿＿ (essen) gern beim Italiener.

    g. Ich ＿＿＿＿＿＿ (verstehen) sechs Sprachen.

    h. Was ＿＿＿＿＿＿ (sein) Sie von Beruf?

    i. ＿＿＿＿＿＿ (haben) ihr auch Hunger?

    j. Die Kinder ＿＿＿＿＿＿ (besuchen) am Wochenende ihre Großeltern.

Ü 7.2) Write down the present tense conjugations for the following verbs:

	MACHEN	WOLLEN	SEHEN	LESEN	WERDEN	SEIN
ich du er/sie/ es wir ihr sie/Sie						

Ü 7.3) Listen to the recording of these 10 verbs. All of them are in the 3rd person singular and are accompanied by the personal pronoun "*er*". Keep possible vowel changes in mind and write down the infinitive of each verb:

＿＿＿＿＿＿＿＿＿＿＿＿＿＿＿＿＿＿＿＿＿＿＿＿＿＿＿＿＿＿＿＿

＿＿＿＿＿＿＿＿＿＿＿＿＿＿＿＿＿＿＿＿＿＿＿＿＿＿＿＿＿＿＿＿

＿＿＿＿＿＿＿＿＿＿＿＿＿＿＿＿＿＿＿＿＿＿＿＿＿＿＿＿＿＿＿＿

CHAPTER 8
THE PAST TENSES

⊘ CHECKBOX – WHAT IS THE PAST TENSE?

Verbs have the ability to express things that happened in the past by being put into their **past tense forms**. There are **three past tenses** in German: the **simple past**, the **present perfect**, and the **past perfect** (*Präteritum, Perfekt, Plusquamperfekt*). They each refer to either a completed action in the past, or an action that happened before another past action. The *Präteritum* is a simple tense, meaning that it is formed by adding certain **endings** to the verb stem. The formation of the *Perfekt* and the *Plusquamperfekt* requires the use of **auxiliary verbs** (📎 **Ch. 23**).

Vor dreihundert Jahren **lebte** in diesem Schloss ein König.
(A king lived in this castle 300 years ago.)

→ *Präteritum* form of "*leben*", describing a **completed** past state of affairs. The simple past **ending** for the 3rd person singular (*-te*) is added to the stem.

Diese Geschichte **hast** du mir schon hundert Mal **erzählt**.
(You've told me that story a hundred times.)

→ *Perfekt* form of "*erzählen*", referring to an action that (repeatedly) took place in the past. The *Perfekt* is composed of the **conjugated auxiliary verb** "*haben*" (2nd person singular) and the **past participle** of "*erzählen*".

Nachdem die Gäste **gegessen hatten**, tranken sie reichlich Wein.
(After the guests had finished eating, they drank plenty of wine.)

→ *Plusquamperfekt* form of "*essen*". The "eating" had taken place before the "drinking", which also took place in the past.

🎧 💬 DIALOGUE – ALTE ZEITEN

(Anna and Lukas, childhood friends, unexpectedly run into each other at the supermarket. They share a warm exchange of memories before resuming their shopping.)

Anna: Erinnerst du dich an unsere Schulzeit?

Lukas: Ja, natürlich. Ich **habe** mich immer **kaputtgelacht**, wenn du zu spät **gekommen bist**.

Anna: O ja! Ich kann mich aber auch noch gut daran erinnern, dass du mir oft **geholfen hast**, wenn ich mir mal weh **getan habe**.

Lukas: Das **war** für mich selbstverständlich. Aber erzähl mal, was **hast** du nach der Schule **gemacht**?

Anna: Nachdem ich das Abitur **geschafft habe**, **bin** ich nach Berlin **gezogen** und **habe** dort **studiert**.

Lukas: Das klingt spannend. Ich **habe** neulich **gehört**, dass du jetzt Lehrerin bist.

Anna: Ja, das stimmt. Ich unterrichte jetzt an einer Grundschule. Und du? Was **hast** du **gemacht**, nachdem du die Universität **abgeschlossen hattest**?

Lukas: Nachdem ich mein Studium **beendet hatte**, **habe** ich ein eigenes Geschäft **eröffnet**. Es läuft gut.

Anna: Das freut mich zu hören. Es **war** schon immer klar, dass du mal etwas ganz Großes machen wirst.

Lukas: Danke Anna. Es **war** schön, über alte Zeiten zu reden.

Anna: Absolut. Hoffentlich sehen wir uns bald wieder.

VOCABULARY LIST – ALTE ZEITEN			
(die) Schulzeit [n.] (-en)	school time	(die) Lehrer /-in [n.] (-nen)	teacher
(das) Abitur [n.] (-e)	a set of examinations taken in the final year of secondary school	erinnern [v.]	(to) remember
		lachen [v.]	(to) laugh
(die) Universität [n.] (-en)	university	zu spät kommen [v.]	(to) come late
(die) Grundschule [n.] (-n)	primary school	helfen [v.]	(to) help
(das) Studium [n.] (Studien)	study	sich verletzen [v.]	(to) get injured
(das) Geschäft [n.] (-e)	business, store	weh tun [v.]	(to) hurt

8.1 INTRODUCTION TO PAST TENSES

German, like many languages, employs various tenses to describe **actions** or **events in the past**. These tenses not only provide a **temporal context** but also convey nuances in terms of **duration**, **sequence**, or the **relevance** of past events to the present.

In the provided dialogue between Anna and Lukas, we see instances of these past tenses in use, as they reminisce about their school days, discuss past life events, and share updates about their current lives. The dialogue aptly captures the essence of how these tenses are interwoven in everyday conversation.

The German language primarily utilizes **three tenses to describe past events**:

· **Simple Past (*Präteritum*)**

Often seen in written German, this tense describes **past actions** or **habits**. For instance, *"Im letzten Jahr machte ich Urlaub in Spanien."* (Last year I went on holiday to Spain.).

- **Present Perfect (*Perfekt*)**

  Commonly used in spoken German, it describes **actions that have been completed in the past but are connected to the present**. For example, *"Ich **habe** mich immer kaputtgelacht"* (I always laughed so hard).

- **Past Perfect (*Plusquamperfekt*)**

  This tense refers to **actions or conditions that were completed before another past action took place**. An example from the dialogue is *"nachdem du die Universität abgeschlossen hattest"* (after you had finished university).

8.2 THE SIMPLE PAST (*PRÄTERITUM*)

8.2.1 Formation of regular verbs in the simple past

The simple past tense in German is formed differently for regular and irregular verbs. For regular verbs, the stem of the verb is taken, and the appropriate ending is added. The stem is obtained by separating the ending "*-en*" or "*-n*" from the nominal form of the verb (❏ Ch. 6).

spielen   →   spiel~~en~~   →   spiel**te**
infinitive   *stem*   *simple*

	ENDING	**EXAMPLE**		**ENGLISH**	
1st person (sing.)	*-te*	*ich*	*spielte*	I	played
2nd person (sing.)	*-test*	*du*	*spieltest*	you	played
3rd person (sing.)	*-te*	*er/sie/es*	*spielte*	he/she/it	played
1st person (pl.)	*-ten*	*wir*	*spielten*	we	played
2nd person (pl.)	*-tet*	*ihr*	*spieltet*	you	played
3rd person (pl.)	*-ten*	*sie*	*spielten*	they	played
Formal (sing. & pl.)	*-ten*	*Sie*	*spielten*	you	played

8.2.2 Irregular verbs in the simple past

The *Präteritum* of irregular verbs is formed by **adding the preterite endings "-st", "-en" and "-t" to the stem**. The *I* and *He* forms do not have a personal ending. In addition, the vowel changes in most irregular verbs.

	PERSON	FORMATION	EXAMPLE 1 *"helfen"*	EXAMPLE 2 *"laufen"*
1st person (sing.)	*ich*	*Basis + Vokal*	*half*	*lief*
2nd person (sing.)	*du*	*Basis + Vokal + -st*	*halfst*	*liefst*
3rd person (sing.)	*er*	*Basis + Vokal*	*half*	*lief*
1st person (pl.)	*wir*	*Basis + Vokal + -en*	*halfen*	*liefen*
2nd person (pl.)	*ihr*	*Basis + Vokal + -t*	*halft*	*lieft*
3rd person (pl.)	*sie*	*Basis + Vokal + -en*	*halfen*	*liefen*
Formal (sing. & pl.)	*Sie*	*Basis + Vokal + -en*	*halfen*	*liefen*

Irregular verbs, however, do not always follow this pattern in the simple past. The stem may undergo a **vowel change**, and the **endings remain similar to the regular verbs**.

VERB	ICH	DU	ER/SIE/ES
sein (to be)	*war*	*warst*	*war*

8.2.3 Usage of the Simple Past

- **Describing past actions and events**

  The simple past is typically used in **written narratives** and **formal speech** to recount **past actions** or **events**. For instance, in a story or news report.

- **Narrating a sequence of events in the past**

  It can also describe a **series of actions** that took place in the past.

  For example: "Er **kam** nach Hause, **aß** zu Abend und **legte** sich schlafen".
  (He came home, ate dinner, and went to bed.)

- **Expressing habits or repeated actions in the past**

  Much like the dialogue's *"Ich habe mich immer kaputtgelacht"*, which suggests that Anna frequently laughed a lot, the simple past can describe **habits** or actions that happened regularly in the past.

- **Comparing the simple past with other past tenses**

  While both the simple past and the present perfect can denote past actions, the simple past is more detached and is often reserved for **formal, written German** or when **talking about distant events**. In contrast, the present perfect, as used in spoken German, connects the past event to the present.

- **Sentence structure and word order in the simple past**

  In main clauses, the conjugated verb is in the second position: *"Ich **spielte** gestern Fußball"* (I played football yesterday). In subordinate clauses, the verb moves to the end: *"Ich wusste, dass er **kam**"* (I knew that he came).

8.3 THE PRESENT PERFECT (*PERFEKT*)

8.3.1 Formation of the present perfect tense

The present perfect in German is formed using the **present tense of an auxiliary verb** (either *"haben"* or *"sein"*) and the **past participle of the main verb**. The choice between *"haben"* and *"sein"* depends on the verb and its semantics.

Conjugation of auxiliary verbs *"haben"* and *"sein":*

	HABEN		SEIN	
1st person (sing.)	ich	**habe**	ich	**bin**
2nd person (sing.)	du	**hast**	du	**bist**
3rd person (sing.)	er/sie/es	**hat**	er/sie/es	**ist**
1st person (pl.)	wir	**haben**	wir	**sind**
2nd person (pl.)	ihr	**habt**	ihr	**seid**
3rd person (pl.)	sie	**haben**	sie	**sind**
Formal (sing. & pl.)	Sie	**haben**	Sie	**sind**

8.3.3 Regular and irregular past participles

For regular verbs, the past participle is formed by adding "*ge-*" to the stem of the verb and then adding "*-t*" at the end.

spielen	→	**ge**spielt
kaufen	→	**ge**kauft
fahren	→	**ge**fahren

Irregular verbs often undergo a vowel change in the stem and end in "*-en*".

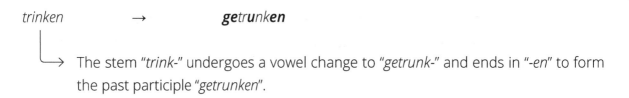

trinken → **ge**trunk**en**

→ The stem "*trink-*" undergoes a vowel change to "*getrunk-*" and ends in "*-en*" to form the past participle "*getrunken*".

Examples from the dialogue:

"*Ich* **habe** *mich immer* **kaputtgelacht**" – Here, "*haben*" is the auxiliary and "*gelacht*" is the past participle of "*lachen.*"

"*Ich* **bin** *nach Berlin* **gezogen**" – "*sein*" is used because "*ziehen*" indicates a change in position or state.

8.3.4 Usage of the Present Perfect

- **Describing recent or ongoing past actions**

  The present perfect is often used in spoken German to describe **events that occurred in the recent past** or **actions whose effects continue into the present**. In the dialogue, Anna's phrase "*Ich **habe** dort **studiert***" suggests that she studied in Berlin and that this fact has relevance now.

- **Expressing past experiences with indefinite time reference**

  Without specifying when exactly something took place, the present perfect is ideal.

  "Ich **habe** das schon einmal **gemacht.**"
  (I have done that before).

- **Talking about past actions with present relevance**

  The event may have taken place in the past, but its **relevance**, **result**, or **effect extends to the present moment**. Anna's statement about moving to Berlin and studying is relevant as it explains her current profession.

- **Differences between the present perfect and simple past**

  While both tenses discuss the past, the present perfect is more **prevalent in spoken German** and **relates past events to the present**. The simple past is more neutral and often found in written language.

8.4 THE PAST PERFECT (*PLUSQUAMPERFEKT*)

8.4.1 Formation of the past perfect tense

The past perfect tense, or *Plusquamperfekt*, indicates an **action that occurred before another action in the past**. It is constructed using the **simple past form of an auxiliary verb** ("*haben*" or "*sein*") and the **past participle of the main verb**.

Conjugation of auxiliary verbs "*haben*" and "*sein*" in the simple past for use in the past perfect:

	HABEN		SEIN	
1st person (sing.)	ich	*hatte*	ich	*war*
2nd person (sing.)	du	*hattest*	du	*warst*
3rd person (sing.)	er/sie/es	*hatte*	er/sie/es	*war*
1st person (pl.)	wir	*hatten*	wir	*waren*
2nd person (pl.)	ihr	*hattet*	ihr	*wart*
3rd person (pl.)	sie	*hatten*	sie	*waren*
Formal (sing. & pl.)	Sie	*hatten*	Sie	*waren*

8.4.2 Regular and irregular past participles

As in the present perfect, regular verbs form the past participle by prefixing the stem with "*ge-*" and adding "-*t*" to the end. Irregular verbs might have a vowel change and typically end in "-*en*."

Examples from the dialogue:

"*Was hast du gemacht, nachdem du die Universität abgeschlossen hattest?*"

⌐→ The part "*nachdem du die Universität abgeschlossen hattest*" employs the past perfect. Lukas had finished university (first action) before doing something else (second action).

8.4.3 Usage of the Past Perfect

- **Describing completed actions before a specific past point**

  It paints a vivid picture of an event that was completed at a certain point in the past.

  "Als ich ankam, **hatte** sie bereits **gekocht**".
  (By the time I arrived, she had already cooked.)

- **Expressing hypothetical past situations**

  This is evident in conditional sentences or with conjunctions like "*wenn*" (if).

  "Wenn du früher **gekommen wärst, hätten** wir noch Zeit **gehabt**".
  (If you had come earlier, we would have had time.)

- **Narrating indirect speech or reported events in the past**

  When you report what someone else said in the past, you might use the past perfect.

  "Er sagte, er **habe** das Buch **gelesen gehabt**".
  (He said he had read the book.)

- **Comparing the past perfect with other past tenses**

  While the simple past and present perfect tenses discuss actions in the past, the past perfect goes a step further to express actions that took place before these other past actions. It is the German equivalent of the English "had done" construction.

- **Sentence structure and word order in the past perfect**

  The auxiliary verb (in its simple past form) is positioned as per the rules of verb placement, and the past participle is placed at the end of the clause.

  "Nachdem ich **gegessen hatte**, ging ich spazieren".
  (After I had eaten, I went for a walk.)

8.5 COMMON MISTAKES TO AVOID

Understanding the intricacies of past tenses in German is crucial, but equally important is to be aware of the common pitfalls learners often fall into. Here are some of the frequent errors and how to sidestep them:

- **Choosing the Wrong Auxiliary Verb**

  Example:

  Incorrect: *Er **hat** nach Hause gegangen.*

  Correct: *Er **ist** nach Hause gegangen.*

  Explanation: *"gehen"* is a motion verb and therefore uses *"sein"* as the auxiliary.

- **Misformation of Past Participles**

  Example:

  Incorrect: *Sie hat das Buch **gelesenen**.*

Correct:	*Sie hat das Buch **gelesen**.*
Explanation:	The past participle of "*lesen*" is "*gelesen*", without an extra "*-en*" at the end.

- **Mixing Simple Past with Present Perfect**

Example:

Incorrect:	*(in a casual conversation)*: Ich **sah** den Film gestern.
Correct:	*(in a casual conversation)*: Ich **habe** den Film gestern **gesehen**.
Explanation:	In spoken German, especially referring to recent events, present perfect is more natural.

- **Incorrect Word Order with Past Perfect**

Example:

Incorrect:	*Weil ich **hatte** meine Schlüssel vergessen, konnte ich nicht das Haus betreten.*
Correct:	*Weil ich meine Schlüssel vergessen **hatte**, konnte ich das Haus nicht betreten.*
Explanation:	The auxiliary verb "*hatte*" should follow the past participle "*vergessen*".

- **Over-relying on One Past Tense**

Example:

Incorrect:	*(for a historical narration)*: Caesar **ist** im Jahr 55 v. Chr. nach Britannien **gekommen**.
Correct:	*(for a historical narration)*: Caesar **kam** im Jahr 55 v. Chr. nach Britannien.
Explanation:	For historical or formal contexts, the simple past is more fitting.

✍ EXERCISES

Ü 8.1) Complete the following sentences with the correct form of the verb in the simple past:

a. Ich _____ (lernen) Deutsch in der Schule.

b. Sie _____ (tanzen) gestern Abend auf der Party.

c. Wir _____ (arbeiten) letztes Jahr in Berlin.

d. Er _____ (spielen) Tennis jeden Samstag.

e. Du _____ (kaufen) ein neues Auto.

f. Sie _____ (wohnen) in einem großen Haus.

g. Wir _____ (hören) das Radio.

h. Er _____ (gehen) ins Kino.

i. Die Kinder _____ (sehen) den Film nicht.

j. Du _____ (schlafen) lange am Wochenende.

k. Sie _____ (lesen) das Buch.

l. Ich _____ (trinken) Kaffee.

m. Wir _____ (finden) den Schlüssel nicht.

n. Du _____ (kommen) spät nach Hause.

Ü 8.2) Use the correct form of "haben" or "sein" and the past participle of the verb to form the present perfect tense:

a. Ich _____ meine Hausaufgaben _____ (haben/sein + machen)

b. Sie _____ nach Paris _____ (haben/sein + fahren)

c. Das Buch _____ auf den Boden _____ (haben/sein + fallen)

d. Er _____ im Park _____ (haben/sein + laufen)

e. Wir _____ Pizza _____ (haben/sein + essen)

f. Du _____ im Meer _____ (haben/sein + schwimmen)

g. Sie _____ ein neues Kleid _____ (haben/sein + tragen)

Ü 8.3) Formulate sentences in the past perfect using the given verbs:

a. Sie _____ (haben/sein + sein) in Berlin _____ bevor sie nach München umzog.

b. Ich _____ (haben/sein + essen) das Essen _____ bevor es kalt wurde.

c. Die Kinder _____ (haben/sein + spielen) draußen _____ bevor es regnete.

d. Er _____ (haben/sein + trinken) den Tee _____ bevor er zu süß wurde.

e. Wir _____ (haben/sein + verlieren) den Ball _____ bevor wir nach Hause gingen.

f. Du _____ (haben/sein + lesen) das Buch _____ bevor der Film startete.

g. Sie _____ (haben/sein + schreiben) den Brief _____ bevor der Postbote kam.

Ü 8.4) Identify and correct the mistake in the following sentences relating to the past tenses:

a. Sie lernt Deutsch letztes Jahr.

_____

b. Er haben gespielt Fußball gestern.

_____

c. Das Buch ist fällt auf den Boden.

_____

d. Wir hatte geschwommen im Meer.

_____

e. Sie bist gefahren nach Berlin.

_____

f. Er hatten getanzt auf der Party.

_____

CHAPTER 9
THE FUTURE TENSES

⊘ CHECKBOX – WHAT IS THE FUTURE TENSE?

In German, verbs also hold the power to convey actions or events that will take place in the future by employing the **two future tenses**. These future tenses provide a means to express forthcoming actions or occurrences with distinct nuances. The first future tense, known as "*Futur I*", is formed by using the **present tense of the auxiliary verb "*werden*"** followed by the **infinitive of the main verb**. It signifies actions that will happen at a specific time or in the future. On the other hand, the second future tense, *Futur II*, is constructed by combining the **present tense of the auxiliary verb "*sein*" or "*haben*"** with the **past participle of the main verb**. "*Futur II*" is employed to describe actions that will have been completed by a certain point in the future.

○ **DIALOGUE – ZUKUNFTSPLÄNE**

(Julia and Max, colleagues in a professional setting, meet in the office cafeteria to catch up on their upcoming plans and exciting endeavors.)

Julia: *Max, **wirst** du die Konferenz nächste Woche **besuchen**?*

Max: *Ja, ich **werde** dort **sein**. Ich **werde** auch einen Vortrag **halten**.*

Julia: *Das klingt interessant! **Wirst** du über das neue Projekt **sprechen**?*

Max: *Genau. Ich **werde** über unsere Fortschritte und die nächsten Schritte **berichten**. Ich bin mir sicher, dass der Vortrag ein Erfolg **wird**.*

Julia: *Ich denke, das **wird** toll! Ich habe gehört, dass sich viele Leute darauf freuen.*

Max: *Danke, Julia. **Wirst** du eigentlich im Sommer Urlaub **machen**?*

Julia: *Ja, das **werde** ich. Ich habe vor, nach Italien zu fahren. Aber ich weiß nicht, ob das Wetter gut **wird**.*

Max: *Ich habe gelesen, dass es in Italien diesen Sommer sehr warm **werden wird**.*

Julia: *Das wird toll! Ich hoffe, ich **werde** die Chance **haben**, viele Orte zu besuchen.*

Max: *Mit Sicherheit! Wenn du zurück bist, **wirst** du uns sicherlich viele Geschichten **erzählen**.*

Julia: *Bestimmt! Und ich **werde** auch viele Fotos **gemacht haben**, die ich euch dann zeigen kann.*

Max: *Darauf freue ich mich schon!*

VOCABULARY LIST – ZUKUNFTSPLÄNE			
(die) Konferenz [*n.*] (-en)	conference	(die) Zukunftspläne [*n.*] (*pl.*)	future plans
(der) Vorträge [*n.*] (-e)	lecture	(der) Urlaub [*n.*] (-e)	vacation
(das) Projekt [*n.*] (-e)	project	fahren [*v.*]	(to) travel
neu [*adj.*]	new	(das) Wetter [*n.*] (-)	weather
(der) Fortschritt [*n.*] (-e)	progress	warm [*adj.*]	warm
(die) nächsten Schritte [*n.*] (*pl.*)	next steps	(die) Chance [*n.*] (-n)	chance
(der) Erfolg [*n.*] (-e)	success	(der) Ort [*n.*] (-e)	place
interessant [*adj.*]	interesting	(die) Geschichte [*n.*] (-n)	story
(die) Leute [*n.*] (*pl.*)	people	(das) Foto [*n.*] (-s)	photo

9.1 INTRODUCTION TO FUTURE TENSES

The future tenses in German are essential tools to articulate events that haven't occurred yet or to speculate about possible situations. While in many contexts, present tense verbs with adverbs can depict the future, using explicit future tenses adds clarity and precision.

German grammar introduces two forms of future tenses:

- **Future I (*Futur I*)**

  Primarily used to express **future events** or actions and make **predictions**.

- **Future II (*Futur II*)**

  Denotes **actions that will have been completed in the future**, often before another event takes place, or to make **assumptions about past events**.

9.2 THE FUTURE I (*FUTUR I*)

The Future I is formed using the **present tense of the auxiliary verb "*werden*"** followed by the **infinitive of the main verb.**

	WERDEN	**ENGLISH**
1st person (sing.) **2nd person** (sing.) **3rd person** (sing.)	*ich werde* *du wirst* *er/sie/es wird*	I will you will he/she/it will
1st person (pl.) **2nd person** (pl.) **3rd person** (pl.) **Formal** (sing. & pl.)	*wir werden* *ihr werdet* *sie werden* *Sie werden*	we will you will they will you will

Examples from the dialogue:

Julia: "Max, **wirst** du die Konferenz nächste Woche **besuchen?**"
(Max, will you be attending the conference next week?)

Max: "Ja, ich **werde** dort sein."
(Yes, I will be there.)

9.2.1 Usage of the Future I

- **Expressing future actions and events**

  Futur I helps to clearly express actions that will happen in the future.

  Max: *"Ich werde auch einen Vortrag halten."*

- **Making predictions and assumptions about the future**

  This tense is often used when the outcome is **uncertain** or **yet to be experienced**.

  Max: *"Ich bin mir sicher, dass der Vortrag ein Erfolg **wird**."*

- **Polite requests and offers in the future**

  Futur I can be used in situations like:

  "Würden Sie das bitte machen?"
  Would you please do that?

9.3 THE FUTURE II (*FUTUR II*)

„WIE NENNT MAN DIE ZEITFORM,
WENN ÖFFENTLICHE
NAHVERKEHRSMITTEL
PÜNKTLICH ANKOMMEN?"

„BUSKAMPERFEKT!"

Futur II is a compound tense that represents **actions expected to be completed in the future**. It's formed by combining the **auxiliary verb "*werden*" in the present tense**, with the **past participle of the main verb** and the **infinitive form of "*haben*" or "*sein*"**. The choice between "*haben*" or "*sein*" depends on the main verb and is in line with the rules of *Perfekt* tense formation (🔗 Ch. 8).

STRUCTURE			
Subject + *werden* + past participle + infinitive ("*haben*" or "*sein*")			

Ich	*werde*	*gegessen*	*haben.*
Subject	werden	past participle	infinitive

(I will have eaten.)

Du	*wirst*	*gelesen*	*haben.*
Subject	werden	past participle	infinitive

(I will have read.)

Er	*wird*	*geschlafen*	*haben.*
Subject	werden	past participle	infinitive

(He will have slept.)

9.3.1 Using the correct past participle in Future II sentences

Just as in *Perfekt*, some verbs use "*sein*" as their auxiliary. For these verbs, "*sein*" replaces "*haben*" in the formation of Futur II.

*Ich werde angekommen **sein**.*
(I will have arrived.)

*Sie wird gegangen **sein**.*
(She will have gone.)

*Ich werde den Brief geschrieben **haben**.*
(I will have written the letter.)

Example from the dialogue:

Julia: "*Und ich **werde** auch viele Fotos **gemacht haben**, die ich euch dann zeigen kann.*"

⌐→ This is a great example of *Futur II* where Julia predicts that by a certain time in the future, she will have taken many photos.

9.3.2 Usage of the Future II

(Please be aware that the Future II is rarely used in spoken German and is reserved primarily for written German.)

- **Describing actions that will be completed in the future before another event**

  Futur II sets the scene for actions or events that will finish before another specified point in the future.

  2   1

  Wenn du ankommst, **werde** *ich die* **Arbeit beendet haben.**
  (By the time you arrive, I will have finished the work.)

- **Expressing assumptions or speculations about past actions from a future perspective**

  When we are uncertain about a past event, we can use *Futur II* to speculate or make an assumption.

  Er **wird** den Zug **verpasst haben**.
  (He might have missed the train.)

- **Imagining hypothetical scenarios in the past from a future viewpoint**

  It's also used to imagine a scenario in the future where one looks back at a hypothetical situation in the past.

  Nächstes Jahr um diese Zeit **wirst** *du dir* **gewünscht haben***, heute angefangen zu haben.*
  (Next year at this time, you will have wished you started today.)

9.4 FUTURE I VS. FUTURE II

While both tenses address the future, their purposes vary:

Future I (*Futur I*):   Indicates events that **will happen** in the future.

Future II (*Futur II*):   Emphasizes actions/events that **will have been completed** by a certain time in the future.

FUTURE I	ENGLISH	FUTURE II	ENGLISH
Ich werde reisen.	I will travel.	*Ich werde gereist sein.*	I will have traveled.

The context determines the usage. *Futur I* is more immediate, often speaking of forthcoming events. *Futur II*, however, presupposes another event that sets a kind of 'deadline'.

9.4.1 Future Tenses in Combination

It's possible, especially in narration, to employ both tenses to convey a sequence of future events.

Julia: "Und ich **werde** *auch viele Fotos* **gemacht haben***, die ich euch dann zeigen kann."*
(And I will have taken many photos, which I can then show you.)

When narrating or planning, one might combine both tenses to illustrate a more intricate relationship between future events.

Wenn du morgen ankommst, **werde** *ich bei der Arbeit* **sein***, aber bis zum Abend* **werde** *ich* **zurückgekehrt sein***.*
(When you arrive tomorrow, I will be at work, but by the evening, I will have returned.)

9.5 COMMON MISTAKES TO AVOID

- **Misplacement of infinitive verbs**

  Especially in *Futur II*, remember that both the auxiliary verb (*haben/sein*) and the main verbs' infinitive come at the end. The auxiliary verb "*werden*" determines the position in the sentence.

- **Incorrect auxiliary verb choice**

  As with the Perfekt tense, ensure you use the correct auxiliary verb (either "*haben*" or "*sein*") when forming the *Futur II*.

- **Overusing the future tenses**

  In German, it's common to use the present tense with a future meaning, especially in casual conversations. Don't overcomplicate by always using the future tenses when they're not required.

✏️ EXERCISES

Ü 9.1) Complete the sentences using the Future I tense.

    a. Morgen _____ ich zum Arzt _____. (gehen)

    b. Sie _____ bald Urlaub _____. (haben)

    c. Nächstes Jahr _____ wir nach Deutschland _____. (reisen)

    d. Meine Schwester _____ das Buch später _____. (lesen)

    e. Die Kinder _____ draußen _____, wenn es warm wird. (spielen)

    f. Ich _____ nächste Woche ein neues Auto _____. (kaufen)

    g. Er _____ einen Brief an seine Freundin _____. (schreiben)

Ü 9.2) Choose the correct form of the verb to complete the sentences in the Future I tense.

    a. Er denkt, dass es morgen _____ (regnen) _____.

    b. Ich hoffe, dass du mir _____ (helfen) _____.

    c. Vielleicht _____ sie zur Party _____. (kommen)

    d. Er _____ es sicherlich nicht _____. (vergessen)

    e. Ich bin sicher, dass du _____ (gewinnen) _____.

    f. Meine Eltern _____ mich nächsten Monat _____. (besuchen)

    g. Sie _____ das Essen bald _____. (bestellen)

Ü 9.3) Formulate sentences in the Future II using the given verbs.

    a. Bis morgen _____ sie alles _____. (haben/sein + lernen)

    b. Ich denke, dass er den Schlüssel _____. (haben/sein + finden)

    c. Nächstes Jahr _____ wir schon _____. (haben/sein + reisen)

    d. Er _____ sein Auto _____. (haben/sein + verkaufen)

    e. Sie _____ bis 10 Uhr _____. (haben/sein + schlafen)

f. Ich _____ bis du zurückkommst. (haben/sein + kochen)

g. Wenn er ankommt, _____ sie schon _____. (haben/sein + essen)

Ü 9.4) Identify whether the sentences are in Future I or Future II.

a. Er wird das Buch gelesen haben. _____

b. Wir werden nach Italien fahren. _____

c. Sie wird gekocht haben. _____

d. Du wirst tanzen. _____

e. Ich werde den Brief geschrieben haben. _____

f. Wir werden morgen studieren. _____

g. Sie wird das Essen gemacht haben. _____

Ü 9.5) Fill in the gaps using the correct tense (Future I or Future II).

a. Wenn ich _____ (ankommen), _____ sie schon _____ (gehen).

b. Bis du _____ (zurückkommen), _____ ich meine Arbeit

_____ (beenden).

c. Er hofft, dass, wenn er älter _____ (werden), er viel _____

(reisen) _____ (haben/sein).

d. Wenn das Wetter gut ist, _____ ich _____ (spazieren gehen).

e. Sie hofft, dass sie bis dahin genug _____ (haben/sein + lernen).

f. Ich denke, wenn du ihn siehst, _____ (werden) er dir die Wahrheit

_____ (sagen).

g. Bis sie ankommt, _____ (werden) wir schon _____ (haben/sein
+ essen).

CHAPTER 10
REFLEXIVE VERBS

⊘ CHECKBOX – WHAT ARE REFLEXIVE VERBS?

Reflexive verbs play a vital role in **expressing actions that are performed by the subject onto themselves**. When using a reflexive verb, the subject becomes both the doer and the receiver of the action, highlighting a self-directed nature. To conjugate a reflexive verb, the appropriate **reflexive pronoun** must be used, which **corresponds to the subjects' person and number**. The reflexive pronouns are "*mich*" (myself), "*dich*" (yourself, singular informal), "*sich*" (yourself, himself, herself, itself, formal singular), "*uns*" (ourselves), "*euch*" (yourselves, plural informal), and "*sich*" (themselves, formal plural).

⊙ **DIALOGUE – TÄGLICHE ROUTINEN**

(Marie and Ben, close friends, find a moment to chat about their daily routines and how they unwind.)

Marie: Ben, wann stehst du normalerweise auf?

Ben: Ich stehe jeden Morgen um 7 Uhr auf. Und du, Marie?

Marie: Normalerweise stehe ich um 8 Uhr auf, aber heute bin ich um 6:30 Uhr aufgestanden, weil ich einen frühen Termin hatte.

Ben: Und **duschst** du **dich** gleich danach?

Marie: Ja, genau. Nachdem ich aufgestanden bin, **dusche** ich **mich** und dann **ziehe** ich **mich an**. Wie sieht dein Morgen aus?

Ben: Zuerst **wasche** ich **mich** und dann **putze** ich **mir** die Zähne. Nach dem Frühstück **kämme** ich **mir** die Haare.

Marie: Ah, ich **schminke mich** immer vor der Arbeit und am Abend **entspanne** ich **mich** gerne bei einem Buch.

Ben: Das klingt schön! Bevor ich ins Bett gehe, **bereite** ich **mir** ein leichtes Abendessen zu und höre Musik.

Marie: O ja, ich **freue mich** auch immer darauf, meine Lieblingslieder zu hören, bevor ich schlafen gehe.

Ben: Musik hilft mir wirklich, **mich zu entspannen**.

Marie: Ja, mir auch!

VOCABULARY LIST – TÄGLICHE ROUTINEN			
aufstehen [*v.*]	(to) stand up	schminken [*v.*]	(to) put on make-up
(der) Termin [*n.*] (-e)	appointment	entspannen [*v.*]	(to) relax
waschen [*v.*]	(to) wash	(das) Buch [*n.*] (Bücher)	book
(das) Frühstück [*n.*] (-e)	breakfast	(das) Abendessen (-)	dinner
(das) Haar [*n.*] (-e)	hair	(das) Lieblingslied [*n.*] (-er)	favorite song
(die) Musik [*n.*] (-)	music	schlafen [*v.*]	(to) sleep
(die) Zähne [*n.*] [*pl.*]	teeth	wirklich [*adv.*]	really
genau [*adv.*] [*coll.*]	right, exactly	schön [*adj.*]	beautiful

10.1 INTRODUCTION TO REFLEXIVE VERBS

Reflexive verbs in German are those **verbs that refer back to the subject of the sentence**, indicating that the **subject is performing an action on themselves**.

For instance, when someone says, "I wash myself", they are both the doer (subject) and the receiver (object) of the action. These verbs are vital for describing daily routines, personal care, and emotions.

In the provided dialogue, for example, Ben asks, "*Und duschst du dich gleich danach?*" (And do you shower right after?). Here, the reflexive verb "*duschen*" is used, with "*dich*" reflecting the action back to the subject "*du*".

10.2 CONJUGATING REFLEXIVE VERBS

Reflexive verbs in German are conjugated similarly to other verbs. The main distinction is the necessary reflexive pronoun. Whether the verb is regular or irregular, this reflexive pronoun remains essential.

For example, a regular reflexive verb like "*sich duschen*" (to shower oneself) and an irregular one like "*sich ziehen*" (to pull oneself) both require reflexive pronouns.

	WERDEN	**ENGLISH**
1ˢᵗ person (sing.) **2ⁿᵈ person** (sing.) **3ʳᵈ person** (sing.)	*ich dusche mich* *du duschst dich* *er/sie/es duscht sich*	I shower myself You (informal) shower yourself He/She/It showers himself/herself/itself
1ˢᵗ person (pl.) **2ⁿᵈ person** (pl.) **3ʳᵈ person** (pl.) **Formal** (sing. & pl.)	*wir duschen uns* *ihr duscht euch* *sie duschen sich* *Sie duschen sich*	We shower ourselves You all shower yourselves They shower themselves You (formal) shower themselves

Reflexive verbs, whether regular or irregular, will conjugate for tense similarly to non-reflexive verbs. The key is to ensure the reflexive pronoun corresponds with the subject.

PRESENT	*Er **freut sich** auf das Fest.*	He is looking forward to the party.
PAST	*Sie hat **sich** gestern **umgezogen**.*	She changed her clothes yesterday.
FUTURE	*Ich werde **mich** morgen **rasieren**.*	I will shave myself tomorrow.

10.3 REFLEXIVE PRONOUNS

Reflexive pronouns **refer back to the subject of the sentence or clause** and **indicate that the action of the verb returns to the subject**. They are used with reflexive verbs to convey actions that subjects perform on themselves. In German, these pronouns often come in a position **right after the conjugated verb**, but their position can change in certain sentence structures. German reflexive pronouns change based on the case they are in (Accusative or Dative) and the gender or number of the noun they refer to.

Reflexive Pronouns in Accusative Case:

	REFLEXIVE PRONOUN	ENGLISH EQUIVALENT
1st person (sing.)	*mich*	myself
2nd person (sing.)	*dich*	yourself (*informal*)
3rd person (sing.)	*sich*	himself/herself/itself
1st person (pl.)	*uns*	ourselves
2nd person (pl.)	*euch*	yourselves
3rd person (pl.)	*sich*	themselves
Formal (sing. & pl.)	*sich*	yourself (*formal*)

Table of Reflexive Pronouns in Dative Case:

	REFLEXIVE PRONOUN	ENGLISH EQUIVALENT
1st person (sing.)	*mir*	to/for myself
2nd person (sing.)	*dir*	to/for yourself (*informal*)
3rd person (sing.)	*sich*	to/for himself/herself/itself
1st person (pl.)	*uns*	to/for ourselves
2nd person (pl.)	*euch*	to/for yourselves
3rd person (pl.)	*sich*	to/for themselves
Formal (sing. & pl.)	*sich*	to/for yourself (*formal*)

*Er **wäscht sich**.*
(He washes himself.)

*Wir haben **uns** im Kino **getroffen**.*
(We met each other at the cinema.)

*Sie **freut sich** auf den Urlaub.*
(She is looking forward to the holiday.)

10.4 PLACEMENT OF REFLEXIVE PRONOUNS

When using reflexive verbs in German, the position of the reflexive pronoun is of paramount importance. Misplacing it can alter the meaning of a sentence or render it nonsensical. Let's explore the positioning of reflexive pronouns in various sentence structures.

- **In Main Clauses (*Hauptsätze*)**

  In main clauses, the <u>reflexive pronoun</u> typically sits **immediately after the conjugated verb**.

  *Ich **freue** <u>mich</u> auf das Wochenende.*
  (I am looking forward to the weekend.)

  *Sie **wäscht** <u>sich</u> jeden Morgen.*
  (She washes herself every morning.)

- **In Subordinate Clauses (*Nebensätze*)**

  When we have a subordinate clause, the <u>reflexive pronoun</u> is positioned **before the verb, at the end of the clause**.

  *Das ist der Film, den ich <u>mir</u> **angesehen habe**.*
  (That's the film I watched.)

  *Sie ist traurig, weil sie <u>sich</u> **verletzt hat**.*
  (She's sad because she injured herself.)

- **With Modal Verbs**

  When using reflexive verbs with modal verbs, the <u>reflexive pronoun</u> is placed **between the <u>modal verb</u> and the infinitive verb**.

  *Ich **<u>kann</u>** <u>mich</u> gut **erinnern**.*
  (I can remember well.)

  *Er **will** <u>sich</u> **verbessern**.*
  (He wants to improve himself.)

- **Separable and Inseparable Prefix Verbs with Reflexive Pronouns**

  For verbs that have separable prefixes, the <u>reflexive pronoun</u> comes **between the verb and its prefix**.

  *Er **zieht** <u>sich</u> **um**.*
  (He changes his clothes.)

  *Sie **reißt** <u>sich</u> **zusammen**.*
  (She pulls herself together.)

However, with **inseparable prefix verbs**, the reflexive pronoun **follows the conjugated verb directly**.

*Sie **beschwert** sich über den Lärm.*
(She complains about the noise.)

*Er **verletzt** sich beim Spielen.*
(He injures himself while playing.)

- **In Questions**

The reflexive pronoun often **follows the subject in questions**.

*Warum freust **du** dich?*
(Why are you happy?)

*Wie fühlen **Sie** sich heute?*
(How do you feel today?)

SENTENCE TYPE	EXAMPLE	TRANSLATION
Main Clauses	*Sie rasiert **sich**.*	She shaves (herself).
Subordinate Clauses	*Das ist der Song, den er **sich** anhört.*	That's the song he listens to.
Modal Verbs	*Du solltest **dich** entschuldigen.*	You should apologize.
Separable Prefix	*Er setzt **sich** hin.*	He sits down.
Inseparable Prefix	*Sie verhält **sich** ruhig.*	She behaves quietly.
Questions	*Was kochst du **dir**?*	What are you cooking for yourself?

10.5 REFLEXIVE VERBS IN THE PRESENT TENSE

Reflexive verbs in the present tense follow the **same conjugation patterns as regular verbs**, with the added element of reflexive pronouns (🔗 Ch. 7). These pronouns match the subject and case of the verb they accompany.

Here's a breakdown of the conjugation pattern, using the verb *"sich freuen"* (to be happy/pleased):

	VERB CONJUGATION	REFLEXIVE PRONOUN	TRANSLATION
1st person (sing.) **2nd person** (sing.) **3rd person** (sing.)	*freue* *freust* *freut*	*mich* *dich* *sich*	*I* am pleased *You (informal)* are pleased *He/She/It* is pleased
1st person (pl.) **2nd person** (pl.) **3rd person** (pl.) **Formal** (sing. & pl.)	*freuen* *freut* *freuen* *freuen*	*uns* *euch* *sich* *sich*	*We* are pleased *You* all are pleased *They* are pleased *You (formal)* are pleased

*Ich **ziehe mich** jetzt **an**.*
(I am getting dressed now.)

*Wie **fühlt** ihr **euch** heute?*
(How do you all feel today?)

10.5.1 Daily Routines with Reflexive Verbs

Reflexive verbs are often used to describe **daily routines** since many of these actions are things we do to ourselves.

*Er **wäscht sich** die Hände.*
(He washes his hands.)

*Wir **putzen uns** die Zähne.*
(We brush our teeth.)

*Sie **kämmt sich** die Haare.*
(She combs her hair.)

10.6 REFLEXIVE VERBS IN THE PAST TENSES

In German, there are mainly two past tenses used with reflexive verbs: the **Simple Past** (*Präteritum*) and the **Present Perfect** (*Perfekt*).

Simple Past with Reflexive Verbs

Reflexive verbs conjugate in the Simple Past just like regular verbs (📖 Ch. 8). The reflexive pronoun remains **right before the verb**.

Using the verb "*sich erinnern*" (to remember) as an example:

	VERB	REFLEXIVE PRONOUN	TRANSLATION
1st person (sing.) **2nd person** (sing.) **3rd person** (sing.)	*erinnerte* *erinnertest* *erinnerte*	*mich* *dich* *sich*	I remembered You *(informal)* remembered He/She/It remembered
1st person (pl.) **2nd person** (pl.) **3rd person** (pl.) **Formal** (sing. & pl.)	*erinnerten* *erinnertet* *erinnerten* *erinnerten*	*uns* *euch* *sich* *sich*	We remembered You all remembered They remembered You *(formal)* remembered

Ich **freute mich** über die gute Nachricht.
(I was happy about the good news.)

Wir **erinnerten uns** an alte Zeiten.
(We remembered the old times.)

Present Perfect with Reflexive Verbs

In the Present Perfect tense, reflexive verbs use either "*haben*" or "*sein*" as the auxiliary verb (📎 Ch. 8). The reflexive pronoun is placed **right before the past participle**.

Here's a table showcasing the conjugation of the verb "*sich waschen*" (to wash oneself) in the Present Perfect tense, which requires the auxiliary verb "*haben*":

SUBJECT	AUXILIARY VERB	REFLEXIVE PRONOUN	PAST PARTICIPLE	TRANSLATION
Ich	*habe*	*mich*	*gewaschen.*	I have washed myself.
Du	*hast*	*dich*	*gewaschen.*	You *(informal)* have washed yourself.
Er/Sie/Es	*hat*	*sich*	*gewaschen.*	He/She/It has washed himself/herself/itself.
Wir	*haben*	*uns*	*gewaschen.*	We have washed ourselves.
Ihr	*habt*	*euch*	*gewaschen.*	You all have washed yourselves.
Sie/Sie	*haben*	*sich*	*gewaschen.*	They have washed themselves.

*Er **hat sich** die Haare **geschnitten**.*
(He has cut his hair.)

*Sie **haben sich** im Spiegel **gesehen**.*
(They saw themselves in the mirror.)

10.7 REFLEXIVE VERBS IN THE FUTURE TENSES

In German, reflexive verbs can also be used in future tenses. There are two primary future tenses: Future I (*Futur I*) and Future II (*Futur II*) (🔗 Ch. 9).

Future I with Reflexive Verbs

Future I is formed with the auxiliary verb *"werden"* and the infinitive form of the main verb. The reflexive pronoun is placed **between *"werden"*** and the **main verb**.

Using the verb *"sich freuen"* (to look forward to) as an example:

SUBJECT	AUXILIARY VERB	REFLEXIVE PRONOUN	INFINITIVE VERB	TRANSLATION
Ich	*werde*	*mich*	*freuen.*	I will look forward to it.
Du	*wirst*	*dich*	*freuen.*	You *(informal)* will look forward to it.
Er/Sie/Es	*wird*	*sich*	*freuen.*	He/She/It will look forward to it.
Wir	*werden*	*uns*	*freuen.*	We will look forward to it.
Ihr	*werdet*	*euch*	*freuen.*	You all will look forward to it.
Sie	*werden*	*sich*	*freuen.*	They will look forward to it.
Sie	*werden*	*sich*	*freuen.*	You *(formal)* will look forward to it.

*Er **wird sich** über das Geschenk **freuen**.*
(He will be happy about the gift.)

*Wir **werden uns** bald **sehen**.*
(We will see each other soon.)

Future II with Reflexive Verbs

For the Future II, the construction involves the use of the auxiliary verb *"werden"*, the past participle of the main verb, and another auxiliary verb (either *"haben"* or *"sein"*) in its infinitive form, based on the verb's requirement. With reflexive verbs, the reflexive pronoun is placed **between *"werden"*** and the **other auxiliary verb.**

Using the verb *"sich erholen"* (to recover) as an example, the construction for Future II is:

SUBJECT	AUXILIARY VERB "WERDEN"	REFLEXIVE PRONOUN	PAST PARTICIPLE	AUXILIARY VERB "HABEN" IN INFINITIVE	TRANSLATION
Ich	*werde*	*mich*	*erholt*	*haben.*	I will have recovered.
Du	*wirst*	*dich*	*erholt*	*haben.*	You *(informal)* will have recovered.
Er/Sie/Es	*wird*	*sich*	*erholt*	*haben.*	He/She/It will have recovered.
Wir	*werden*	*uns*	*erholt*	*haben.*	We will have recovered.
Ihr	*werdet*	*euch*	*erholt*	*haben.*	You all will have recovered.
Sie	*werden*	*sich*	*erholt*	*haben.*	They will have recovered.
Sie	*werden*	*sich*	*erholt*	*haben.*	You *(formal)* will have recovered.

Note: Not all reflexive verbs use *"haben"* in the Future II tense. Some, depending on their nature (such as movement or change of state), will use *"sein"*. However, *"sich erholen"* uses *"haben"* as it's not associated with movement or a state change in the same sense as verbs like *"fahren"* or *"gehen"*.

10.8 REFLEXIVE VERBS FOR RECIPROCAL ACTIONS

Reciprocal actions refer to **actions done by two or more people to each other**. In German, reflexive verbs can also be used to express such actions. This use creates a sense of "each other" or "one another" in English.

Differentiating Between Reflexive and Reciprocal Actions

REFLEXIVE ACTION	RECIPROCAL ACTION
The subject and object are the same. For instance, "*Ich wasche mich*" (I wash myself).	Two or more subjects perform the action on each other. For instance, "*Wir sehen uns*" can mean "We see ourselves" (reflexive) or "We see each other" (reciprocal), depending on context.

Examples of Reciprocal Verbs:

sich treffen (to meet):

Sie treffen sich jeden Sonntag.
(They meet (each other) every Sunday.)

sich verstehen (to understand each other):

Die beiden Schwestern verstehen sich gut.
(The two sisters understand each other well.)

sich helfen (to help each other):

Die Kinder helfen sich bei den Hausaufgaben.
(The children help each other with their homework.)

sich küssen (to kiss each other):

Sie küssen sich jeden Morgen.
(They kiss each other every morning.)

10.9 REFLEXIVE VERBS IN IMPERATIVE MOOD

Imperative mood in German serves the purpose of giving commands, making requests, or offering suggestions (⬇ Ch. 13). When dealing with reflexive verbs in the imperative, the reflexive pronoun typically **follows the verb**.

PERSON	VERB EXAMPLE: SICH SETZEN (TO SIT DOWN)	STRUCTURE	IMPERATIVE FORM
du	*Setz dich!*	Verb + *dich*	*Beeil dich!*
ihr	*Setzt euch!*	Verb + *euch*	*Beeilt euch!*
Sie	*Setzen Sie sich!*	Verb + *Sie sich*	*Beeilen Sie sich!*

sich beeilen (to hurry):

du: *Beil dich!*
ihr: *Beeilt euch!*
Sie: *Beeilen Sie sich!*

sich entspannen (to relax):

du: *Entspann dich!*
ihr: *Entspannt euch!*
Sie: *Entspannen Sie sich!*

10.10 REFLEXIVE VERBS IN SUBORDINATE CLAUSES

Subordinate or dependent clauses **add additional information to the main clause** and are typically introduced by subordinating conjunctions (e.g., *weil, wenn, obwohl*) (⬙ Ch. 21). When reflexive verbs are used in subordinate clauses, there are two key aspects to remember.

· **Word Order**

In subordinate clauses, the conjugated verb (and the auxiliary verb, if present) is moved **to the end of the clause**.

· **Reflexive Pronoun Placement**

The reflexive pronoun remains **next to its corresponding verb**, coming **before the conjugated or auxiliary verb**.

MAIN CLAUSE	CONJUNCTION	SUBORDINATE CLAUSE WITH REFLEXIVE VERB
Ich weiß,	*dass*	*du **dich** gut **fühlst**.*
Es ist toll,	*wenn*	*man **sich entspannen** kann.*

*Nachdem ich **aufgestanden bin**, **dusche** ich **mich** und dann **ziehe** ich **mich an**.*

✏️ EXERCISES

Ü 10.1) Conjugate the given reflexive verbs in the present tense:

a. Ich _____ (sich freuen) auf den Urlaub.

b. Du _____ (sich waschen) die Hände.

c. Sie _____ (sich erinnern) an ihre Kindheit.

d. Wir _____ (sich treffen) im Café.

e. Ihr _____ (sich langweilen) ohne Fernsehen.

f. Es _____ (sich lohnen) nicht.

g. (Sich setzen) _____ Sie (formal) _____ bitte!

Ü 10.2) Fill in the gaps with the correct reflexive pronoun:

a. Er hat _____ beim Sport verletzt.

b. Sie interessiert _____ für Kunst.

c. Sie (plural) freuen _____ auf die Party.

d. Ich putze _____ jeden Morgen die Zähne.

e. Es hat _____ schnell verkauft.

f. Ihr zieht _____ warm an.

g. Wir beeilen _____, damit wir pünktlich sind.

h. Er rasiert _____ jeden Tag.

i. Du solltest _____ mehr entspannen.

j. Sie (formal) können _____ hier ausruhen.

k. Das Kind wäscht _____ alleine.

l. Ihr habt _____ für das Konzert angezogen.

m. Die Katze putzt _____ nach dem Essen.

Ü 10.3) Match the reflexive verbs in Column A with their English meanings in Column B:

Column A	Column B
sich erholen	to get dressed
sich beschweren	to introduce oneself
sich entscheiden	to fall in love
sich vorstellen	to recover
sich anziehen	to complain
sich verspäten	to make an effort
sich bemühen	to decide
sich verlieben	to be late

Ü 10.4) Using the given reflexive verbs, complete the sentences describing daily routines. Ensure that you conjugate the verbs correctly based on the context:

a. Jeden Morgen _____ (sich duschen) Martin und dann _____ (sich anziehen).

b. Bevor sie zur Arbeit geht, _____ (sich schminken) Sandra.

c. Nach der Arbeit _____ (sich entspannen) ich _____ gerne mit einem Buch.

d. In der Mittagspause _____ (sich treffen) die Kollegen immer im Park.

e. Am Wochenende _____ (sich ausschlafen) Petra und Tom immer lange _____.

f. Abends vor dem Schlafen _____ (sich die Zähne putzen) die Kinder _____.

g. Bei Stress _____ (sich erholen) Herr Müller oft in der Sauna.

Ü 10.5) Read the following short dialogues. Based on the context, fill in the gaps with the correct conjugated form of the given reflexive verb:

a. A: Warum kommt Lisa zu spät zur Party?

B: Sie hat _____ (sich verlaufen) und findet den Weg nicht.

b. A: Wie fühlst du dich heute?

B: Ich _____ (sich fühlen) ein bisschen müde.

c. A: Wo trefft ihr euch vor dem Konzert?

B: Wir _____ (sich treffen) am Haupteingang.

d. A: Willst du nicht tanzen?

B: Nein, ich _____ (sich schämen) für meine Tanzfähigkeiten.

e. A: Warum schaut ihr den Film nicht?

B: Wir _____ (sich für etwas interessieren) nicht für Horrorfilme.

f. A: Warum hat Paul diesen Job angenommen?

B: Er _____ (sich auf etwas freuen) auf die Herausforderungen und Möglichkeiten.

g. A: Hast du Sarah gesehen?

B: Ja, sie _____ (sich sonnen) drüben im Garten.

h. A: Warum rennst du so?

B: Ich _____ (sich beeilen), weil mein Zug in 10 Minuten fährt.

Ü 10.6) Listen to the following short passages. As you listen, fill in the gaps using the correct reflexive pronoun or verb form.

a. Meine Schwester hat _____ heute Morgen sehr lange im Bad aufgehalten.

b. Peter und Maria wollen _____ in Berlin treffen.

c. In der Pause habe ich _____ ein Sandwich gemacht.

d. Die Kinder ziehen _____ schnell an, wenn es kalt ist.

e. Thomas freut _____ über das schöne Geschenk.

f. Wir setzen _____ neben die Großeltern im Theater.

g. Lisa, beeil _____! Der Bus kommt gleich.

h. Bei der Meditation versuchen viele, _____ zu entspannen.

CHAPTER 11
TRANSITIVE AND INTRANSITIVE VERBS

⊘ **CHECKBOX – WHAT ARE TRANSITIVE AND INTRANSITIVE VERBS?**

Verbs can be classified as transitive or intransitive, based on their usage and relation to the direct object in a sentence. **Transitive verbs require a direct object** to complete their meaning and convey the action performed by the subject onto something or someone else. On the other hand, **intransitive verbs do not take a direct object** and express a complete action without affecting anything else.

For example, the verb "*lesen*" (to read) is transitive, as it needs a direct object to make sense. We say "*Ich lese ein Buch*" (I am reading a book), where "*ein Buch*" (a book) is the direct object. In contrast, the verb "*gehen*" (to go) is intransitive because it doesn't require a direct object. We can say "*Ich gehe*" (I am going) without any additional object.

DIALOGUE – TAGESABLAUF UND HOBBYS

(Julia and Tim, friends enjoying a casual conversation, discuss their daily routines and hobbies. The dialogue takes place in the present tense.)

Julia: Tim, **hast** du heute schon **gefrühstückt**?

Tim: Ja, ich **habe** heute Morgen Brot mit Marmelade **gegessen**.

Julia: Ich **liebe** Marmelade! Aber heute Morgen **habe** ich nur Kaffee **getrunken**.

Tim: Du **trinkst** immer nur Kaffee am Morgen! Ich **verstehe** das nicht. Ich **schlafe** immer besser, wenn ich Tee trinke.

Julia: Wir **haben** alle unsere Angewohnheiten. Was **machst** du heute Nachmittag?

Tim: Ich **gehe** ins Kino. Und du?

Julia: Ich **lese** ein gutes Buch. Es **handelt** von einem Detektiv, der Geheimnisse lüftet.

Tim: Das **klingt** spannend! Ich **liebe** Krimis.

Julia: Du solltest es auch **lesen**! Vielleicht **leihst** du es dir später aus?

Tim: Sicher! Ich **freue** mich darauf.

VOCABULARY LIST – TAGESABLAUF UND HOBBYS			
frühstücken [*v.*]	(to) have breakfast	alle [*indef. pron.*]	all
(das) Brot [*n.*] (-e)	bread	handeln [*v.*]	(to) act
trinken [*v.*]	(to) drink	spannend [*adj.*]	exciting, thrilling
verstehen [*v.*]	(to) understand	lieben [*v.*]	(to) love
(der) Kaffee [*n.*] (-)	coffee	(der) Krimi [*n.*] (-s)	detective novel
(der) Tee [*n.*] (-s)	tea	ausleihen [*v.*]	(to) borrow

11.1 INTRODUCTION TO TRANSITIVE AND INTRANSITIVE VERBS

Transitive verbs inherently require a direct object to complete their essence. The crux of a transitive verb is its ability to **transfer the action onto something or someone**. For example, in the sentence, "*Er trinkt einen Kaffee*" (He drinks a coffee), "*trinkt*" is a transitive verb, and "*einen Kaffee*" becomes the direct object, clarifying what is being drunk.

Conversely, **intransitive verbs** can stand independently, without the need for a direct object. Their essence is self-contained. For instance, in the statement "*Er schläft*" (He sleeps), there's no indication of a direct object being affected by the verb. Here, "*schläft*" is intransitive, expressing a complete thought by itself.

Drawing from the dialogue, "*Tim, hast du heute schon gefrühstückt?*" exemplifies the intransitive "*gefrühstückt*", which doesn't necessitate a direct object. On the other hand, "*Ja, ich habe heute Morgen Brot mit Marmelade gegessen*" showcases the transitive "*gegessen*" with "*Brot mit Marmelade*" as its direct object.

TRANSITIVE VERB EXAMPLE	INTRANSITIVE VERB EXAMPLE
*Ich **esse** <u>den Apfel</u>.* (I eat the apple.)	*Sie **lacht**.* (She laughs.)
*Er **liebt** <u>seine Frau</u>.* (He loves his wife.)	*Das Baby **weint**.* (The baby cries.)
*Du **öffnest** <u>das Fenster</u>.* (You open the window.)	*Der Hund **rennt**.* (The dog runs.)

11.2 TRANSITIVE VERBS AND DIRECT OBJECTS

Transitive verbs are foundational to understanding sentence construction. Their name itself suggests their function. "Transitive" comes from the Latin verb "*transire*", which means "to pass over". Essentially, the action of the verb passes over to the object.

- **Word Order Variations in Sentences with Direct Objects**

  In German, the basic word order is Subject–Verb–Direct Object (SVO). For instance: "*Der Junge* (subject) **isst** (verb) *Pizza* (direct object)."

- **Strategies for Identifying Direct Objects in Sentences**

  Direct objects answer the questions *"wen?"* (whom?) or *"was?"* (what?) with regard to the verb. They can often be identified by their case; they usually appear in the accusative case in German.

- **Conjugation of Transitive Verbs in Different Tenses**

  Just like other verbs, transitive verbs are conjugated based on their tenses and the subject. The presence of a direct object doesn't change the conjugation of the verb itself.

VERB	SENTENCE EXAMPLE	DIRECT OBJECT
kaufen (to buy)	*Ich kaufe **ein Buch**.*	*ein Buch* (a book)
sehen (to see)	*Sie sieht **den Film**.*	*den Film* (the movie)
hören (to hear)	*Er hört **die Musik**.*	*die Musik* (the music)

*Sie **schreibt** einen langen Brief.* →	*"schreibt"* acts as a transitive verb, having *"einen langen Brief"* serve as the direct object of the action.
*Er **trinkt** einen heißen Tee.* →	In this case, *"trinkt"* functions as a transitive verb, with *"einen heißen Tee"* being the object that receives the action.
*Wir **kaufen** ein neues Auto.* →	Here, the verb *"kaufen"* is transitive, and it takes *"ein neues Auto"* as the object directly affected by the action.

11.3 TRANSITIVE VERBS AND DIRECT OBJECTS

Intransitive verbs are unique in that they don't require a direct object to convey a full meaning. This is essential for learners of German to understand, as these verbs often follow different rules and structures compared to their transitive counterparts.

- **Positioning of Intransitive Verbs in Sentences**

  In a main clause, intransitive verbs typically **follow the subject**, conforming to the Subject-Verb order. In a compound tense, the auxiliary verb (*haben or sein*) usually occupies the second position, pushing the intransitive verb to the end, often in its past participle form.

- **Using Intransitive Verbs with Reflexive Pronouns**

  Some intransitive verbs are reflexive, meaning the action is done to oneself. In these cases, a reflexive pronoun is used (🔗 Ch. 10). For instance: *"Ich freue mich"* (I am happy). Here, *"freuen"* is an intransitive verb used reflexively.

- **Ambitransitive Verbs and Their Meaning Variations**

  Ambitransitive verbs can be both transitive and intransitive depending on the context. Their meaning can slightly vary based on how they're used. For example, *"essen"* can be transitive as in *"Ich esse den Apfel"* (I eat the apple) or intransitive as in *"Ich esse"* (I eat).

INTRANSITIVE VERB	WITH REFLEXIVE PRONOUN	AMBITRANSITIVE VERB USAGE
Er **schläft**. (He sleeps.)	*Sie* **erinnert sich**. (She remembers.)	*Ich* **esse**. (I eat.) *Ich* **esse** *Pfannkuchen.* (I eat pancakes.)
Die Blumen **blühen**. (The flowers bloom.)	*Er* **freut sich**. (He is happy.)	*Sie* **läuft**. (She runs.) *Sie* **läuft** *den Marathon.* (She runs the marathon.)

11.4 DITRANSITIVE VERBS

Ditransitive verbs are special because they require not just one, but **two objects to convey a full meaning** – a direct object and an indirect object. This characteristic presents an interesting dimension to sentence formation in German.

Ditransitive verbs inherently carry the action across to two different objects. This means, in one action, there is a receiver (indirect object) and something being received (direct object). A classic example is the verb *"geben"* (to give). *"Ich gebe <u>ihm</u> <u>das Buch</u>"* (I give him the book). Here, *"Buch"* is the direct object, and *"ihm"* (to him) is the indirect object.

Some ditransitive verbs use prepositions to introduce one or both of their objects, adding to the complexity of the sentence.

Ich vertraue <u>dem Mann</u> mit <u>meinem Geheimnis</u>.

          dative   accusative

(I trust the man with my secret).

VERB	SENTENCE	DIRECT OBJECT	INDIRECT OBJECT
geben (to give)	*Ich gebe <u>ihr</u> **das Buch**.*	*das Buch*	*ihr*
sagen (to tell)	*Er sagt <u>mir</u> **die Wahrheit**.*	*die Wahrheit*	*mir*
kaufen (to buy)	*Sie kauft <u>ihrem Bruder</u> **ein Geschenk**.*	*ein Geschenk*	*ihrem Bruder*

11.5 PASSIVE VOICE WITH TRANSITIVE VERBS

In German, as in many languages, the passive voice is a way of shifting the focus from the agent (the doer of the action) to the recipient of the action (often the direct object in the active voice) (🔖 Ch. 12). When using passive constructions in German, the verb *"werden"* becomes crucial.

The passive in German is formed with the **auxiliary verb *"werden"*** plus the **past participle of the main verb**. In passive constructions, the **verb always remains in its infinitive form at the end of the clause**. The verb *"werden"* is conjugated in accordance with the subject of the sentence. The past participle of the main verb is then added at the end of the clause. In an active voice sentence, the subject performs the action. In passive voice, the focus is shifted to the receiver of the action.

Active: *Der Künstler <u>malt</u> das Bild.*
(The artist paints the picture.)

↓

Passive: *Das Bild <u>wird</u> vom Künstler <u>gemalt</u>.*
(The picture is painted by the artist.)

ACTIVE VOICE	PASSIVE VOICE
*Der Lehrer **lehrt** die Studenten.* (The teacher teaches the students.)	*Die Studenten **werden** vom Lehrer **gelehrt**.* (The students are taught by the teacher.)
*Die Köchin **bereitet** das Essen **zu**.* (The chef prepares the meal.)	*Das Essen **wird** von der Köchin **zubereitet**.* (The meal is prepared by the chef.)
*Die Katze **jagt** die Maus.* (The cat chases the mouse.)	*Die Maus **wird** von der Katze **gejagt**.* (The mouse is chased by the cat.)

✍️ EXERCISES

Ü 11.1) Determine whether the verb in each sentence is *transitive (T)* or *intransitive (I)*. Write *T* or *I* next to each sentence:

a. Die Blumen blühen im Garten. _____

b. Der Junge liest ein Buch. _____

c. Der Vogel singt. _____

d. Sie trinkt einen Tee. _____

e. Das Baby schläft. _____

f. Er öffnet die Tür. _____

g. Die Kinder spielen im Park. _____

h. Sie kauft ein neues Kleid. _____

i. Der Kater schnurrt. _____

j. Der Mann baut ein Haus. _____

Ü 11.2) For each of the following transitive sentences, <u>underline</u> the direct object:

a. Die Lehrerin korrigiert die Hausaufgaben.

b. Maria bestellt eine Pizza.

c. Der Vater liest seinem Sohn eine Geschichte vor.

d. Die Schüler schreiben den Test.

e. Wir beobachten die Sterne in der Nacht.

f. Der Kellner serviert das Essen.

g. Sie versteht die Frage nicht.

h. Der Mechaniker repariert das Auto.

i. Mein Bruder spielt die Gitarre jeden Abend.

j. Der Direktor präsentiert den neuen Plan.

Ü 11.3) Some verbs can be both transitive and intransitive, depending on the context. Given the verb, construct two sentences: one using the verb transitively and the other using it intransitively:

a. essen (to eat)

_____

_____

b. fahren (to drive/ride)

_____

_____

c. beginnen (to begin)

_____

_____

d. schreiben (to write)

_____

_____

e. spielen (to play)

_____

_____

Ü 11.4) For each sentence, <u>underline</u> the direct object and <u>circle</u> the indirect object:

a. Der Lehrer gibt dem Schüler ein Buch.

b. Meine Mutter kocht mir ein leckeres Abendessen.

c. Der Chef zeigt der Assistentin den Bericht.

d. Er erzählt seinem Freund eine interessante Geschichte.

e. Das Mädchen kauft ihrer Mutter einen Blumenstrauß.

f. Der Verkäufer bietet dem Kunden einen Rabatt an.

g. Sie schickt ihrem Bruder eine Postkarte.

h. Der Kellner serviert dem Gast ein Glas Wasser.

i. Die Großmutter strickt ihrem Enkel einen Pullover.

j. Der Direktor erklärt den Angestellten das neue Projekt.

Ü 11.5) Transform the following active voice sentences into passive voice. Remember to use the auxiliary verb *"werden"* and the past participle of the transitive verb:

a. Die Lehrerin erklärt den Stoff.

_____

b. Der Bäcker backt das Brot.

_____

c. Der Mechaniker repariert das Fahrrad.

_____

d. Die Schauspielerin spielt die Hauptrolle.

_____

e. Der Künstler malt das Bild.

_____

f. Die Autorin schreibt den Artikel.

_____

g. Der Gärtner pflanzt die Blumen.

_____

h. Die Köchin bereitet das Essen zu.

_____

i. Der Fotograf nimmt das Foto auf.

_____

j. Der Direktor stellt den neuen Mitarbeiter ein.

_____

Unit 3

MOOD & VOICE

Mood and voice are integral components in the art of communication in any language, determining not just what we say, but how we say it and the intended impact. In German, just like in other languages, moods provide insight into the attitude or feeling of the speaker, whether it's a simple statement of fact, a command, a wish, or a hypothetical situation. Voice, on the other hand, signals who is performing the action of the verb, allowing for the differentiation between actions done by the subject (active) and actions received by the subject (passive).

Though there are parallels between German and English in terms of mood and voice, their usage and formation can differ notably. For instance, the German subjunctive mood has its own unique characteristics that are essential for expressing wishes, unreal situations, or indirect speech.

In this unit, we delve into the depths of German moods and voices. You'll discover the intricacies of the indicative, imperative, and subjunctive moods, as well as the active and passive voices. Through the chapters, you will grasp the nuances of their application and formation, paving the way for richer, more varied expressions in your German conversations.

CHAPTER 12
THE PASSIVE VOICE

⊘ CHECKBOX – WHAT IS THE PASSIVE VOICE?

The passive voice represents an essential aspect of sentence construction, offering an alternative perspective to the active voice. While the active voice emphasizes the subject as the doer of an action, the **passive voice shifts the focus onto the object, making it the receiver of the action**. This change in perspective often results in a **more formal or objective tone** in the sentence.

There are three main types of passive voice constructions: **process passive**, **status passive**, and **personal/impersonal passive**. To form the passive voice, German speakers use different auxiliary verbs (Ch. 23) depending on the tense and mood of the sentence. The most frequently used auxiliary verbs in the passive voice are *"werden"* (to become) for the present and future tenses and *"sein"* (to be) for the past tense. These auxiliary verbs are combined with the past participle of the main verb to create the passive form.

🎧 ○ DIALOGUE – DAS PROJEKT

(Erik and Lena, colleagues working on a project, discuss its progress and upcoming presentation. The dialogue involves various passive voice forms and active voice for contrast.)

*Erik: Lena, **wird** das Projekt bis Freitag **abgeschlossen**?*

*Lena: Ja, es **wird** gerade von der IT-Abteilung **bearbeitet**.*

*Erik: Super! Und **wurde** die Präsentation schon **erstellt**?*

*Lena: Nein, sie **ist** noch nicht **fertiggestellt**.*

*Erik: Wer **wird** sie dann **vorstellen**?*

*Lena: Sie **wird** von Julia **vorgestellt**.*

*Erik: Ah, okay. **Wird** ein Meeting dafür **gegeben**?*

*Lena: Ja, ein Meeting **wird organisiert**.*

Erik: Gut zu wissen. Danke für die Info!

VOCABULARY LIST – DAS PROJEKT			
(das) Projekt [n.] (-e)	project	erstellen [v.]	(to) create
abschließen [v.]	(to) finalize	fertigstellen [v.]	(to) finish
(die) Abteilung [n.] (-en)	department	vorstellen [v.]	(to) present
(die) Präsentation [n.] (-en)	presentation	(die) Info [n.] (-s)	info

12.1 INTRODUCTION TO THE PASSIVE VOICE

In German, just like in English, the passive voice is used when the focus of a sentence is on the action rather than who or what performed it. It allows for a shift from the subject (the doer) to the object (what is acted upon).

While an active voice sentence focuses on the subject performing the action (*Erik fragt*), the passive voice emphasizes the action itself or the recipient of the action (*Eine Frage wird gestellt*).

Active

Wer wird sie dann vorstellen?
(Who will then present it?)

Passive (Status)

Sie ist noch nicht fertiggestellt.
(It hasn't been completed yet.)

12.2 FORMATION OF THE PROCESS PASSIVE (*VORGANGSPASSIV*)

The key to forming the process passive in German is the auxiliary verb "*werden*" paired with the past participle of the main verb. This structure primarily highlights actions that are in progress or underway.

Tense	ich 1st person	du 2nd person	er/sie/es 3rd person	wir 1st person	ihr 2nd person	sie/Sie 3rd person/ Formal
Present	werde	wirst	wird	werden	werdet	werden
Simple Past	wurde	wurdest	wurde	wurden	wurdet	wurden
Future	werde	wirst	wird	werden	werdet	werden

CONJUGATION OF "WERDEN" IN DIFFERENT TENSES

Formation of past participles for regular and irregular verbs

Regular verbs typically derive their past participles by adding a "**ge-**" prefix and an "**-t**" suffix (e.g., "*arbeiten*" becomes "*gearbeitet*"). Irregular verbs, on the other hand, can be more unpredictable. Some might use the "**ge-**" prefix and an "**-en**" suffix (e.g., "*sehen*" becomes "*gesehen*"), while others may omit the "**ge-**" prefix entirely.

VERB TYPE	BASE VERB	PAST PARTICIPLE
Regular	*arbeiten*	*gearbeitet*
Irregular (Type 1)	*sehen*	*gesehen*
Irregular (Type 2)	*nehmen*	*genommen*

Example from the dialogue:
"Es wird von Julia vorgestellt."

> → Here, "*wird*" is the present tense form of "*werden*", and "*vorgestellt*" is the past participle of "*vorstellen*".

12.2.1 Usage of the Process Passive

- **Purpose of the Process Passive**

  The process passive in German serves a pivotal role in **shifting the focal point of a sentence from the subject**, traditionally the doer of the action, **to** either **the action itself** or the recipient of that action. The fundamental advantage lies in its flexibility: we can utilize the passive voice when the agent is either unknown or when it's more strategic to underscore the action or its beneficiary.

  For example, consider the active sentence "*Der Direktor startet das Projekt*" (The director starts the project). Here, the spotlight is on "*Der Direktor*". In the passive transformation "*Das Projekt wird gestartet*", the attention shifts squarely onto the action of the project being initiated.

- Contextual Applications of the Process Passive

Different situations can necessitate the use of the passive voice. Formal settings, especially in news reports or official announcements, often lean on the passive form to maintain a tone of **objectivity and impartiality**. For instance, *"Das Fenster wurde zerbrochen"* (The window was broken) emphasizes the state of the window without dwelling on the culprit. **Scientific writing** is another domain where the passive voice reigns supreme. It allows emphasis on process or result, sidelining the researcher for a tone of neutrality.

While the passive voice offers a fresh perspective and can enrich expression, it might render sentences more circuitous or indirect. Discerning its apt usage, especially with reintroducing the agent using *"von"* or *"durch"*, becomes vital. Notably, *"von"* is prevalent, while *"durch"* usually indicates the means through which an action occurs.

12.3 FORMATION OF THE STATUS PASSIVE (*ZUSTANDSPASSIV*)

The Status Passive, as the name suggests, **focuses more on the state or condition resulting from a previous action**, rather than the action itself. This is different from the Process Passive, which highlights the ongoing action or an action that took place.

In German, the Status Passive is formed using the auxiliary verb *"sein"* combined with the past participle of the main verb. The conjugation of *"sein"* will change according to the tense, while the past participle remains consistent.

Active:

Der Mechaniker repariert das Auto.
(The mechanic is repairing the car.)

Status Passive:

Das Auto ist repariert.
(The car is repaired.)

The above example perfectly showcases the utility of the Status Passive. In the active sentence, the focus is on the mechanic and his action of repairing. However, in the passive version, the emphasis shifts entirely to the car and its state of being repaired.

It's important to differentiate the Status Passive from the Process Passive. While both are passive structures, they emphasize different aspects. For instance, while *"Das Auto wird repariert"* (The car is being repaired) indicates an ongoing process, *"Das Auto ist repariert"* points towards a completed state.

The following table showcases the transformation of sentences from active voice in the present tense to the status passive.

ACTIVE VOICE (PRESENT)	STATUS PASSIVE (PRESENT)	PAST PARTICIPLE
Der Mechaniker **repariert** *das Auto.*	*Das Auto* **ist repariert.**	**repariert**
Die Bauarbeiter **bauen** *das Haus.*	*Das Haus* **ist gebaut.**	**gebaut**
Der Koch **bereitet** *das Essen* **zu.**	*Das Essen* **ist zubereitet.**	**zubereitet**
Die Lehrerin **korrigiert** *die Tests.*	*Die Tests* **sind korrigiert.**	**korrigiert**
Der Gärtner **pflanzt** *die Blumen.*	*Die Blumen* **sind gepflanzt.**	**gepflanzt**

12.3.1 Usage of the Status Passive

To form the status passive, the **auxiliary verb** "*sein*" is combined with a **past participle**.

For example, consider the verb "*öffnen*" (to open). In the active voice, you might say "*Der Laden* **öffnet** *um 9 Uhr*" (The store opens at 9 o'clock). In the status passive, this becomes "*Der Laden* **ist geöffnet**" (The store is open), indicating the state of the store as a result of the action.

In constructing the status passive:

- The verb "*sein*" is conjugated **according to the subject**.

- The main verb's past participle is placed at the **end of the sentence**.

- There's usually **no mention of the doer** of the action, since the emphasis is on the state or result.

Erik: Super! Und wurde die Präsentation schon erstellt?

Lena: Nein, sie **ist noch nicht fertiggestellt.**

In this exchange, Erik is asking about the creation of the presentation, and Lena replies emphasizing the state of the presentation – it's not yet complete. The main interest here is not who's responsible for completing it, but the presentation's current status.

Other scenarios for the status passive include:

- **When discussing art or historical monuments**

  Das Bild ist gemalt.
  (The picture is painted.)

- **When referring to buildings or construction**

  Das Gebäude ist renoviert.
  (The building is renovated).

12.4 PERSONAL PASSIVE AND IMPERSONAL PASSIVE

The German passive voice can manifest in two primary forms: the **personal passive** and the **impersonal passive**.

- **Personal Passive**

  The personal passive emphasizes an action on an object, where the agent (or doer) of the action can be included but isn't always. In these cases, the sentence can be transformed from an active voice, where the agent performs the action, to the passive voice, where the focus shifts to the action's receiver. An example from the dialogue illustrates this:

  Lena: Sie (die Präsentation) **wird von Julia vorgestellt**.

  Here, the action (the presentation) is the focus. The agent, Julia, is mentioned but isn't the primary emphasis of the sentence.

  To form a personal passive sentence, the formula to keep in mind is:

Subject + *"werden"* conjugated + past participle of main verb + (optional) von + agent

  Active:

  Der Lehrer **erklärt** *die Regel.*
  (The teacher explains the rule.)

  Personal Passive:

  Die Regel **wird** *vom Lehrer* **erklärt**.
  (The rule is explained by the teacher.)

- **Impersonal Passive**

The impersonal passive voice is used when the action's performer is general or unspecified, often represented by *"man"* in active sentences. This passive form is especially useful when discussing rules, general facts, or when the exact agent isn't crucial to the message.

Lena: Ja, ein Treffen wird organisiert.

This doesn't specify who organizes the meeting – the important thing is that it's being set up. To transform an active voice sentence with *"man"* into an impersonal passive, use this formula:

Object + *"werden"* conjugated + past participle of main verb

Active:	**Impersonal Passive:**
***Man** organisiert ein Treffen.*	*Ein Treffen wird organisiert.*
(One organizes a meeting.)	(A meeting is organized.)

It's important to understand when to use each form. **Personal passive** is best when the agent's possible **identity may be relevant to the listener**, even if it's not the central focus. **Impersonal passive**, meanwhile, **depersonalizes the action entirely**, which can be handy in many contexts, especially when offering general information or discussing broadly applicable situations.

12.5 USING THE PASSIVE VOICE WITH MODALS AND MODAL-PASSIVE CONSTRUCTIONS

Incorporating modal verbs with passive voice can be a bit tricky, but understanding the nuances allows for more sophisticated expressions in German. Modal verbs like *müssen* (must), *können* (can), *dürfen* (may), *wollen* (want to), *sollen* (should), and *mögen* (like to) bring a shade of possibility, obligation, or desire into passive constructions (🔗 Ch. 22).

For a modal-passive construction, the following structure is used:

Subject + modal verb (conjugated) + *"werden"* in infinitive
form + past participle of the main verb

Active:

*Man **muss** die Regeln befolgen.*
(One must follow the rules.)

Active:

*Man **kann** das Buch lesen.*
(One can read the book.)

Modal-Passive:

*Die Regeln **müssen** befolgt werden.*
(The rules must be followed.)

Modal-Passive:

*Das Buch **kann** gelesen werden.*
(The book can be read.)

12.6 ACTIVE VS. PASSIVE VOICE IN DIFFERENT TENSES

When discussing actions or events, the choice between the active and passive voice is crucial in German, as it is in many languages. It's not only about what happened but also about the **perspective** from which the event is presented.

In the **active voice**, the subject performs the action on the object:

Der Lehrer (subject) unterrichtet (verb) die Schüler (object).

↳ Here, the focus is on the doer (the teacher).

In contrast, the **passive voice** places emphasis on the action or the recipient, often omitting the doer altogether:

Die Schüler (new subject) werden (auxiliary verb) unterrichtet (past participle).

↳ In this case, the students (previously the object) become the center of attention.

To see how this works across tenses, let's examine a verb – say, *"bauen"* (to build) – in both its active and passive forms:

TENSE	VOICE	GERMAN SENTENCE	ENGLISH TRANSLATION
Present (*Präsens*)	Active	*Der Bauarbeiter baut das Haus.*	The construction worker builds the house.
	Passive	*Das Haus wird gebaut.*	The house is being built.
Simple Past (*Präteritum*)	Active	*Der Bauarbeiter baute das Haus.*	The construction worker built the house.
	Passive	*Das Haus wurde gebaut.*	The house was built.
Present Perfect (*Perfekt*)	Active	*Der Bauarbeiter hat das Haus gebaut.*	The construction worker has built the house.
	Passive	*Das Haus ist gebaut worden.*	The house has been built.
Past Perfect (*Plusquamperfekt*)	Active	*Der Bauarbeiter hatte das Haus gebaut.*	The construction worker had built the house.
	Passive	*Das Haus war gebaut worden.*	The house had been built.
Future I (*Futur I*)	Active	*Der Bauarbeiter wird das Haus bauen.*	The construction worker will build the house.
	Passive	*Das Haus wird gebaut werden.*	The house will be built.
Future II (*Futur II*)	Active	*Der Bauarbeiter wird das Haus gebaut haben.*	The construction worker will have built the house.
	Passive	*Das Haus wird gebaut worden sein.*	The house will have been built.

✏️ EXERCISES

Ü 12.1) Determine whether the following sentences are written in the passive or active (P/A) voice.

Example: Das Lied wird gesungen.   P

a. Das Buch wird von ihr gelesen. _____   **f.** Sie kauft ein Kleid. _____

b. Er spielt Fußball. _____   **g.** Das Haus wurde von ihm gebaut. _____

c. Die Türen wurden geschlossen. _____   **h.** Wir besuchen den Zoo. _____

d. Ich schreibe den Brief. _____   **i.** Die Suppe wird serviert. _____

e. Das Fenster wird geöffnet. _____   **j.** Er wird von dem Hund gejagt. _____

Ü 12.2) Change the following active voice sentences to passive voice.

Example: Er schreibt den Artikel.   →   Der Artikel wird von ihm geschrieben.

a. Sie macht die Hausaufgaben.

_____

b. Der Koch bereitet das Essen zu.

_____

c. Die Lehrerin korrigiert die Tests.

_____

d. Der Junge füttert den Hund.

_____

e. Die Mutter singt das Lied.

_____

f. Er öffnet das Fenster.

_____

g. Sie kauft das Auto.

_____

h. Der Lehrer erklärt die Regel.

_____

i. Wir trinken den Saft.

_____

j. Die Kinder spielen das Spiel.

_____

Ü 12.3) Complete the sentences using the passive voice.

Example: Das Bild ___ von ihm___. (malen)   →   Das Bild wird von ihm gemalt.

a. Die Tür _____ von ihm _____ (schließen)

b. Das Essen _____ von der Köchin _____ (zubereiten)

c. Das Fahrrad _____ in der Werkstatt _____ (reparieren)

d. Der Vertrag _____ vom Chef _____ (unterschreiben)

e. Die Bücher _____ in der Buchhandlung _____ (verkaufen)

f. Der Garten _____ von der Gärtnerin _____ (pflegen)

g. Die Musik _____ von den Nachbarn _____ (hören)

h. Die Kleidung _____ im Waschsalon _____ (waschen)

i. Die Worte _____ von den Schülern _____ (aufschreiben)

j. Das Wasser _____ von den Tieren _____ (trinken)

Ü 12.4) Identify the doer in each passive sentence.

Example: Das Buch wird von Paul gelesen.   →   Das Buch wird von **Paul** gelesen.

    a. Das Lied wird von Lara gesungen.

    b. Das Auto wird von meinem Vater gefahren.

    c. Die Geschichte wird von einem alten Mann erzählt.

    d. Die Suppe wird von der Köchin gekocht.

    e. Die Aufgabe wird vom Schüler gelöst.

    f. Der Ball wird von den Spielern geworfen.

    g. Der Artikel wird von der Journalistin geschrieben.

    h. Das Theaterstück wird von einer bekannten Gruppe aufgeführt.

    i. Die Schokolade wird von dem Kind gegessen.

    j. Die Bilder werden von einem talentierten Künstler gemalt.

Ü 12.5) Imagine a busy city street. Using passive voice, describe what is happening.

Example: Der Kaffee wird in dem Café serviert.

_____

_____

_____

_____

_____

_____

_____

_____

Ü 12.6) Rewrite the passive sentences without mentioning the doer.

Example: Das Essen wird vom Koch zubereitet.   →   Das Essen wird zubereitet.

a. Das Haus wird von meinen Eltern gekauft.

_____

b. Das Lied wird von einem berühmten Sänger gesungen.

_____

c. Die Türen werden vom Wächter geschlossen.

_____

d. Der Film wird von einem berühmten Regisseur gedreht.

_____

e. Das Buch wird von einem bekannten Autor geschrieben.

_____

f. Das Essen wird von einem Sternekoch zubereitet.

_____

g. Die Bilder werden von einem professionellen Fotografen aufgenommen.

_____

h. Die Kleidung wird von einem Designer entworfen.

_____

Ü 12.7) Fill in the blanks using the passive voice combined with modal verbs.

Example: Der Raum _____ (sollen) regelmäßig gereinigt _____ (werden).

→ Der Raum soll regelmäßig gereinigt werden.

a. Das Buch _____ (müssen) von den Schülern gelesen _____ (werden).

b. Das Zimmer _____ (sollen) regelmäßig gereinigt _____ (werden).

c. Das Essen _____ (können) um 18 Uhr serviert _____ (werden).

d. Der Bericht _____ (müssen) bis Freitag fertiggestellt _____ (werden).

e. Der Müll _____ (sollen) jeden Tag herausgenommen _____ (werden).

f. Das Projekt _____ (können) nächste Woche gestartet _____ (werden).

g. Die Tiere _____ (dürfen) nicht gefüttert _____ (werden).

h. Die Tickets _____ (sollen) im Voraus gekauft _____ (werden).

i. Die Blumen _____ (müssen) täglich gewässert _____ (werden).

j. Das Auto _____ (können) in der Garage geparkt _____ (werden).

Ü 12.8) Match the first half of each sentence with its correct ending to form a complete passive voice sentence.

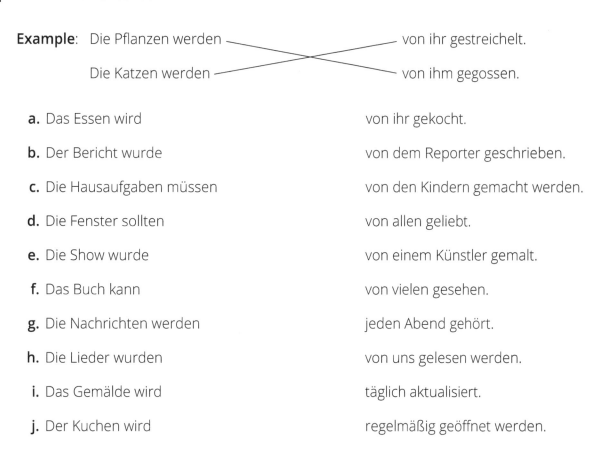

Example: Die Pflanzen werden — von ihr gestreichelt.

Die Katzen werden — von ihm gegossen.

a. Das Essen wird   von ihr gekocht.

b. Der Bericht wurde   von dem Reporter geschrieben.

c. Die Hausaufgaben müssen   von den Kindern gemacht werden.

d. Die Fenster sollten   von allen geliebt.

e. Die Show wurde   von einem Künstler gemalt.

f. Das Buch kann   von vielen gesehen.

g. Die Nachrichten werden   jeden Abend gehört.

h. Die Lieder wurden   von uns gelesen werden.

i. Das Gemälde wird   täglich aktualisiert.

j. Der Kuchen wird   regelmäßig geöffnet werden.

CHAPTER 13
THE IMPERATIVE

⊘ CHECKBOX – WHAT IS THE IMPERATIVE?

The imperative mood serves as a powerful tool for **issuing commands**, **making requests**, or **giving instructions**. There are five ways to express the imperative: **singular familiar**, **singular formal**, **plural familiar**, **plural formal**, and **mixed group**. Each form is used to address different audiences, whether informally or formally.

In German, the imperative singular familiar form is usually formed by using the base form of the verb, and the pronoun "*du*" is often omitted.

Komm bitte hierher!　　　　　　　　　Geh jetzt!
(Come here, please!)　　　　　　　　　(Go now!)

The singular formal and plural imperative use the polite form of "*Sie*" and the base form of the verb.

Singular Formal:　　　　　　　　　**Plural Informal:**

Kommen Sie bitte.　　　　　　　　　Kommt alle her!
(Please come.)　　　　　　　　　　　(Come here, all of you!)

The plural formal imperative is formed by using the polite form of "*Sie*" followed by the base form of the verb when addressing multiple people formally.

Kommen Sie bitte alle.　　　　　　　Helft uns, bitte!
(Please come, all of you.)　　　　　　(Please help us.)

In a mixed group, the formal imperative is commonly used as a sign of respect when addressing both familiar and formal individuals.

Kommen Sie alle her!　　　　　　　　Helft mir, bitte.
(All of you, please come.)　　　　　　(Help me, please.)

⊃ **DIALOGUE – ANWEISUNGEN IM BÜRO**

(Marie and Paul, coworkers in the office, exchange instructions and interact with their colleague Herr Müller. The dialogue includes imperative forms in both singular and plural, and in familiar and formal contexts.)

Marie:	*Paul, **komm** bitte hierher.*
Paul:	*Ja, Marie?*
Marie:	***Schau** dir diese Akte **an** und **gib** sie mir **zurück**, wenn du fertig bist.*
Paul:	*In Ordnung.* *(A coworker, Herr Müller, enters the scene.)*
Marie:	*Herr Müller, **kommen** Sie bitte einen Moment zu mir.*
Herr Müller:	*Selbstverständlich.*
Marie:	***Lesen Sie** diesen Bericht und **lassen Sie** mich wissen, was Sie denken.*
Herr Müller:	*Werde ich machen.*
Marie:	*Paul, **geh** mit Herrn Müller und **zeig** ihm, wo das Konferenzzimmer ist.*
Paul:	*Klar, **folgen** Sie mir, Herr Müller.*
Marie:	*Und alle anderen, **arbeiten** Sie weiter und **stören** Sie die beiden nicht!*

VOCABULARY LIST – ANWEISUNGEN IM BÜRO			
(die) Anweisung [*n.*] (-en)	instruction	(der) Bericht [*n.*] (-e)	report
(die) Akte [*n.*] (-n)	file	lassen [*v.*]	(to) leave
in Ordnung [*adj.*] / [*adv.*]	all right	folgen [*v.*]	(to) follow
herkommen [*v.*]	(to) come here	stören [*v.*]	(to) disturb
selbstverständlich [*adv.*]	of course	beide [*pron.*]	both
(das) Konferenzzimmer [*n.*] (-)	conference room	hierher [*adv.*]	here

13.1 INTRODUCTION TO THE IMPERATIVE

The imperative mood, or *"Befehlsform"* in German, is the linguistic tool we wield when issuing **commands**, **requests**, or **giving instructions**. To understand the essence of the imperative, imagine a spectrum. At one end, we have singular commands targeting an individual, and at the other, plural commands directed at a group.

· **Singular Commands**

   (e.g., *"Komm hierher!"* meaning "Come here!")

· **Plural Commands**

   (e.g., *"Kommt hierher!"* meaning "Come here!" addressing multiple people)

Furthermore, within this spectrum, there's a distinction based on formality: the familiar *"du"* form versus the formal *"Sie"* form. Let's illustrate this with a table:

TYPE	EXAMPLE	TRANSLATION
Singular, familiar	*Komm hierher, Paul!*	Come here, Paul!
Singular, formal	*Kommen Sie bitte, Herr Müller.*	Please come, Mr. Müller.
Plural, familiar	*Kommt hierher!*	Come here!
Plural, formal	*Kommen Sie hierher!*	Come here!

Considering the dialogue between Marie, Paul, and Herr Müller, we can identify various imperative instances that display both singular and plural commands, as well as familiar and formal interactions. Marie's interaction with Paul is informal, so she uses the familiar form, while her dialogue with Herr Müller adheres to the formal imperative due to their professional relationship.

13.2 FORMING THE IMPERATIVE SINGULAR

The German imperative singular is primarily used to address one individual informally. For regular verbs, the formation is quite straightforward. Begin with the base form of the verb (also known as the stem) and, in most cases, remove the "-en" or "-n" ending. For example, the verb "machen" (to do/make) becomes "mach!" in the singular imperative.

REGULAR VERB	IMPERATIVE SINGULAR	TRANSLATION
machen	Mach!	do/make!
lesen	Lies!	read!

IRREGULAR VERB	IMPERATIVE SINGULAR	TRANSLATION
sein	Sei!	be!
haben	Hab!	have!

Some imperatives might sound abrupt in isolation. To soften the tone or make the request more polite, you can add "bitte" (please) at the beginning or end of the command, e.g., "Komm **bitte**!" (Please come!) or "**Bitte** komm!".

13.3 FORMING THE IMPERATIVE PLURAL

When addressing multiple people or using a more formal approach, the imperative plural comes into play. This is divided into the familiar form, which typically uses the "ihr" conjugation, and the formal form that aligns with the "Sie" conjugation.

To form the familiar imperative plural for regular verbs, start with the base form of the verb, maintaining the "-en" or "-t" ending and add the "ihr" form without the pronoun itself. For instance, "machen" (to do/make) becomes "macht!".

IRREGULAR VERB	IMPERATIVE PLURAL (FAMILIAR)	TRANSLATION
haben	*Habt!*	have!
essen	*Esst!*	eat!

FLACHWITZE

„STERB!"

„Der Imperativ von 'sterben' wird mit 'i' gebildet, du bildungsresistenter Intelligenzallergiker!"

„Sterbi?"

On the other hand, for the formal imperative plural, begin with the "*Sie*" form of the verb, but place the "*Sie*" after the verb. For instance, "*machen*" transforms to "*Machen Sie!*"

As with the singular imperative, the tone can be softened using "*bitte*". For instance, "*Kommen Sie bitte hierher!*" (Please come here!) or "*Bitte kommen Sie hierher!*"

The choice between familiar and formal imperative is not just about the number of people you're addressing, but also about the **degree of familiarity or respect**. The **familiar imperative** is used with close **friends, family**, or **peers**. In contrast, the **formal imperative** is used with **strangers, elders**, or in **professional settings**.

13.4 FAMILIAR AND FORMAL IMPERATIVE

In the German language, the way we issue commands or make requests varies depending on our relationship with the listener. The two main forms for expressing the imperative mood are **familiar** (informal) and **formal**.

- **Familiar Imperative (*du-form*)**

  The familiar imperative is used with people whom you know well, like **close friends**, **family**, or **children**. Its tone is informal. To form the familiar imperative for most verbs, drop the "*-en*" ending from the infinitive and use the verb stem. For example, the verb "*sprechen*" (to speak) becomes "*sprich!*" For the imperative plural familiar (*ihr-form*), keep the "*-t*" ending from the present tense conjugation: "*sprecht!*".

- **Formal Imperative (*Sie-form*)**

  The formal imperative is reserved for situations requiring politeness or formality, such as **addressing strangers**, **seniors**, or in **professional settings**. The formation is straightforward. Use the verb's infinitive form followed by "*Sie*". For the verb "*sprechen*", the formal imperative becomes "*Sprechen Sie!*"

VERB	IMPERATIVE SINGULAR (FAMILIAR)	IMPERATIVE PLURAL (FORMAL)	IMPERATIVE FORMAL	TRANSLATION
sprechen	*Sprich!*	*Sprecht!*	*Sprechen Sie!*	speak
machen	*Mach!*	*Macht!*	*Machen Sie!*	make/do!
kommen	*Komm!*	*Kommt!*	*Kommen Sie!*	come!

It's important to recognize when to use which form. Using the familiar imperative with a stranger might be considered rude, while using the formal imperative with a close friend might sound overly distant.

13.5 USING PRONOUNS WITH THE IMPERATIVE

In German, it's often clear who the command is directed at, especially given the formal and informal distinctions we've already discussed. However, sometimes pronouns are incorporated for clarity or emphasis.

In the Familiar Imperative:

Pronouns are typically not needed, as the verb form itself makes the intended audience clear. However, they can be added for emphasis. In the singular form, "*du*" can follow the verb, while in the plural form, "*ihr*" can follow. For example:

Hör (du) zu!   *Kommt (ihr) hierher!*
(Listen!)   (Come over here!)

COMMAND WITHOUT PRONOUN	COMMAND WITH PRONOUN	TRANSLATION
Geh weg!	*Geh du weg!*	*Go away!*
Kommt her!	*Kommt ihr her!*	*Come here!*

In the Formal Imperative:

Including "*Sie*" at the end of the command is standard, as we've seen, but sometimes it's placed in the middle of the sentence for a change in emphasis or when additional information is added:

Öffnen Sie die Tür!   *Öffnen Sie bitte die Tür!*   *Öffnen Sie die Tür, bitte!*
(Open the door!)   (Please open the door!)   (Open the door, please!)

13.6 NEGATIVE IMPERATIVE

Forming negative commands in German is quite straightforward. The key component here is the word "*nicht*", which is **placed before the verb or at the end of the command**. Whether you're making a command in the familiar or formal form, "*nicht*" remains the key element in constructing a negative imperative.

For the familiar form, the pattern is as follows:

Singular (du):   *Nicht* + verb *(or verb +* nicht*)*
Example: *Nicht schmatzen!* or *Schmatz nicht!*
                    (Don't smack!)

Plural (ihr):   Verb + *nicht*
Example: *Redet nicht!*
                    (Don't talk!)

Formal (Sie):   *Nicht* + verb + *Sie* (or verb + *Sie* + *nicht*)
Example: *Machen Sie nicht!* or *Machen Sie das nicht!*
                    (Don't do it!)

IMPERATIVE TYPE	POSITIVE COMMAND	NEGATIVE COMMAND
Singular (du)	*Komm!* (Come!)	*Komm nicht!* (Don't come!)
Plural (ihr)	*Lernt!* (Learn!)	*Lernt nicht!* (Don't learn!)
Formal (Sie)	*Nehmen Sie!* (Take!)	*Nehmen Sie nicht!* (Don't take!)

When giving negative commands involving separable-prefix verbs, the "***nicht***" is typically positioned between the prefix and the base verb:

*Schalte den Fernseher **nicht** ein!*
(Don't turn on the TV!)

 **EXERCISES**

Ü 13.1) Create the imperative form for the given verbs. For each verb, form both the informal imperative (using "du") and the formal imperative (using "Sie").

Example: sehen   Imperative: Sieh! (informal)   Sehen Sie! (formal)
                                  Informal imperative   Formal imperative

a. gehen   _____   _____

b. essen   _____   _____

c. trinken   _____   _____

d. hören   _____   _____

e. schreiben   _____   _____

f. lesen   _____   _____

g. spielen   _____   _____

h. nehmen   _____   _____

i. sprechen   _____   _____

j. fahren   _____   _____

Ü 13.2) Fill in the blanks using the imperative form (using "du") of the verb in brackets.

Example: _____ bitte den Tisch! (decken)   →   **Decke** bitte den Tisch!

a. _____ bitte das Buch!   (geben)

b. _____ nicht so laut!   (sprechen)

c. _____ das Fenster!   (öffnen)

d. _____ die Hausaufgaben!   (machen)

e. _____ mir das Salz!   (geben)

f. _____ hier!   (bleiben)

g. _____ schneller!   (laufen)

h. _____ das Auto!   (parken)

i. _____ zu Hause!   (bleiben)

j. _____ das Licht aus!   (machen)

Ü 13.3) Determine whether the imperative form is informal (du) or formal (Sie).

Example: Fahren Sie!   →   ____formal____

a. Komm!   _____   **e.** Gehen Sie!   _____

b. Arbeiten Sie!   _____   **f.** Trink!   _____

c. Denken Sie!   _____   **g.** Lächeln Sie!   _____

d. Setz dich!   _____

Ü 13.4) Turn the following statements into imperative commands.

Example: Du hörst den Vogel.   Hör den Vogel!

a. Du siehst den Film.   _____

b. Sie probieren die Suppe.   _____

c. Du nimmst den Schirm.   _____

d. Sie fragen den Lehrer.   _____

e. Du schließt die Tür.   _____

f. Sie buchen das Hotelzimmer.   _____

g. Du hörst die Musik.   _____

h. Sie überprüfen die E-Mails.   _____

i. Du triffst deine Freunde.   _____

j. Sie füllen das Formular aus.   _____

Ü 13.5) Turn the following positive commands into negative ones.

Example: Lauf! → Lauf nicht!

a. Geh! _____

b. Essen Sie! _____

c. Schreib! _____

d. Hören Sie! _____

e. Spiel! _____

f. Lesen Sie! _____

g. Nimm! _____

Ü 13.6) Given a situation, respond using an appropriate imperative.

Example: The music is too loud.

⌐→ Mach die Musik leiser!

a. The room is dark.

_____

b. Someone is speaking loudly in the library.

_____

c. You want someone to give you a pen.

_____

d. You're cold, and the window is open.

_____

e. You're at a restaurant and ready to order.

_____

Ü 13.7) Complete the dialogues using the imperative form of the verbs in brackets.

Example: A: Ich kann nicht gut sehen.

             B: _____ die Brille! (tragen)   →   Trage die Brille!

a. A: Ich habe Durst.

   B: Dann _____! (trinken)

b. A: Es ist so kalt hier.

   B: _____ das Fenster! (schließen)

c. A: Wo ist die Toilette?

   B: _____ nach rechts und dann die zweite Tür links. (gehen)

d. A: Ich verstehe diese Regel nicht.

   B: _____ sie noch einmal. (lesen)

e. A: Das Radio ist so leise.

   B: _____ es lauter! (machen)

Ü 13.8) In pairs, one person will describe a place in the room, and the other must guess it using only imperative commands. This will help practice the imperative while also improving listening skills. For example, "Go forward, stop, look right."

CHAPTER 14
THE *KONJUNKTIV I* AND *II*

⊘ CHECKBOX – WHAT IS THE *KONJUNKTIV*?

The *Konjunktiv I* and *II* are two essential mood forms used to express indirect speech, possibilities, unfulfillable wishes, or conditions. Each *Konjunktiv* has its distinct functions and is employed in different contexts.

The *Konjunktiv I* is primarily used in indirect speech, where the speaker reports someone else's words or thoughts without quoting them directly. It is also utilized in formal writing, such as news articles or official documents.

Indirect Speech:

Er sagte, er sei müde.
(He said he is tired.)

Formal Writing:

Es sei darauf hingewiesen, dass …
(It should be pointed out that …)

The *Konjunktiv II* is employed to express possibilities, hypothetical situations, wishes, or unfulfilled conditions in the present or past. It is frequently used in "if" clauses (conditional sentences) and for polite requests.

Possibility:

Wenn ich (die) Zeit hätte, würde ich kommen.
(If I had time, I would come.)

Wishes:

Ich wünschte, du wärst hier.
(I wish you were here.)

Polite Request:

Können Sie mir bitte helfen?
(Could you please help me?)

💬 TEXT – EIN WUNSCHZETTEL

(The following text tells the story of Maria, who sits by the window observing the starry sky and wishes that stars could fulfill her desires.)

Maria saß am Fenster und beobachtete den Sternenhimmel. Es wäre (Konjunktiv II) wunderschön, dachte sie, wenn Sterne Wünsche erfüllen könnten (Konjunktiv II). Sie hätte (Konjunktiv II) so viele Wünsche, die sie in ihrem Leben gerne erfüllt sähe (Konjunktiv II).

Am nächsten Morgen erzählte sie ihrer besten Freundin Lena von ihrem nächtlichen Gedanken. Lena sagte, Maria habe (Konjunktiv I) gesagt, sie wünsche (Konjunktiv I) sich, dass Sterne Wünsche erfüllen könnten (Konjunktiv II). Maria lachte und bestätigte, dass sie das tatsächlich gesagt hätte (Konjunktiv II).

Lena meinte dann, es sei (Konjunktiv I) zwar schön zu träumen, aber es wäre (Konjunktiv II) auch wichtig, sich auf die wirkliche Welt zu konzentrieren. Maria stimmte zu, doch in ihrem Herzen würde (Konjunktiv II) sie immer an die Magie der Sterne glauben.

VOCABULARY LIST – EIN WUNSCHZETTEL			
(der) Wunschzettel [*n.*] (-)	wish list	nächtlich [*adj.*]	nocturnal
(das) Fenster [*n.*] (-)	window	(der) Gedanke [*n.*] (-n)	thought
beobachten [*v.*]	(to) observe	tatsächlich [*adv.*]	actually
(der) Sternenhimmel [*n.*] (-)	starry sky	träumen [*v.*]	(to) dream
wunderschön [*adj.*]	beautiful	konzentrieren [*v.*]	(to) concentrate
(der) Stern [*n.*] (-e)	star	bestätigen [*v.*]	(to) confirm
(der) Wunsch [*n.*] (Wünsche)	wish	(die) Welt [*n.*] (-en)	world
erfüllen [*v.*]	(to) fulfill	(das) Herz [*n.*] (-en)	heart
(die) Magie [*n.*] (-n)	magic		

> # Wäre ich der Konjunktiv, hätte ich mehr würde.

The German language is rich and diverse, offering speakers a plethora of tools to convey various nuances of thought and emotion. One such tool is the *Konjunktiv* mood, a mode of verb conjugation that captures everything from **indirect speech** to the expression of **wishes, desires,** and **hypothetical situations**.

In essence, the *Konjunktiv* mood allows a speaker to transport their audience into the world of "what could be" or "what someone said". It's a realm where reality melds with possibility, and facts intertwine with beliefs. For instance, while the indicative mood would state a fact such as "He says he is coming", the *Konjunktiv* can modify this to "He said he would come." This shift, subtle yet profound, encapsulates the heart of the *Konjunktiv* mood's purpose in German: to transport the listener to a realm of speculation, possibility, or indirect reporting.

Maria's contemplative gaze at the starry expanse and her ensuing conversation with Lena in the provided text, *"Ein Wunschzettel"*, perfectly encapsulate the nuanced role of the *Konjunktiv* mood. The story is sprinkled with instances of *Konjunktiv II*, conveying Maria's unfulfilled wishes and hypothetical thoughts. Then, as Lena recounts Maria's wishes, the narrative seamlessly shifts to *Konjunktiv I*, illustrating the role of this mood in reported speech.

14.2 FORMING THE *KONJUNKTIV I* (PRESENT TENSE FORM)

The *Konjunktiv I*, primarily used for indirect speech, is formed by **adding special endings to the verb's stem**. This mood is particularly prevalent in **formal writing**, such as newspapers or reports, where statements made by others are paraphrased or cited without direct quotation.

Let's take a closer look at the formation process. The **verb stem**, derived from the infinitive, is **combined with specific *Konjunktiv I* endings**. For most verbs, these endings are quite similar to the indicative present tense, with slight alterations. However, it's essential to remember that for many commonly used verbs, especially irregular ones, the *Konjunktiv I* form might resemble the indicative form, leading to potential confusion. In such cases, the *Konjunktiv II* is often preferred for clarity.

Regular Verb Formation

	INDICATIVE MOOD (PRESENT)	KONJUNKTIV I
1ˢᵗ **person** (sing.) 2ⁿᵈ **person** (sing.) 3ʳᵈ **person** (sing.)	*ich spiele* *du spielst* *er/sie/es spielt*	*ich spiele* *du spielest* *er/sie/es spiele*
1ˢᵗ **person** (pl.) 2ⁿᵈ **person** (pl.) 3ʳᵈ **person** (pl.) **Formal** (sing. & pl.)	*wir spielen* *ihr spielt* *sie spielen* *Sie spielen*	*wir spielen* *ihr spielet* *sie spielen* *Sie spielen*

Irregular Verb Formation

	INDICATIVE MOOD (PRESENT)	KONJUNKTIV I
1ˢᵗ **person** (sing.) 2ⁿᵈ **person** (sing.) 3ʳᵈ **person** (sing.)	*ich bin* *du bist* *er/sie/es ist*	*ich sei* *du seist* *er/sie/es sei*
1ˢᵗ **person** (pl.) 2ⁿᵈ **person** (pl.) 3ʳᵈ **person** (pl.) **Formal** (sing. & pl.)	*wir sind* *ihr seid* *sie sind* *Sie sind*	*wir seien* *ihr seiet* *sie seien* *Sie seien*

In the provided narrative, *"Ein Wunschzettel"*, when Lena recounts Maria's thoughts, she uses the *Konjunktiv I* form *"Maria habe gesagt"* (Maria is said to have said) and *"sie wünsche sich"* (she is said to wish). These constructions capture the essence of indirect speech, signaling to the listener that these are not Lena's direct words but her **interpretation or recounting** of Maria's sentiments.

14.3 THE *KONJUNKTIV II*

14.3.1 Expressing Possibilities and Uncertainty with *Konjunktiv II*

> **IHR TUT SO,
> ALS GIBT
> ES KEINEN
> KONJUNKTIV.**

German's **Konjunktiv II** offers an intriguing linguistic avenue to convey hypothetical scenarios, unfulfilled desires, or situations steeped in uncertainty. While English might use phrases like "would" or "could" to hint at such notions, German utilizes *Konjunktiv II* to encapsulate the entire sentiment.

Imagine a world where every wish or wonder can be framed in a sentence. That's precisely the power *Konjunktiv II* grants. It's as if this mode paints German phrases with a layer of "what-ifs", providing them with a unique shade of speculation.

For instance, the phrase "*Ich **würde** das machen*" translates to "I would do that." Here, the inclusion of "**würde**" (the *Konjunktiv II* form of "*werden*") adds the uncertainty to the action.

While *Konjunktiv I* is often reserved for indirect speech, *Konjunktiv II* takes a broader stage, dealing with **possibilities, politeness**, and even **doubts**. But how do you differentiate it from the indicative mood or *Konjunktiv I*?

- **Formation**

  Most verbs in *Konjunktiv II* are formed using the **simple past tense of the verb** and **changing the vowel to its *Umlaut*** (where applicable). For example, "*ging*" (went) becomes "*ginge*" (would go).

  For many commonly used verbs, there's a unique *Konjunktiv II* form. For example, "*war*" (was) becomes "*wäre*" (would be).

· *Modals and Konjunktiv II*

Modal verbs play well with *Konjunktiv II*, adding further layers of speculation or politeness. For instance, *"könnten"* (could), *"sollten"* (should), or *"möchten"* (would like to) are common in polite requests or hypothetical situations.

MOOD	FORMATION	EXAMPLE SENTENCE	ENGLISH TRANSLATION
Indicative	Uses the regular verb form.	*Ich weiß das.*	I know that.
Konjunktiv I	Alters the verb form slightly for indirect speech.	*Er sagte, ich wisse das.*	He said I knew that.
Konjunktiv II	Often uses the simple past tense of the verb, potentially changing the vowel to its *Umlaut*.	*Ich wüsste das gerne.*	I would like to know that.

14.3.2 *Konjunktiv II* in Conditional Sentences

Conditional sentences are often used to express hypothetical situations or conditions that might have been true under different circumstances. These "if… then…" statements in German often employ the *Konjunktiv II*.

CONDITION (IF...)	RESULT (THEN...)
Wenn ich Geld hätte,	*würde ich verreisen.*
(If I had money,)	(I would travel.)

In this table, the left column showcases the hypothetical condition using *Konjunktiv II* (*"hätte"* – had). The right column demonstrates the result that would arise from this condition, again using *Konjunktiv II* (*"würde"* + infinitive verb–would + verb).

14.3.3 Konjunktiv II in Polite Requests and Offers

In German, politeness can be conveyed using the *Konjunktiv II*. This mood softens requests, making them less direct, and therefore, more polite.

DIRECT (INDICATIVE)	POLITE (KONJUNKTIV II)
Kannst du mir helfen?	*Könntest du mir helfen?*
(Can you help me?)	(Could you help me?)

→ This table contrasts the direct request in the indicative mood with the polite version in the *Konjunktiv II*. The latter uses "*könntest*", the *Konjunktiv II* form of "*können*", to make the request softer and more courteous.

14.3.4 Expressing Doubt and Subjunctive in *Konjunktiv II*

The *Konjunktiv II* isn't solely for hypotheticals or polite speech; it also effectively communicates doubt, skepticism, or speculation.

INDICATIVE (STATEMENT OF FACT)	KONJUNKTIV II (EXPRESSION OF DOUBT)
Das ist wahr.	*Es könnte wahr sein.*
(That's true.)	(That could be true.)

14.4 MIXED CONJUNCTIONS WITH *KONJUNKTIV I* AND *II*

Mixed conjunctions introduce both main and subordinate clauses (🔗 Ch. 17). When using them in German, the verb in the main clause can be in the indicative mood, while the subordinate clause verb can be in the *Konjunktiv I* or *II*.

Anna sagt, dass, wenn sie Geld hätte (Konjunktiv II), sie nach Paris reisen würde (Konjunktiv II).
(Anna says that if she had money, she would travel to Paris.)

→ In this example, while "*sagt*" (says) introduces indirect speech and could be followed by *Konjunktiv I*, the hypothetical nature of Anna's statement necessitates the use of *Konjunktiv II*.

MAIN CLAUSE (INDICATIVE)	SUBORDINATE CLAUSE (*KONJUNKTIV II*)
Ich bin (mir) sicher,	*dass er kommen würde.*
(I am sure,)	(that he would come.)

$\hookrightarrow$ Here, the main clause expresses certainty (indicative mood), while the subordinate clause conveys a hypothetical scenario (*Konjunktiv II*).

The best way to distinguish *Konjunktiv II* from Indicative and *Konjunktiv I* is by direct comparison:

SITUATION	INDICATIVE	KONJUNKTIV I	KONJUNKTIV II
Statement of fact	*Er geht ins Kino.*	-	-
(He is going to the cinema.)	(Actual event)	-	-
Reporting someone else's statement	-	*Er sagt, er gehe ins Kino.*	-
(You heard he's going to the cinema.)	-	(Indirect report)	-
Hypothetical scenario	-	-	*Er würde ins Kino gehen.*
(If he had time, he would go to the cinema.)	-	-	(Unreal or contrary-to-fact)
Expressing doubt	*Das ist sein Buch.*	-	*Das könnte sein Buch sein.*
(That's his book.)	(Statement of fact)	-	(This might be his book.)

- **Indicative**

  Represents factual statements and actual events.

- ***Konjunktiv I***

  Typically used for indirect or reported speech. It relays someone else's words or thoughts without directly quoting them.

- ***Konjunktiv II***

  Describes contrary-to-fact situations, expresses doubt, and is employed for polite requests and offers.

 **EXERCISES**

Ü 14.1) Determine whether the verb in each sentence is in *Konjunktiv I* **or** *Konjunktiv II.*

> **Example:** *Sie sagte, **sie** sei krank.*   →   *Konjunktiv I*

    a. Ich wünschte, ich **hätte** mehr Geld.   _____

    b. Er behauptet, dass er im Park **sei**.   _____

    c. Wenn ich Zeit **hätte**, würde ich reisen.   _____

    d. Sie fragt, ob er **komme**.   _____

    e. Er würde gehen, wenn er **könnte**.   _____

    f. Sie sagte, sie **möchte** ein Eis.   _____

    g. Sie fragte, ob wir müde **seien**.   _____

    h. Ich würde es kaufen, wenn es billiger **wäre**.   _____

    i. Er meint, dass sie **gehe**.   _____

    j. Wenn ich du **wäre**, würde ich das tun.   _____

Ü 14.2) Change the following sentences into indirect speech using *Konjunktiv I.*

> **Example**: *Sie sagt, „Ich bin müde."*   →   *Sie sagt, sie sei müde.*

    a. Er sagt, „Ich **gehe** ins Kino."

    _____

    b. Maria behauptet, „Das **ist** mein Buch."

    _____

    c. „Wir **kommen** später", meint Peter.

    _____

    d. Sie erzählt, „Ich **habe** einen Hund."

    _____

e. „Sie **sind** im Park", sagt er.

_____

f. „Ich **werde** bald reisen", sagt sie.

_____

g. Thomas meint, „Das **war** mein Fehler."

_____

h. „Ich **kann** das tun", sagt er.

_____

i. Maria sagt, „Ich **mag** Schokolade."

_____

j. „Das **ergibt** keinen Sinn", behauptet er.

_____

Ü 14.3) Change the following sentences to express hypothetical situations using
Konjunktiv II.

Example: _Ich habe Geld._ → _Wenn ich Geld hätte ..._

a. Ich **gehe** zur Party. _____

b. Sie **kennen** den Weg. _____

c. Wir **haben** ein Auto. _____

d. Du **bist** hier. _____

e. Er **kauft** das Haus. _____

f. Sie **arbeitet** im Büro. _____

g. Ich **esse** den Kuchen. _____

Ü 14.4) Choose the correct form of the verb in parentheses to complete each sentence.

Example: *Er sagte, ich _____ (weiß) das.*

⤷ *Er sagte, ich wisse das. = He said I knew that.*

a. Er behauptet, dass er das Geld nicht _____ (haben).

b. Ich wünschte, ich _____ (sein) im Urlaub.

c. Sie sagte, sie _____ (kommen) später.

d. Wenn du es mir früher _____ (sagen), hätte ich geholfen.

e. Er meint, dass sie zu Hause _____ (bleiben).

f. Ich wäre glücklich, wenn er kommen _____ (können).

g. Es wäre besser, wenn er es _____ (wüsste).

h. Sie fragte, ob das Buch interessant _____ (sein).

i. Wenn sie mehr Zeit _____ (haben), würde sie ein Buch lesen.

Ü 14.5) Use the context to determine whether *Konjunktiv I* **(indirect speech) or** *Konjunktiv II* **(hypotheticals/wishes) is needed.**

Example: *Sie sagt, sie _____ (sein) krank.*

⤷ *Sie sagt, sie __sei__ krank.*

a. Ich wünschte, ich _____ (können) fliegen.

b. Er sagt, er _____ (machen) seine Hausaufgaben.

c. Wenn sie das Geld _____ (haben), würde sie ein Haus kaufen.

d. Sie fragt, ob er das Buch _____ (lesen).

e. Wenn ich ein Vogel _____ (sein), flöge ich hoch.

f. Er meint, das _____ (sein) ein gutes Restaurant.

g. Sie würde mehr trainieren, wenn sie mehr Zeit _____ (haben).

h. Er erzählt, dass sein Bruder in Berlin _____ (wohnen).

i. Würdest du mir helfen, wenn ich dich _____ (fragen)?

j. Sie sagt, sie _____ (wollen) einen Kaffee.

Ü 14.6) Each of the following sentences contains a mistake in the verb form. Rewrite them correctly.

Example: *Sie sagt, sie ist krank.* → *Sie sagt, sie sei krank.*

a. Er glaubt, dass sie kennen die Antwort.

_____

b. Wenn ich ein Auto hätte, ich fahren zur Arbeit.

_____

c. Sie meint, dass sie können das tun.

_____

d. Wenn er hier wäre, er kaufen ein Eis.

_____

e. Sie sagt, dass sie mag Hunde.

_____

f. Er hofft, dass er sein in der Schule morgen.

_____

g. Wenn ich mehr Geld, ich kaufen ein neues Haus.

_____

h. Sie denkt, dass er machen seine Hausaufgaben.

_____

Unit 4

CASES, CLAUSES & WORD ORDER

Language is an intricate tapestry, and the threads that weave it together in German are its cases, clauses, and word order. These elements serve as the building blocks of structured and meaningful communication. They dictate not only what words we choose but also where we place them and how they relate to each other in a sentence.

While English also employs cases and clauses, German's utilization of them, coupled with its specific word order rules, creates a unique rhythmic structure. This might seem challenging initially, but with understanding comes appreciation for the nuances it brings to the language.

This unit journeys through the fascinating world of German cases, the dynamic interplay of clauses, and the rhythmic dance of word order. As you navigate each chapter, you'll uncover the logic behind the structure, enhancing both your comprehension and expression. By the end of this unit, the seeming complexity will translate into a symphony of clarity and confidence in your German communication.

CHAPTER 15
SUBJECT, PREDICATE AND OBJECT

⊘ CHECKBOX – WHAT ARE SUBJECT, PREDICATE AND OBJECT?

In German grammar, sentences are constructed with three key elements: the **subject**, representing the **doer or topic**; the **predicate**, expressing the **action or state**; and the **object**, signifying the **receiver of the action**. Maintaining a typical word order, the subject appears at the beginning of the sentence, followed by the predicate and, if present, the object(s).

◯ TEXT – EIN BESUCH IM ZOO

(The following text describes a boy named Lukas, who has a deep fondness for animals and enjoys visiting the zoo regularly.)

Lukas, der Junge mit den blauen Augen, liebt Tiere. Deshalb ist der Zoo sein Lieblingsort. Jeden Samstag besucht er diesen wunderbaren Ort und lässt sich von der Vielfalt der Natur verzaubern. Die bunten Papageien singen immer die schönsten Lieder. Seine Schwester Clara füttert oft die Ziegen, während Lukas von einer Bank aus zusieht. Am meisten faszinieren ihn aber die majestätischen Löwen, die er stundenlang beim Ruhen und Spielen beobachtet.

Die Tierpfleger im Zoo kennen Lukas gut. Oft erzählen sie ihm spannende Geschichten über die Tiere und ihre Abenteuer. Für Lukas sind diese Geschichten immer der Höhepunkt seines Besuchs und er geht jedes Mal mit einem Lächeln nach Hause.

VOCABULARY LIST – EIN BESUCH IM ZOO			
(der) Junge [*n.*] (-n)	boy	(die) Natur [*n.*] (-)	nature
(das) Auge [*n.*] (-n)	eye	verzaubern [*v.*]	(to) enchant
deshalb [*adv.*]	therefore	bunt [*adj.*]	colorful
(der) Lieblingsort [*n.*] (-e)	favorite place	singen [*v.*]	(to) sing
jeden [*adj.*]	each	(die) Schwester [*n.*] (-n)	sister
wunderbar [*adj.*]	wonderful	faszinieren [*v.*]	(to) fascinate
(die) Vielfalt [*n.*] (-)	variety	majestätisch [*adj.*]	majestic
ruhen [*v.*]	(to) rest	(der) Löwe [*n.*] (-n)	lion
(der/die) Tierpfleger/-in [*n.*] (-nen)	animal keeper	stundenlang [*adj.*]	hour-long
(das) Abenteuer [*n.*] (-)	adventure	(der) Besuch [*n.*] (-e)	visit
(der) Höhepunkt [*n.*] (-e)	highlight		

15.1 INTRODUCTION TO SENTENCE ELEMENTS

Every sentence we formulate consists of core elements that convey the crux of the message. These elements are the building blocks, helping in comprehending and constructing meaningful statements. The three foundational pillars of any sentence are the **subject**, **predicate**, and **object**.

- **Subject**

  This is the "who" or "what" the sentence is about. It generally dictates the verb form and hence the agreement in number and person.

- **Predicate**

  This encompasses the verb and what comes after it, illustrating what the subject is doing or the state of the subject.

- **Object**

  Provides more details about the verb. There can be direct objects (what the verb acts upon) and indirect objects (to whom or for whom the action is done).

While these components might appear straightforward, the complexity arises in languages like German, where cases and word order can drastically change their appearances and positions.

15.2 THE SUBJECT

In a sentence, the subject typically answers the questions "**Who?**" or "**What?**" It refers to the person, animal, thing, or idea that is doing or being. In the context of German, the subject always dictates the conjugation of the verb, ensuring agreement in terms of gender, number, and person.

- **Definition**

  The subject can be a noun, pronoun, or any phrase that generally performs the action of or which the sentence speaks about.

- **Characteristics**

  Subjects will often be in the nominative case in German. Moreover, they often come at the beginning of a declarative sentence but can shift in position with different sentence structures or types.

- **Subjects in Different Tenses and Mood**

  The position of the subject can vary, especially when dealing with different verb tenses and moods. For instance, in a question or in the second position with certain modal verbs.

| "*Lukas besucht den Zoo.*" | → | Here, "*Lukas*" is the <u>subject</u>. |
| "*Die bunten Papageien singen.*" | → | "*Die bunten Papageien*" is the <u>subject</u>. |

In a sentence, nouns can either perform the action (as the subject) or be acted upon/receive the action (as the object). For instance, in the text, "*Lukas*" acts as the subject, while "*Zoo*" is an object.

Another example is "***Die Tierpfleger** erzählen <u>Geschichten</u>.*" Here, "*Die Tierpfleger*" is the **subject**, and "*Geschichten*" is the <u>direct object</u>.

15.3 THE PREDICATE

Central to any sentence is the **predicate**, which essentially tells what the subject does or what happens to the subject. It comprises the verb and any accompanying structures, such as objects or modifiers.

- **Definition**

  The predicate is the part of the sentence that provides information about what the subject is doing or what is happening to the subject. It encompasses the verb and often expands to include objects, complements, and other modifiers.

- **Recognizing the Main Verb**

  At the heart of every predicate is the main verb. This verb conveys the main action or state of being in the sentence. In German, the main verb can appear in different positions within the sentence, depending on the sentence structure. For instance, in a typical statement, the main verb is second, but in a question, it often comes first.

- **Predicate Verbs in Different Tenses and Moods**

  The verb in the predicate agrees with the subject in number and person. Additionally, its form can change depending on the tense (present, past, future) or mood (indicative, imperative, subjunctive) of the sentence.

| "*Lukas <u>besucht</u> den Zoo.*" | → | The verb "*besucht*" is the <u>predicate</u>, indicating Lukas' action. |

"Die Tierpfleger erzählen Geschichten." → Here, *"erzählen"* is the <u>predicate</u>, denoting the action of the zookeepers.

15.4 THE OBJECT

When we talk about the object within a sentence, we're discussing the component that usually receives the action of the verb. German, like many languages, distinguishes between different types of objects, with the two most common being direct and indirect objects.

- **Definition**

  An object in a sentence typically refers to the entity that is acted upon by the verb. This entity might receive, feel, or experience the action directly (direct object) or might benefit from or be affected by the action in a secondary manner (indirect object).

- **Distinguishing Direct and Indirect Objects**

  The direct object answers the question "What?" or "Whom?", while the indirect object often answers the question "To whom?" or "For whom?". In German, the direct object is typically in the accusative case, while the indirect object is in the dative case.

- **Identifying Objects in Sentences**

  Spotting objects becomes easier with practice. Look for nouns or pronouns that seem to be on the receiving end of the action. For instance, in the sentence *"Lukas besucht den Zoo"* *"den Zoo"* is a direct object, receiving the action of the verb *"besucht"*.

*"Die Tierpfleger erzählen **ihm** spannende* <u>*Geschichten*</u>*."* → Here, *"Geschichten"* is a <u>direct object</u> (What do they tell?), and *"ihm"* (to him) is an **indirect object**.

"Seine Schwester füttert <u>die Ziegen</u>." → In this case, *"die Ziegen"* is the <u>direct object</u>.

✎ EXERCISES

Ü 15.1) Underline the subject in each of the following sentences.

Example: Der Junge spielt Fußball. → <u>Der Junge</u> spielt Fußball.

a. Die Sonne scheint hell.

b. Der Hund bellt laut.

c. Der Lehrer erklärt den Stoff.

d. Die Vögel singen im Wald.

e. Meine Schwester kocht Pasta.

f. Der Computer funktioniert nicht.

g. Die Katzen schlafen.

h. Der Apfel fällt vom Baum.

i. Sie lernen Deutsch.

Ü 15.2) Underline the predicate verb in each of the following sentences.

Example: Der Junge <u>spielt</u> Fußball. (spielen)

a. Anna liest ein Buch.

b. Der Baum wächst schnell.

c. Der Zug kommt an.

d. Die Blumen blühen.

e. Peter und Maria tanzen.

f. Das Auto fährt.

g. Sie schreibt einen Brief.

h. Die Kinder lachen.

i. Die Vögel fliegen.

j. Der Regen fällt.

Ü 15.3) Underline the object in each of the following sentences.

Example: Der Junge spielt <u>Fußball</u>.

a. Sie trinkt Tee.

b. Ich liebe meine Familie.

c. Der Lehrer unterrichtet Mathematik.

d. Meine Mutter kauft das Kleid.

e. Er sieht den Film.

f. Das Mädchen gibt dem Hund einen Knochen.

g. Der Bäcker verkauft Brot.

h. Er liest das Magazin.

i. Sie hört Musik.

j. Die Kinder essen Kuchen.

Ü 15.4) Using the provided subjects, predicates, and objects, construct meaningful sentences.

a. (Die Blume / duften / süß)

_____

b. (Der Mann / tragen / Hut)

_____

c. (Die Studenten / lernen / Geschichte)

_____

d. (Das Auto / haben / Panne)

_____

e. (Die Vögel / suchen / Futter)

_____

f. (Das Mädchen / mögen / Eis)

_____

g. (Der Opa / erzählen / Geschichte)

_____

h. (Der Lehrer / korrigieren / Tests)

_____

i. (Die Katze / jagen / Maus)

_____

j. (Der Tourist / fotografieren / Sehenswürdigkeiten)

_____

Ü 15.5) Rearrange the words to form a coherent sentence.

Example: spielt / der / Junge / Fußball   →   Der Junge spielt Fußball.

a. Apfel / der / fällt / Baum / vom

_____

b. im / die / Katze / schläft / Korb

_____

c. essen / die / Kinder / Schokolade

_____

d. der / fliegt / Himmel / Vogel / im

_____

e. Buch / liest / Anna / das

_____

f. in / der / regnet / Es / Stadt

_____

g. hört / der / Mann / Radio

_____

h. die / im / schwimmen / Fische / Teich

_____

i. Frau / kauft / die / Schuhe / rote

_____

j. singt / im / das / Mädchen / Chor

_____

Ü 15.6) Choose the correct object for each sentence.

Example: *Er liest _____.*   *(A) eine Zeitung*   *(B) ein Brot*   *(C) ein Tuch*
↳ *A*

a. Sie isst _____.   (A) einen Apfel   (B) einen Stuhl   (C) ein Fenster

b. Er fährt _____.   (A) die Blume   (B) den Tisch   (C) das Auto

c. Wir hören _____.   (A) den Hut   (B) die Musik   (C) den Teppich

d. Die Katze jagt _____.   (A) die Maus   (B) die Lampe   (C) die Tasse

e. Der Bäcker verkauft _____.   (A) die Uhr   (B) den Stift   (C) das Brot

f. Sie trinkt _____.   (A) die Karte   (B) den Tee   (C) das Sofa

g. Die Schüler schreiben _____.   (A) die Tasse   (B) die Aufsätze   (C) den Schrank

h. Der Fotograf macht _____.   (A) die Bilder   (B) den Ball   (C) den Schal

i. Der Arzt untersucht _____.   (A) die Patienten   (B) die Teller   (C) den Baum

Ü 15.7) Complete the sentences with a suitable subject, predicate, or object from the box.

Example: Der _____ backt Brot.   →   Der <u>Bäcker</u> backt Brot.

wachsen, Lehrer, wünscht, schenkt, Tante, backt, näht, Rosen, kauft, Großmutter

a. Meine _____ feiert Geburtstag.

b. Die Blumen _____ im Garten.

c. Der Bäcker _____ Kuchen.

d. Sie _____ ihrem Neffen ein Geschenk.

e. Die _____ blühen schön.

f. Er _____ Brot beim Bäcker.

g. Der Schneider _____ täglich.

h. Sie pflegt ihre_____.

i. Meine Mutter _____ sich Kuchen zum Geburtstag.

j. Der _____ bringt den Schülern neuen Stoff bei.

Ü 15.8) Find and correct the mistake in each sentence.

Example: Der Junge <u>spielen</u> Fußball.   →   Der Junge <u>spielt</u> Fußball.

a. Das Kindern spielen im Garten.   _____

b. Er lieben Pizza.   _____

c. Die Lehrerin erklär die Regel.   _____

d. Der Hunde bellt laut.   _____

e. Sie haben ein rotes Kleider.   _____

f. Das Bücher ist spannend.   _____

g. Der Mädchen singt ein Lied.   _____

h. Die Blume duftet guter.   _____

i. Der Autos fahren schnell.   _____

j. Ich mag Eiscremes.   _____

Ü 15.9) Change the sentences from singular to plural and from plural to singular.

Example: Die Jungen essen das Eis.　　→　　　Der Junge isst das Eis.

a. Der Vogel fliegt hoch.

_____

b. Die Kinder lernen im Klassenzimmer.

_____

c. Das Auto ist schnell.

_____

d. Die Äpfel sind saftig.

_____

e. Die Frau kauft Gemüse.

_____

f. Das Pferd galoppiert auf der Wiese.

_____

g. Die Bücher sind auf dem Tisch.

_____

h. Der Stuhl ist alt.

_____

i. Die Fenster sind offen.

_____

j. Der Lehrer korrigiert die Tests.

_____

CHAPTER 16
WORD ORDER IN DECLARATIVE SENTENCES AND QUESTIONS

⊘ CHECKBOX – WHAT ARE THE GENERAL RULES FOR WORD ORDER IN GERMAN?

In **declarative sentences**, the standard word order is **Subject-Verb-Object** (SVO). The subject typically appears first, followed by the verb, and then the object(s). However, adverbial phrases, such as time expressions or adverbs, may alter the word order to emphasize specific details within the sentence.

In **questions**, the word order changes to **Verb-Subject-Object** (VSO). The verb precedes the subject, and the rest of the sentence retains the standard SVO order. Additionally, question words (interrogative pronouns) introduce specific information in questions.

Handling word order in declarative sentences and questions requires attention to the context and the intended emphasis. Adverbial phrases and other elements may be placed in different positions within the sentence to highlight particular details or add clarity.

○ **DIALOGUE – WOCHENENDPLÄNE**

(Anna and Lukas, friends catching up on their weekend plans, discuss Lukas' upcoming visit to his grandparents.)

Anna: *Lukas, was machst du am Wochenende?*

Lukas: *Am Samstag fahre ich zu meinen Großeltern.*

Anna: *Wann fährst du zu ihnen?*

Lukas: *Um 10 Uhr morgens fahre ich los.*

Anna: *Mit dem Zug oder mit dem Auto?*

Lukas: *Mit dem Auto, das geht schneller.*

Anna: *Warum fährst du am Wochenende zu ihnen?*

Lukas: *Sie feiern ihren 50. Hochzeitstag.*

Anna: *Das ist schön. Und wo wird gefeiert?*

Lukas: *Sie feiern im Garten bei sich zu Hause.*

Anna: *Dann wünsche ich euch viel Spaß!*

VOCABULARY LIST – WOCHENENDPLÄNE			
(die) Großeltern [*n.*] [*pl.*]	grandparents	(der) Hochzeitstag [*n.*] (-e)	wedding day
fahren [*v.*]	(to) ride	feiern [*v.*]	(to) celebrate
(der) Zug [*n.*] (Züge)	train	(der) Garten [*n.*] (Gärten)	garden
(das) Auto [*n.*] (-s)	car	zu Hause [*adv.*]	at home
morgens [*adv.*]	morning	(der) Spaß [*n.*] (Späße)	fun
schneller [*adj.*]	faster	wünschen [*v.*]	(to) wish

16.1 BASIC WORD ORDER IN DECLARATIVE SENTENCES

German follows a standard word order for declarative sentences, often termed as the **Subject-Verb-Object** (SVO) order. This structure ensures the subject usually comes before the verb and the object follows the verb. Let's take a simple sentence: *"Der Hund beißt den Mann"* (The dog bites the man). Here, *"Der Hund"* is the subject, *"beißt"* is the verb, and *"den Mann"* is the object.

However, German also features flexibility in its word order to **emphasize different elements** or to **fit the rhythmic flow** of the language. For instance, the sentence *"Den Mann beißt der Hund"* emphasizes *"Den Mann"* and changes the meaning slightly to stress the man as the bitten one.

In our dialogue, Anna's first question *"Lukas, was machst du am Wochenende?"* exhibits the standard SVO order with *"du"* (you) as the subject, *"machst"* (do) as the verb, and *"am Wochenende"* (on the weekend) as the object.

GERMAN SENTENCE	ENGLISH TRANSLATION	SUBJECT	VERB	OBJECT
Der Hund beißt den Mann.	The dog bites the man.	*Der Hund*	*beißt*	*den Mann.*
Lukas fährt zu seinen Großeltern.	Lukas is driving to his grandparents.	*Lukas*	*fährt*	*zu seinen Großeltern.*

16.2 POSITION OF ADVERBIAL PHRASES

The placement of adverbial phrases in a German sentence can be influenced by what kind of information the adverbial provides. Adverbials can convey details about time, manner, place, reason, or frequency, among others.

One basic rule in German is the **TMP rule**: **Time**, **Manner**, and **Place**. This rule dictates the preferred order for adverbials when they appear in a sentence together. Let's break it down:

- **Time (*Zeit*)**
  When an event occurs.
- **Manner (*Art und Weise*)**
  How an event occurs.
- **Place (*Ort*)**
  Where an event occurs.

Am Samstag fahre ich mit dem Auto zu meinen Großeltern.
(On Saturday, I am driving by car to my grandparents.)

  → **Time**: "*Am Samstag*" (On Saturday)
  Manner: "*mit dem Auto*" (by car)
  Place: "*zu meinen Großeltern*" (to my grandparents)

If we analyze Lukas' statement in the dialogue: "*Um 10 Uhr morgens fahre ich los*" it starts with a time element "*Um 10 Uhr morgens*" (At 10 in the morning). This conforms to the tendency to place time details at the beginning for clarity.

GERMAN SENTENCE	ENGLISH TRANSLATION	TIME	MANNER	PLACE
Am Samstag fahre ich mit dem Auto zu meinen Großeltern.	On Saturday, I am driving by car to my grandparents.	*Am Samstag*	*mit dem Auto*	*zu meinen Großeltern*
Um 10 Uhr morgens fahre ich los.	I am leaving at 10 in the morning.	*Um 10 Uhr morgens*		
Er fährt im Sommer oft mit dem Rad ins Büro.	He often rides his bike to the office in the summer.	*im Sommer*	*mit dem Rad*	*ins Büro*
Im Winter fahre ich selten mit dem Bus zur Schule.	In winter, I rarely take the bus to school.	*Im Winter*	*mit dem Bus*	*zur Schule*
Jeden Freitag essen wir zu Hause mit Freunden.	Every Friday, we eat at home with friends.	*Jeden Freitag*	*mit Freunden*	*zu Hause*

While the TMP rule is a guideline, German speakers sometimes rearrange these elements to emphasize a particular detail. The verb, however, often remains the anchor in the second position, ensuring clarity even when other elements move around.

16.3 VERB PLACEMENT IN QUESTIONS

The way verbs are positioned in German questions is fundamentally different from declarative sentences and plays a crucial role in word order.

In German, there are mainly two types of questions: yes-no questions and information questions.

- **Yes-No Questions**

  These are questions that expect either a *"ja"* (yes) or *"nein"* (no) as an answer. The word order in such questions is characterized by the **verb taking the first position, followed by the subject**. Consider the dialogue example: *"**Fährst du** zu ihnen?"* Here, *"fährst"* (drive) is the verb, and *"du"* (you) is the subject.

- **Information Questions**

  These questions aim to gather specific details and are usually initiated by question words like *"wer"* (who), *"was"* (what), *"wann"* (when), *"wo"* (where), *"warum"* (why), etc. In these questions, the **question word often starts the sentence, followed by the verb and then the subject**. The dialogue provides an apt example with *"**Was machst du** am Wochenende?"* Here, *"**was**"* (what) is the question word, *"**machst**"* (do) is the verb, and *"**du**"* (you) is the subject.

QUESTION TYPE	GERMAN EXAMPLE	ENGLISH EQUIVALENT	STRUCTURE
Yes-No	*Fährst du zu ihnen?*	Are you driving to them?	Verb-Subject-Object
Information	*Was machst du am Wochenende?*	What are you doing on the weekend?	Question Word-Verb-Subject-Object

A handy trick to remember is that in most yes-no questions, if you can insert *"ja"* or *"nein"* at the beginning of an answer, then you're on the right track. For instance, answering the question *"Fährst du zu ihnen?"* with *"Ja, ich fahre zu ihnen"* is appropriate.

16.4 QUESTION WORDS AND WORD ORDER

The magic of German question words, often referred to as *"**W-Fragen**"* (due to most starting with the letter *"W"*), resides in their power to extract specific information. These words act as tools to frame questions aiming for more than just a *"yes"* or *"no"*.

Let's look at some common German question words:

- **Wer? (Who?)**

  Asks about a person. For instance, *"Wer ist das?"* translates to "Who is that?"

- **Was? (What?)**

  Seeks details about a thing or idea. In the dialogue, *"Was machst du am Wochenende?"* is inquiring about weekend plans.

- **Wann? (When?):**

  Targets time details. *"Wann fährst du zu ihnen?"* from our dialogue precisely asks about the timing of Lukas's visit.

- **Wo? (Where?):**

  Asks about location. For instance, *"Wo wohnst du?"* means "Where do you live?"

- **Warum? (Why?):**

  Seeks reasons or causes. As in, *"Warum fährst du am Wochenende zu ihnen?"* from our dialogue, Anna is curious about the reason for Lukas's weekend trip.

When forming questions using these words, the typical structure is the **question word at the beginning, followed by the verb, and then the subject**. However, if another element like an **adverbial phrase** (e.g., *"am Wochenende"*) is included, it often comes **after the subject**. This structure ensures clarity in the question while also placing emphasis on the specific information being sought.

QUESTION WORD	GERMAN EXAMPLE	ENGLISH TRANSLATION	STRUCTURE
Wer	*Wer ist das?*	Who is that?	Question Word-Verb-Subject
Was	*Was machst du am Wochenende?*	What are you doing on the weekend?	Question Word-Verb-Subject-Adverbial Phrase
Wann	*Wann fährst du zu ihnen?*	When are you going to them?	Question Word-Verb-Subject-Object
Wo	*Wo wohnst du?*	Where do you live?	Question Word-Verb-Subject
Warum	*Warum fährst du am Wochenende zu ihnen?*	Why are you going to them on the weekend?	Question Word-Verb-Subject-Adverbial Phrase-Object

16.5 HANDLING DIRECT AND INDIRECT OBJECTS IN WORD ORDER

The interplay between direct and indirect objects is crucial in German, as it has a direct impact on word order and, ultimately, sentence clarity. To truly grasp their placement, one must first recognize them.

In English, the **direct object receives the action of the verb directly**, while the **indirect object indirectly benefits from that action**. German follows the same principle. For instance, in the sentence *"Ich gebe dem Mann das Buch" "das Buch"* is the direct object (the item being given) and *"dem Mann"* is the indirect object (the recipient of the item).

In standard German **declarative sentences**, the **word order** usually **prioritizes the direct object over the indirect object when both are noun phrases**. However, when the indirect object is a pronoun, it often comes before the direct object.

SENTENCE STRUCTURE	GERMAN EXAMPLE	ENGLISH TRANSLATION
Verb-Direct Object-Indirect Object	*Ich schenke das Buch dem Mann.*	I give the book to the man.
Verb-Indirect Object (Pronoun)-Direct Object	*Ich schenke ihm das Buch.*	I give him the book.

Note the switch in the order when the indirect object, "*dem Mann*" is replaced with the pronoun "*ihm*."

Furthermore, when framing **questions** involving direct and indirect objects, it's essential to ensure that the **verb** (usually in second position) **is followed immediately by the subject**. Subsequent placements of direct and indirect objects can then follow based on the focus of the question.

Direct Object Question:

Was schenkst du dem Mann?
(What are you giving to the man?)

Indirect Object Question:

Wem schenkst du das Buch?
(To whom are you giving the book?)

16.6 WORD ORDER IN SUBORDINATE CLAUSES

Subordinate clauses, also known as dependent clauses, are a unique feature of German grammar, especially concerning word order. These clauses cannot stand alone and typically provide additional information to a main clause.

In German, the **key identifier** of a subordinate clause is the **position of the conjugated verb**: it always comes **at the end**. This is a notable departure from main clauses where the verb typically occupies the second position.

Ich weiß, **dass** *du Recht* **hast**.
(I know that you are right.)

In the sentence above, "**dass**" (that) is a **subordinating conjunction** which introduces the subordinate clause. The verb "*hast*" (have) is at the end of the clause.

Subordinating conjunctions that can introduce these clauses include: **weil** (because), **obwohl** (although), **wenn** (if/when), **sobald** (as soon as), and others.

MAIN CLAUSE	SUBORDINATING CONJUNCTION	SUBJECT	OTHER ELEMENTS	CONJUGATED VERB	ENGLISH TRANSLATION
Ich glaube,	dass	er	ein Buch	liest.	I believe that he reads a book.
Sie fragt,	ob	ich	zum Fußballspiel	gehe.	She asks if I go to the soccer match.
Anna bleibt zu Hause,	obwohl	sie	eigentlich ins Kino	wollte.	Anna stays at home although she wanted to go to the cinema.

Another vital aspect to note about subordinate clauses is that they can appear either at the beginning or the end of a main clause. However, when the subordinate clause begins the sentence, it is followed by a comma and the main clause, and the main verb of the main clause directly follows the comma.

- **Subordinate Clause first:**

  Weil er müde war, ging er früh ins Bett.
  (Because he was tired, he went to bed early.)

- **Main Clause first:**

  *Er ging früh ins Bett, **weil er müde war**.*
  (He went to bed early because he was tired.)

16.7 EMPHASIZING ELEMENTS WITH WORD ORDER

The flexibility of German word order allows for emphasizing different parts of a sentence to adjust the meaning or to add emphasis to a particular element.

- **Fronting for Emphasis**

  In German, when you move elements to the beginning of a sentence (a process known as "fronting"), you give them added emphasis. For instance, if you want to emphasize the time aspect of an action, you can start the sentence with the time element.

  Standard:

  Ich sehe den Film am Freitag.
  (I'll watch the movie on Friday.)

  Emphasized:

  Am Freitag sehe ich den Film
  (On Friday, I'll watch the movie.)

  In the second example, by fronting "*Am Freitag*", you emphasize the time frame over the action.

- **Emphasizing Objects**

  Just as with time, you can front objects to give them more prominence in a sentence. This does not change the meaning but can offer subtle differences in emphasis.

  Standard:

  Ich habe den Schlüssel verloren.
  (I have lost the key.)

  Emphasized:

  Den Schlüssel habe ich verloren.
  (The key, I have lost.)

  The latter construction can be especially effective in a conversation where you are discussing multiple items, and you want to emphasize the importance or specificity of one of them.

📝 EXERCISES

Ü 16.1) Choose the sentence with the correct word order.

Example: **a.** *Ich in Berlin wohne.* _____

            b. *Wohne ich in Berlin.* _____

            c. *Ich wohne in Berlin.* ___✓___

a. Oft er spielt Fußball. _____

b. Er spielt oft Fußball. _____

c. Er oft spielt Fußball. _____

a. Sie liebt Musik hören. _____

b. Musik liebt sie hören. _____

c. Sie liebt es, Musik zu hören. _____

a. Schokolade sie mag sehr. _____

b. Sie mag Schokolade sehr. _____

c. Sie Schokolade mag sehr. _____

a. Er hat einen Apfel gegessen. _____

b. Gegessen einen Apfel hat er. _____

c. Er einen Apfel hat gegessen. _____

a. Immer ins Kino sie geht. _____

b. Sie geht immer ins Kino. _____

c. Sie immer geht ins Kino. _____

a. Er liest das Buch. _____

b. Das Buch er liest. _____

c. Er das Buch liest. _____

a. Der Hund schläft im Haus. _____

b. Im Haus der Hund schläft. _____

c. Schläft im Haus der Hund. _____

a. In einem Büro sie arbeiten. _____

b. Einem Büro sie arbeiten in. _____

c. Sie arbeiten in einem Büro. _____

Ü 16.2) Rearrange the given words to form a coherent sentence.

Example: Apfel | den | isst | er → Er isst den Apfel.

a. Blumen | die | schön | sind

_____

b. heute | gegrillt | wir | zu Hause | haben

_____

c. trinke | Kaffee | morgens | ich | immer

_____

d. sie | Haus | ein | großes | hat

_____

e. Berlin | in | wohnt | er | nicht

_____

f. arbeitet | er | wo | weiß | ich | nicht

_____

g. Pizza | isst | gerne | sie

_____

h. im | lese | Bett | ich | gerne | Bücher

_____

i. oft | nach | fährt | er | Berlin

_____

j. im | Garten | Kinder | die | spielen

_____

Ü 16.3) Change the following declarative sentences into questions.

Example: Wir gehen auf eine Party. → Gehen wir auf eine Party?

a. Sie besucht das Museum. _____

b. Er lernt Deutsch. _____

c. Sie haben ein neues Auto. _____

d. Die Vögel singen. _____

e. Es regnet heute. _____

f. Sie essen Pizza. _____

g. Die Kinder schlafen. _____

h. Er schreibt einen Brief. _____

i. Das Flugzeug landet. _____

j. Sie tanzt im Club. _____

Ü 16.4) Fill in the blanks.

a. _____ möchtest du trinken?

b. Sie _____ nach Paris geflogen.

c. _____ gehen sie ins Kino?

d. _____ trinkt sie immer Tee.

e. _____ spielt er Klavier.

f. Wann _____ du ins Bett?

g. Warum _____ sie so spät?

h. Wie _____ sie das gemacht?

i. _____ lernen sie Deutsch?

j. _____ hat er so viel Geld?

Ü 16.5) Match the subject with the correct predicate to form a coherent sentence.

Example:

Die Kinder *liest sich gut.*
Das Buch *fliegen nach London.*

a. Das Mädchen   hat ein neues Kleid.

b. Die Katze   spielen Fußball.

c. Die Eltern   isst den Fisch.

d. Der Mann   schlafen schon.

e. Der Zug   kauft ein Buch.

f. Die Jungs   fährt um fünf Uhr ab.

g. Die Oma   kocht Suppe.

h. Der Vogel   singt ein Lied.

i. Die Lehrerin   lesen die Zeitung.

j. Die Schüler   erklärt die Aufgabe.

Ü 16.6) Identify and underline the time element in each sentence.

a. Im Winter fahre ich Ski.

b. Letzten Sommer waren wir in Italien.

c. Sie besucht uns jeden Sonntag.

d. Morgen wird es regnen.

e. Nächstes Jahr werde ich studieren.

f. Er ruft mich jeden Abend an.

g. Im April blühen die Blumen.

h. Sie haben vor zwei Wochen geheiratet.

i. Ich sehe sie einmal im Monat.

j. Am Wochenende gehen wir wandern.

Ü 16.7) Fill in the blanks with the correct auxiliary verb: "*haben*" or "*sein*".

a. Die Kinder _____ im Park gespielt.

b. Sie _____ nach Spanien gereist.

c. Er _____ ein Eis gegessen.

d. Die Blumen _____ gewachsen.

e. Wir _____ ins Kino gegangen.

f. Ich _____ ein Buch gelesen.

g. Die Tasse _____ zerbrochen.

h. Sie _____ aufgestanden.

i. Er _____ ins Wasser gesprungen.

j. Sie _____ einkaufen gewesen.

Ü 16.8) Identify and underline the modal verb in each sentence.

Example: Du <u>solltest</u> mehr Wasser trinken.

a. Er darf nicht ins Kino gehen.

b. Sie können gut singen.

c. Ich möchte ein Eis.

d. Wir müssen jetzt gehen.

e. Sie will ins Theater.

f. Er mag keinen Käse.

g. Du darfst das nicht tun.

h. Ich kann das Fenster öffnen.

i. Sie müssen das Formular ausfüllen.

CHAPTER 17
SUBCLAUSES

⊘ CHECKBOX – WHAT IS A SUBCLAUSE?

A subclause, also known as a subordinate clause, functions as a **dependent clause** within a sentence. It **relies on the main clause** to provide complete meaning and **cannot stand alone as an independent sentence**. Subclauses often introduce **additional information**, **conditions**, or **reasons**, and they are typically **introduced by subordinating conjunctions** such as *"weil"* (because), *"obwohl"* (although), *"dass"* (that), etc.

Compound clauses consist of **two or more subclauses connected by coordinating conjunctions** like *"und"* (and), *"aber"* (but), *"oder"* (or), etc. Each subclause in a compound clause contributes to the overall meaning, and their arrangement impacts the flow and coherence of the sentence.

Ich gehe ins Kino, <u>falls es nicht zu spät ist</u> <u>und wenn der Film interessant ist.</u>
(I will go to the cinema if it's not too late and if the movie is interesting.)

Er kam, <u>weil er eingeladen war</u> <u>und blieb bis zum Ende der Party.</u>
(He came because he was invited and stayed until the end of the party.)

Relative clauses provide **additional information about a noun in the main clause** and are **introduced by relative pronouns** such as *"der"*, *"die"*, *"das"* (who, which, that) or *"dessen"* *"deren"* (whose). They serve to specify or describe the noun more precisely and are an integral part of the sentence structure.

*Das Buch, **das** <u>ich gestern gekauft habe, ist sehr interessant.</u>*
(The book that I bought yesterday is very interesting.)

*Das Auto, **das** <u>vor dem Haus parkt, gehört meinem Bruder.</u>*
(The car that is parked in front of the house belongs to my brother.)

⌕ **DIALOGUE – DAS NEUE BUCH**

(Mia and Jan, friends who share a love for books, discuss a captivating new novel that Mia is currently reading.)

Mia: Jan, ich lese gerade ein Buch, **das mir sehr gefällt.**

Jan: Wirklich? Erzähl mir von dem Buch, **das du liest.**

Mia: Es handelt von einem Mädchen, **das in einer Fantasiewelt lebt.** Sie trifft auf Kreaturen, **die ihr bei ihrer Reise helfen.**

Jan: Das klingt nach einem Buch, **das ich auch gerne lesen würde.** Ist es das Buch, **dessen Autor letztes Jahr einen Preis gewonnen hat**?

Mia: Genau! Das Buch, **das ich meine,** wurde von ihm geschrieben.

Jan: Ich liebe Geschichten, **in denen es um Abenteuer und Fantasie geht.**

Mia: Ich auch! Bücher, **die solche Themen haben,** sind immer meine Favoriten.

Jan: Nun, da du es erwähnt hast, werde ich es lesen, **sobald ich Zeit habe.**

VOCABULARY LIST – DAS NEUE BUCH			
gefallen [*v.*]	(to) like	(der) Preis [*n.*] (-e)	prize, award
handeln [*v.*]	(to) act	gewinnen [*v.*]	(to) win
(das) Mädchen [*n.*] (-)	girl	schreiben [*v.*]	(to) write
(die) Fantasiewelt [*n.*] (-en)	fantasy world	(die) Geschichte [*n.*](-n)	story
klingen [*v.*]	(to) sound	(die) Fantasie [*n.*] (-n)	fantasy
(der) Autor/-in [*n.*] (-en/-nen)	author	(das) Thema [*n.*] (Themen)	topic
(die) Zeit [*n.*] (-en)	time	(der) Favorit [*n.*] (-en)	favorite
letzte /-r /-s [*adj.*]	last	erwähnen [*v.*]	(to) mention

17.1 INTRODUCTION TO SUBCLAUSES

Subclauses, also known as subordinate clauses or "*Nebensätze*" in German, are an intrinsic part of the German sentence structure. Unlike main clauses ("*Hauptsätze*"), which can stand alone as sentences, **subclauses cannot**. They rely on a main clause to provide context and meaning. These clauses allow for richer, more complex expressions in the language. For example, in the sentence "*Ich denke, dass du recht hast*" (I think that you are right), "*dass du recht hast*" is the subclause providing further detail on what is being thought.

Main clause:

Ich liebe Bücher.
(I love books.)

With subclause:

Ich lese Bücher, weil sie spannend sind.
(I read books because they are exciting.)

17.2 TYPES OF SUBCLAUSES

German subclauses come in various types, each serving a unique function within the sentence. The main categories are noun clauses, adverbial clauses, and relative clauses.

- **Noun Clauses**

  A noun clause can **function as a subject, object, or complement in a sentence**, often providing more **detail** or **clarification**. For instance, in the sentence "*Ich glaube, dass du recht hast.*" the phrase "*dass du recht hast*" is a noun clause serving as the object of the verb "*glaube*".

  Common conjunctions that introduce noun clauses include "dass" (that), "ob" (whether/if), and "*wer/was*" (who/what). Each of these sets the stage for more information to follow.

- **Adverbial Clauses**

  These clauses **provide additional context or details regarding the timing, reason, condition, or manner of an action**. For instance, in the sentence "*Er kam, weil er Hunger hatte.*" ("He came because he was hungry"), "*weil er Hunger hatte*" is an adverbial clause explaining the reason for the action.

  Essential subordinating conjunctions that signal adverbial clauses include "*weil*" (because), "*wenn*" (when/if), "*obwohl*" (although), and "*da*" (since/because). Each of these imparts specific nuances to the main action described in the *Hauptsatz*.

- **Relative Clauses**

Relative clauses are particularly important in German, as they allow for the integration of **additional information about a noun or pronoun** from the main clause. **Introduced by relative pronouns** like "*der, die, das*" (who, which), these clauses are versatile tools for description.

For instance, in our dialogue, Mia mentions "*ein Buch, **das** mir sehr gefällt.*" Here, "***das** mir sehr gefällt*" is a relative clause, offering more details about the book in question.

17.3 COMPOUND SENTENCES WITH SUBCLAUSES

Die Möglichkeiten der deutschen Grammatik können einen, wenn man sich darauf, was man ruhig, wenn man möchte, sollte, einlässt, überraschen.

In German, compound sentences, or "*zusammengesetzte Sätze*", play a vital role in expanding on simple ideas and introducing more detailed information. These sentences often **consist of a combination of main clauses and subclauses**.

The main distinction between a compound sentence and a simple sentence is the **presence of more than one subject and predicate**. These can be in the form of two main clauses combined using coordinating conjunctions or a main clause combined with a subclause.

Coordinating Conjunctions:

In German, coordinating conjunctions like *"und"* (and), *"oder"* (or), *"aber"* (but), *"denn"* (for/because), and *"sondern"* (but rather) are frequently used to join two main clauses. When two main clauses are linked with these conjunctions, the word order remains unchanged in each clause.

> *Ich wollte ins Kino gehen,* **aber** *er hatte keine Zeit.*
> (I wanted to go to the cinema, but he didn't have time.)

Main Clauses and Subclauses:

The intricate nature of compound sentences becomes even more evident when combining a main clause with a subclause. A subclause, as mentioned previously, cannot stand alone. It provides additional information to the main clause and is often introduced by subordinating conjunctions. When a **subclause** is **added to the beginning of a main clause**, it's **separated by a comma**, and **the <u>verb</u> in the main clause moves to the first position right after the comma**.

> *<u>Wenn es regnet</u>, <u>gehe</u> ich nicht spazieren.*
> (If it rains, I won't go for a walk.)

✍ EXERCISES

Ü 17.1) Spot the subclause in each of the following sentences.

Example: Ich weiß, <u>dass du Recht hast</u>.

    a. Er sagte, dass er morgen kommen würde.

    b. Ich gehe schwimmen, obwohl es kalt ist.

    c. Wenn es regnet, bleibe ich zu Hause.

    d. Sie fragte, ob ich Kaffee möchte.

    e. Bevor du gehst, ruf mich an.

    f. Er kann nicht kommen, weil er krank ist.

    g. Sie hat geübt, damit sie den Test besteht.

    h. Ich schlafe, wenn du fernsiehst.

    i. Obwohl er müde war, hat er weitergearbeitet.

    j. Das ist der Mann, den sie geheiratet hat.

Ü 17.2) Complete the sentence with a suitable subclause.

Example: Ich bin froh, ...

        ↳ ... dass du gekommen bist.

    a. Sie geht spazieren,   _____

    b. Obwohl er Geld hat,   _____

    c. Wenn sie Zeit hat,   _____

    d. Er hat gelacht,   _____

    e. Ich werde es tun,   _____

    f. Bevor du einschläfst,   _____

    g. Sie hat geweint,   _____

h. Wenn es schneit, _____

i. Nachdem sie gegessen hatte, _____

j. Sie schreibt ihm, _____

Ü 17.3) Select the correct conjunction to complete the subclause.

Example: Ich bleibe zu Hause, _____ ich krank bin.

       ↳ Ich bleibe zu Hause, _weil_ ich krank bin.

a. _____ es regnet, habe ich meinen Schirm genommen.

b. Sie geht ins Kino, _____ sie den Film sehen möchte.

c. _____ du das sagst, werde ich es tun.

d. Ich bin froh, _____ du da bist.

e. Er hat geübt, _____ er den Test bestehen will.

f. _____ du schläfst, werde ich lesen.

g. _____ ich genug Geld habe, werde ich reisen.

h. _____ er müde ist, geht er ins Bett.

i. _____ sie ihre Hausaufgaben gemacht hat, darf sie spielen.

j. _____ du das Buch liest, wirst du es verstehen.

Ü 17.4) Use the given words to create a subclause. Make sure to put the words in the correct order.

Example: hat, sie, weil, geweint, traurig, sie, war

       ↳ weil sie traurig war, hat sie geweint

a. gegangen, er, weil, spät, ist, es, ist

_____

b. sie, ich, angerufen, weil, habe, besorgt, war, ich

_____

c. wir, wenn, Pizza, bestellen, hungrig, sind, wir

_____

d. ich, es, tun, werde, wenn, Zeit, habe, ich

_____

e. sie, wenn, fernsehen, schlafen, ich, gehe, wird

_____

f. du, ob, fragte, sie, kommen, würdest

_____

g. er, Geld, hat, obwohl, kaufen, es, nicht, will, er

_____

h. ich, werde, dich, sehen, hoffe, dass, ich

_____

Ü 17.5) Combine the two given sentences into one using a subclause.

Example: Ich bin glücklich.   Du bist hier.

      ↳   Ich bin glücklich, dass du hier bist.

a. Er hat Hunger.   Er isst einen Apfel.

_____

b. Es regnet.   Sie nimmt einen Schirm.

_____

c. Sie möchte Tee.   Sie kocht Wasser.

_____

d. Ich habe einen Traum.   Ich fliege.

_____

e. Du bist müde.   Du gehst ins Bett.

_____

f. Sie hat Angst.   Sie schreit.

_____

g. Es ist spät.   Er geht nach Hause.

_____

h. Er hat Geld.   Er gibt mir keins.

_____

i. Ich sehe einen Film.   Du schläfst.

_____

j. Sie liest ein Buch.   Sie lernt viel.

_____

Ü 17.6) Translate the following sentences with subclauses into German.

Example: I'm happy because you're here.

         ↳   Ich bin glücklich, weil du hier bist.

a. I'll come if you invite me.

_____

b. Although he's tired, he's still working.

_____

c. After she finished her meal, she left.

_____

d. I don't understand why she's upset.

_____

e. He asked if I had seen the movie.

_____

Ü 17.7) Rearrange the sentences so that the subclause comes at the beginning.

Example: Ich kaufe ein Auto, <u>weil ich viel Geld habe</u>.
                 <u>Weil ich viel Geld habe</u>, kaufe ich ein Auto.

a. Ich gehe nicht aus, <u>weil es regnet</u>.

_____

b. Er liest ein Buch, <u>während sie schläft</u>.

_____

c. Sie spielt Klavier, <u>obwohl sie müde ist</u>.

_____

d. Er geht schwimmen, <u>wenn es warm ist</u>.

_____

e. Sie kocht, weil sie Hunger hat.

_____

f. Ich werde fernsehen, nachdem ich Hausaufgaben gemacht habe.

_____

Ü 17.8) Convert the main clause into a subclause by adding an appropriate main clause.

Example: Du bist hier.   →   Ich bin froh, dass du hier bist.

a. Es regnet.

_____

b. Sie hat ein neues Auto.

_____

c. Er kann Deutsch sprechen.

_____

d. Das Museum ist geschlossen.

_____

e. Sie hat ihre Hausaufgaben gemacht.

_____

f. Das Essen ist fertig.

_____

g. Du verstehst die Aufgabe.

_____

h. Der Film war spannend.

_____

i. Das Wetter wird kälter.

_____

j. Er hat sein Buch verloren.

_____

Unit 5

MODIFIERS

Modifiers in a language serve as the unsung heroes of expression. These words or groups of words subtly adjust, qualify, or alter our sentences, adding layers of detail and color to our statements. In German, modifiers play a pivotal role in enhancing the specificity and depth of a conversation, ensuring that listeners receive a clearer and richer picture of the narrative.

While the concept of modifiers exists in both English and German, their placement, variety, and usage can vary distinctly between the two languages. For instance, German adjectives can change form depending on their function in a sentence, a feature not always mirrored in English.

This unit embarks on a detailed exploration of modifiers in the German language. We'll dive into the world of adjectives, adverbs, relative clauses, and prepositions, uncovering how they work individually and in concert to refine the meaning of a statement. As you progress through the chapters, you will gain insights into the intricacies of German modifiers, from their comparative and superlative forms to their precise positioning in complex sentences. By mastering these elements, you will be equipped to craft more descriptive, nuanced, and vibrant expressions in your German dialogues.

CHAPTER 18
ADJECTIVES

⊘ CHECKBOX – WHAT IS AN ADJECTIVE?

Adjectives play a vital role in **providing descriptive qualities to nouns**. They can function as **predicate adjectives** after linking verbs like "*sein*" (to be) or attributive adjectives preceding the noun they modify. Adjectives are also declined based on gender, case, and number, with three **declension patterns**: **strong**, **weak**, and **mixed**.

 ⊘ DIALOGUE – EIN SPAZIERGANG IM PARK

(Clara and Max, friends enjoying a leisurely stroll in the park, marvel at the natural beauty around them.)

Clara: *Max, sieh dir diesen **großen** Baum an!*

Max: *Wow, er ist wirklich **hoch**!*

Clara: *Und die Blumen dort drüben sind so **farbenfroh**.*

Max: *Ja, die **gelben** Tulpen neben den **roten** Rosen sehen **beeindruckend** aus.*

Clara: *Der **kleine** Teich hier ist immer so **ruhig**.*

Max: *Ja, und die **grünen** Bäume darum bieten einen **schönen** Kontrast.*

Clara: *Siehst du die Kinder dort? Ihre **neuen** Bälle sind **hellblau** und **pink**.*

Max: *Stimmt, und ihre Jacken sind **dunkelblau**. Das ist eine **interessante** Farbkombination.*

Clara: *Dieser Park hat immer so eine **friedliche** Atmosphäre.*

Max: *Ja, alles hier wirkt so **harmonisch** und **entspannt**.*

VOCABULARY LIST – EIN SPAZIERGANG IM PARK			
groß [adj.]	large	immer [adv.]	always
ansehen [v.]	(to) look at	(das) Kind [n.] (-er)	child
(die) Blume [n.] (-n)	flower	(der) Ball [n.] (Bälle)	ball
farbenfroh [adj.]	colorful	(die) Jacke [n.] (-n)	jacket
dort drüben [adv.]	over there	interessant [adj.]	interesting
(der) Teich [n.] (-e)	pond	(die) Farbkombination [n.] (-en)	color combination
beeindruckend [adj.]	impressive	(die) Atmosphäre [n.] (-n)	atmosphere
ruhig [adj.]	quiet	friedlich [adj.]	peaceful
(der) Park [n.] (-s)	park	harmonisch [adj.]	harmonious
zustimmen [v.]	(to) agree	entspannt [adj.]	relaxed

18.1 INTRODUCTION TO ADJECTIVES

Adjectives, in German as in many other languages, serve a crucial purpose: they describe and provide information about nouns. Adjectives **give depth to descriptions**, making them more vivid, exact, and interesting. In German, the term "*Adjektiv*" encompasses words that depict characteristics or properties of nouns.

For instance, let's consider the dialogue between Clara and Max during their stroll in the park. Clara points out, *"Max, sieh dir diesen **großen** Baum an!"* The word *"großen"* (big) is the adjective here. It doesn't just inform Max about a tree; it tells him about a notably large one. By adding this adjective, Clara paints a clearer picture for Max.

Functionally, adjectives can be utilized in various roles within German sentences. They can be positioned right before a noun, as in *"roter Apfel"* (red apple), or they can be used predicatively after a verb, like *"Der Apfel ist rot"* (The apple is red).

18.2 PREDICATE AND ATTRIBUTIVE ADJECTIVES

German adjectives typically serve **two primary roles**, where they can appear either as **attributive adjectives** or as **predicate adjectives**. Let's delve deeper into these two categories and their characteristics:

Attributive Adjectives

↳ Attributive adjectives **directly describe the noun they precede**, providing specific information about that noun. These adjectives can be found directly before the noun in a sentence.

Example from Dialogue:

In the sentence *"Die **gelben** Tulpen neben den **roten** Rosen sehen beeindruckend aus"* the adjectives *"gelben"* (yellow) and *"roten"* (red) are attributive adjectives. They directly modify *"Tulpen"* (tulips) and *"Rosen"* (roses) respectively.

Predicate Adjectives

↳ Predicate adjectives, on the other hand, are **separate from the noun they are referring to**. They typically follow the verb, especially when that verb is a form of *"sein"* (to be).

Example from Dialogue:

Take the sentence *"Er ist wirklich **hoch**"* as an example. Here, *"hoch"* (tall) is a predicate adjective, offering a description about the tree. It is not directly preceding the noun; instead, it comes after the verb *"ist"* (is).

18.3 DECLENSION OF ADJECTIVES

In the German language, adjectives alter their form to match the gender, case, and number of the nouns they modify. This is termed as adjective declension.

German adjectives adopt one of three declension patterns: strong, weak, or mixed, determined by the preceding article or pronoun.

DECLENSION TYPE	DESCRIPTION	EXAMPLE
Strong	Distinctive endings indicating gender, case, and number. Usually follows indefinite articles or no article.	*ein* **guter** *Freund* (a good friend – masc. nominative) *ein* **gutes** *Buch* (a good book – neut. nominative)
Weak	Less distinctive endings, as definite articles already give gender, case, and number cues.	*die* **gelben** *Tulpen* (The yellow tulips – fem. nominative)
Mixed	A fusion of strong and weak declensions. Typically follows indefinite pronouns like "*jeder*" or "*manche*".	*jeder* **kleine** *Schritt* (every small step – masc. nominative)

Context is crucial. The article or pronoun preceding the adjective usually provides hints to the correct adjective ending.

18.4 ADJECTIVE ENDINGS

While understanding the declension patterns is crucial, putting it into practice requires knowledge of the specific endings. These endings hinge largely upon the articles preceding the adjective, whether definite, indefinite, or absent.

18.4.1 Adjective Endings with Definite and Indefinite Articles

	NOMINATIVE	ACCUSATIVE	DATIVE	GENITIVE
Masculine	der alte Mann	den alten Mann	dem alten Mann	des alten Mannes
Feminine	die alte Frau	die alte Frau	der alten Frau	der alten Frau
Neuter	das alte Buch	das alte Buch	dem alten Buch	des alten Buches
Plural	die alten Leute	die alten Leute	den alten Leuten	der alten Leute

	NOMINATIVE	ACCUSATIVE	DATIVE	GENITIVE
Masculine	ein alter Mann	einen alten Mann	einem alten Mann	eines alten Mannes
Feminine	eine alte Frau	eine alte Frau	einer alten Frau	einer alten Frau
Neuter	ein altes Buch	ein altes Buch	einem alten Buch	eines alten Buches
Plural				

18.4.2 Adjective Endings without Articles

In absence of articles, adjectives usually adopt the strong declension pattern, bearing the responsibility of showcasing gender, case, and number.

	NOMINATIVE	ACCUSATIVE	DATIVE	GENITIVE
Masculine	alter Mann	alten Mann	altem Mann	alten Mannes
Feminine	alte Frau	alte Frau	alter Frau	alter Frau
Neuter	altes Buch	altes Buch	altem Buch	alten Buches
Plural	alte Leute	alte Leute	alten Leuten	alter Leute

18.4.3 Adjective Endings with Indefinite Pronouns

As mentioned earlier, indefinite pronouns like "*jeder*" adopt the mixed declension pattern.

	NOMINATIVE	ACCUSATIVE	DATIVE	GENITIVE
Masculine	jeder alte Mann	jeden alten Mann	jedem alten Mann	jedes alten Mannes
Feminine	jede alte Frau	jede alte Frau	jeder alten Frau	jeder alten Frau
Neuter	jedes altes Buch	jedes altes Buch	jedem alten Buch	jedes alten Buches
Plural	alle alten Leute	alle alten Leute	allen alten Leuten	aller alten Leute

18.4.4 Adjective Endings with Indefinite Pronouns

When adjectives follow possessive pronouns (like *mein, dein, sein, ihr, unser,* etc.), they take endings that are similar to those following indefinite articles.

Below is the declension table for adjective endings following possessive pronouns in the neuter gender:

CASE	WITH "*MEIN*" (MY)	EXAMPLE
Nominative	*mein altes Buch*	*Das ist mein altes Buch.*
Accusative	*mein altes Buch*	*Ich lese mein altes Buch.*
Dative	*meinem alten Buch*	*Ich verpasse meinem alten Buch einen neuen Umschlag.*
Genitive	*meines alten Buches*	*Die Seiten meines alten Buches sind wie neu.*

Here, the declension pattern in the neuter gender for adjectives following possessive pronouns remains similar to the pattern for indefinite articles.

Let's look back at the dialogue for examples:

Clara points out a significant tree, mentioning: **"Max, sieh dir diesen großen Baum an!"**. Here "*großen*" is an adjective in accusative masculine form.

Max replies with admiration: **"Wow, er ist wirklich hoch!"**. In this instance, "*hoch*" serves as a predicate adjective, reflecting the height of the tree.

Clara draws attention to vibrant flowers: **"Und die Blumen dort drüben sind so farbenfroh."** The adjective "*farbenfroh*" doesn't have an ending since it's used predicatively.

✍ EXERCISES

Ü 18.1) Find the adjective(s) in each sentence.

Example: Der <u>grüne</u> Apfel schmeckt <u>süß</u>.

a. Das blaue Meer ist wunderschön.

b. Sie hat langes, lockiges Haar.

c. Der alte Mann sitzt auf einer Bank.

d. Er kauft ein neues Auto.

e. Die kleinen Kinder lachen laut.

f. Der Film war wirklich interessant.

g. Die kalte Limonade ist erfrischend.

h. Ich habe großen Hunger.

i. Ihr Zimmer ist immer ordentlich.

j. Das ist ein schwieriges Rätsel.

Ü 18.2) Match the adjective with its opposite.

Example: *alt*   *laut*
              leise   *jung*

a. schnell		leise
b. hell		kalt
c. schwer		dunkel
d. glücklich		tief
e. warm		unglücklich
f. sauber		leicht
g. voll		schmutzig
h. laut		langsam
i. hoch		hart
j. weich		leer

Ü 18.3) Using the adjective in brackets, complete the sentence.

Example: Das ist ein ___ (alt) Buch.   →   <u>Answer</u>: altes

a. Er hat einen _____ (rot) Ball.

b. Sie trägt eine _____ (schön) Bluse.

c. Das ist ein _____ (teuer) Auto.

d. Sie haben _____ (kalt) Wasser getrunken.

e. Er wohnt in einem _____ (groß) Haus.

f. Die _____ (neu) Schüler sind freundlich.

g. Das war eine _____ (spannend) Geschichte.

h. Es ist ein _____ (lang) Film.

i. Sie hat _____ (kurz) Haare.

j. Das ist ein _____ (lecker) Kuchen.

Ü 18.4) Form the comparative and superlative of the given adjective.

Example: alt   →   älter   →   am ältesten

	comparative	superlative
a. klein	_____	_____
b. lang	_____	_____
c. schnell	_____	_____
d. kalt	_____	_____
e. jung	_____	_____
f. groß	_____	_____
g. hoch	_____	_____
h. schwer	_____	_____
i. kurz	_____	_____
j. teuer	_____	_____

Ü 18.5) Fill in with the correct adjective from the box.

Example: Ein <u>kaltes</u> Getränk ist im Sommer erfrischend.

klar, laut, grün, stark, hungrig, schmal, voll, sauer, faul, traurig

a. Er behält einen ＿＿＿＿＿＿＿ Kopf.

b. Das Radio spielt ＿＿＿＿＿＿＿ Musik.

c. Ich bin nicht müde, ich bin nur ＿＿＿＿＿＿＿.

d. Die Zitrone schmeckt ＿＿＿＿＿＿＿.

e. Die Tasche ist ＿＿＿＿＿＿＿ mit Büchern.

f. Mein Bruder ist sehr ＿＿＿＿＿＿＿; er macht nie seine Hausaufgaben.

g. Sie ist ein bisschen ＿＿＿＿＿＿＿ heute.

h. Der Fluss ist sehr ＿＿＿＿＿＿＿ und schnell.

i. Der Baum hat ＿＿＿＿＿＿＿ Blätter.

j. Ich habe einen ＿＿＿＿＿＿＿ Appetit.

Ü 18.6) Determine if the adjective correctly describes the noun.

Example: Eine schnelle Schildkröte. (False)

	True	False
a. Ein kalter Kamin.	＿＿＿＿＿＿	＿＿＿＿＿＿
b. Eine schwere Feder.	＿＿＿＿＿＿	＿＿＿＿＿＿
c. Ein glücklicher Gewinner.	＿＿＿＿＿＿	＿＿＿＿＿＿
d. Ein lautes Flüstern.	＿＿＿＿＿＿	＿＿＿＿＿＿
e. Ein warmes Eis.	＿＿＿＿＿＿	＿＿＿＿＿＿
f. Ein roter Apfel.	＿＿＿＿＿＿	＿＿＿＿＿＿
g. Ein kleiner Riese.	＿＿＿＿＿＿	＿＿＿＿＿＿
h. Ein nasses Handtuch.	＿＿＿＿＿＿	＿＿＿＿＿＿
i. Ein kurzer Roman.	＿＿＿＿＿＿	＿＿＿＿＿＿
j. Ein weiches Metall.	＿＿＿＿＿＿	＿＿＿＿＿＿

CHAPTER 19
ADVERBS

⊘ CHECKBOX – WHAT IS AN ADVERB?

Adverbs play a significant role in enriching sentences by **providing valuable information about actions, adjectives, or other adverbs**. Adverbs serve various functions, indicating how an action is performed (**manner**), when it occurs (**time**), where it takes place (**place**), how often it happens (**frequency**), or to what extent (**degree**).

Manner:	*"Sie tanzt wunderschön."*	(She dances beautifully.)
Time:	*"Ich komme morgen."*	(I'm coming tomorrow.)
Place:	*"Das Buch liegt hier."*	(The book is here.)
Frequency:	*"Er liest oft."*	(He reads often.)
Degree:	*"Es ist sehr heiß."*	(It is very hot.)

⬭ **DIALOGUE – EIN NEUER FILM**

(Lena and Jonas, friends who recently watched a movie together, discuss their opinions about it. The dialogue takes place in the past tense.)

Lena: Jonas, **wie** fandest du den Film gestern?

Jonas: **Ehrlich gesagt**, ich fand ihn **wirklich** gut. Die Handlung war **ziemlich** spannend.

Lena: Ja, die Schauspieler haben **besonders** gut gespielt. Aber **manchmal** war der Ton **leider** zu leise.

Jonas: Stimmt. **Übrigens**, hast du bemerkt, **wie oft** der Hauptcharakter **plötzlich** seine Meinung geändert hat?

Lena: Ja, das war seltsam. Aber **insgesamt** war der Film doch **ziemlich** beeindruckend.

Jonas: Absolut. Und die Kulissen waren auch **wunderbar** detailliert.

Lena: Das habe ich auch gedacht. Die Szenen im Wald waren **offensichtlich** an echten Orten gedreht.

Jonas: Genau. Ich würde mir den Film **sicherlich** noch einmal ansehen.

Lena: Ich auch, aber **vielleicht** zu Hause, wo ich die Lautstärke kontrollieren kann.

VOCABULARY LIST – EIN NEUER FILM			
finden [*v.*]	(to) find	übrigens [*adv.*]	by the way
(der) Film [*n.*] (-e)	film	besonders [*adv.*]	particular
(die) Handlung [*n.*] (-en)	plot	detailliert [*adj.*]	detailed
(der) Schauspieler/-in [*n.*] (-nen)	actor	(die) Szene [*n.*] (-n)	scene
(der) Hauptcharakter/-in [*n.*] (-nen)	main character	echt [*adj.*]	genuine
(die) Meinung [*n.*] (-en)	opinion	sicherlich [*adv.*]	certainly
bemerken [*v.*]	(to) notice	kontrollieren [*v.*]	(to) control
ändern [*v.*]	(to) change	(die) Kulisse [*n.*] (-n)	scenery
(die) Lautstärke [*n.*] (-n)	volume	spielen [*v.*]	(to) play
(der) Wald [*n.*] (Wälder)	forest	manchmal [*adv.*]	sometimes

19.1 INTRODUCTION TO ADVERBS

Adverbs are a vital component of the German language, adding flavor and precision to a sentence. By definition, an adverb is a word that m**odifies or qualifies an adjective, verb, or other adverb or word group**, expressing a relation of **place, time, manner, cause, degree**, etc.

In German, adverbs can be recognized often by their placement within a sentence, and their function of providing additional information about how, when, where, or to what degree an action takes place. For instance, consider the simple sentence "*Sie singt*" (She sings). By adding the adverb "*laut*" (loudly), the sentence "*Sie singt laut*" gives more depth, explaining how she sings.

From our dialogue, Lena and Jonas's exchange about the film provides numerous adverbial insights. Let's take the opening line, "*Jonas, wie fandest du den Film gestern?*" Here, "*wie*" (how) and "*gestern*" (yesterday) serve as adverbs, indicating the manner of Jonas's opinion and the time of the film viewing, respectively.

SENTENCE	ADVERB	FUNCTION
Jonas, wie fandest du den Film gestern?	*wie, gestern*	manner, time
Ich fand ihn wirklich gut.	*wirklich*	degree
Die Handlung war ziemlich spannend.	*ziemlich*	degree
Die Schauspieler haben besonders gut gespielt.	*besonders*	manner
... der Ton war leider zu leise.	*leider*	manner
... wie oft der Hauptcharakter ...	*oft*	frequency
... der Film doch ziemlich beeindruckend.	*doch*	manner
... die Kulissen waren auch wunderbar detailliert.	*auch*	degree
... im Wald waren offensichtlich an echten Orten gedreht.	*offensichtlich*	manner

19.2 TYPES OF ADVERBS

19.2.1 Adverbs of Manner

Definition: These adverbs describe the way or manner in which an action is performed.

schnell	*laut*	*besonders*
(quickly)	(loudly)	(especially)

Function: By employing adverbs of manner, you can convey additional details about the method or style of an action, thereby enriching your statement's descriptive quality.

Sample Sentence from Dialogue: "*Die Schauspieler haben **besonders** gut gespielt.*" (The actors performed **especially** well.) This hints at the exceptional quality of the actor's performance.

Further Explanation: The placement of adverbs of manner in German sentences usually follows the direct object. For instance, "*Sie spielt das Klavier **schön**.*" (She plays the piano **beautifully**).

19.2.2 Adverbs of Time

Definition: Time adverbs give information about when a particular action occurred.

gestern	*heute*	*morgen*
(yesterday)	(today)	(tomorrow)

Function: They're pivotal for clarifying the timeline of events, making narratives and recounts clearer.

Sample Sentence from Dialogue: *"Jonas, wie fandest du den Film **gestern**?"* (Jonas, how did you like the film **yesterday**?)

Further Explanation: In German, adverbs of time are flexible in their positioning. They can begin a sentence to emphasize the timing, as in *"Morgen gehe ich ins Kino"* (Tomorrow, I'm going to the cinema), or can be placed after the verb, like *"Ich gehe **morgen** ins Kino."*

19.2.3 Adverbs of Place

Definition: These adverbs highlight the location or direction of an action.

hier	*dort*	*überall*
(here)	(there)	(everywhere)

Function: Vital for pinpointing locations, navigating, and giving or seeking directions.

Further Explanation: While not exemplified in the dialogue, understanding these adverbs is paramount for daily interactions. In German, the placement often follows the verb, such as *"Das Buch liegt **hier**."* (The book is **here**).

19.2.4 Adverbs of Degree

Definition: These describe the intensity, quantity, or degree of the action.

ziemlich	*sehr*	*kaum*
(quite)	(very)	(hardly)

Function: They enhance or diminish the impact of the accompanying verb, adjective, or other adverb.

Sample Sentence from Dialogue: *"Die Handlung war **ziemlich** spannend."* (The plot was **quite** thrilling.)

Further Explanation: Degree adverbs generally precede the adjective or adverb they modify. For instance, *"Das Essen ist **sehr** lecker."* (The food is **very** delicious).

19.2.5 Adverbs of Frequency

Definition: They denote how often a particular action takes place.

oft	*selten*	*immer*
(often)	(rarely)	(always)

Function: Vital for setting routines, habits, or recurrent events in context.

Sample Sentence from Dialogue: *"… wie **oft** der Hauptcharakter plötzlich seine Meinung geändert hat?"* (…how **often** did the main character suddenly change his mind?)

Further Explanation: In German sentences, frequency adverbs typically appear before the main verb in main clauses. For instance, *"Ich lese **oft** Bücher."* (I **often** read books).

ADVERB TYPE	EXAMPLES	FUNCTION	SAMPLE SENTENCE FROM DIALOGUE
Manner	*besonders, laut*	Describes how an action is done	Die Schauspieler haben **besonders** gut gespielt.
Time	*gestern, heute*	Specifies when an action occurs	Jonas, wie fandest du den Film **gestern**?
Place	*hier, dort*	Indicates the location or direction	Der Schauspieler steht **dort** drüben.
Degree	*ziemlich, sehr*	Modifies the intensity of an action	Die Handlung war **ziemlich** spannend.
Frequency	*oft, selten*	Denotes how often an action happens	… wie **oft** der Hauptcharakter …

19.3 INTERROGATIVE ADVERBS

DEUTSCH	ENGLISH
Wieso?	**Why?**
Weshalb?	**Why?**
Warum?	**Why?**
Wofür?	**Why?**
Wozu?	**Why?**

Interrogative adverbs are used to introduce questions and play an instrumental role in inquiring about certain elements of a sentence, such as time, place, manner, and reason.

For instance, the adverb *"wie"* (how) is perhaps the most common interrogative adverb in German. It's utilized to ask about the state, condition, or quality of something. In the dialogue shared, Lena begins her conversation with Jonas asking, *"Jonas, wie fandest du den Film gestern?"* Here, "wie" is used to inquire about Jonas's opinion on the film.

Another interrogative adverb, *"wo"* (where), is used to ask about location. For instance, *"Wo ist das Kino?"* (Where is the cinema?). Though not present in the dialogue, it's a quintessential example of inquiring about place.

In addition, *"wann"* (when) is employed to pose questions about time. A hypothetical example might be, *"Wann beginnt der Film?"* (When does the film start?).

ADVERB	MEANING	FUNCTION	SAMPLE SENTENCE
wie	how	Asks about manner or state	*Jonas, **wie** fandest du den Film?*
wo	where	Inquires about location	*Wo ist das Kino?*
wann	when	Poses questions about time	*Wann beginnt der Film?*
warum	why	Seeks reason or explanation	*Warum mochtest du den Film?*
wohin	where to	Asks about direction or destination	*Wohin gehst du?*

 **EXERCISES**

Ü 19.1) Underline the adverb in each sentence.

Example: Sie spricht <u>leise</u> in der Bibliothek.

a. Er läuft schnell.

b. Sie singt wunderschön.

c. Der Hund bellt laut.

d. Sie schreibt oft Briefe.

e. Er liest selten Bücher.

f. Wir arbeiten hart für das Projekt.

g. Sie denkt immer an ihre Familie.

h. Er kommt nie zu spät.

i. Sie spricht deutlich.

j. Er isst gerne Schokolade.

Ü 19.2) Determine whether the highlighted word is an adverb or an adjective.

Example: Sie ist <u>oft</u> müde.　　→　　Adverb

	Adverb	Adjective
a. Er ist ein **schneller** Läufer.	☐	☐
b. Sie singt **klar**.	☐	☐
c. Das ist ein **hartes** Brot.	☐	☐
d. Er spricht **laut**.	☐	☐
e. Das **alte** Haus ist schön.	☐	☐
f. Sie arbeitet **effizient**.	☐	☐
g. Die **kalte** Suppe schmeckt nicht.	☐	☐

h. Er hört **aufmerksam** zu. ☐ ☐

i. Das **schöne** Lied berührt mich. ☐ ☐

j. Sie lachen **lautlos**. ☐ ☐

Ü 19.3) Using the given adverbs, create your own sentences.

Example: vielleicht → Ich komme vielleicht morgen.

a. selten _____

b. leise _____

c. manchmal _____

d. besonders _____

e. schlecht _____

f. klar _____

g. direkt _____

h. tatsächlich _____

i. genauso _____

j. zufällig _____

Ü 19.4) Rearrange the words to form correct sentences.

Example: oft / Sie / ins / Kino / geht → Sie geht oft ins Kino.

a. morgen / er / vielleicht / kommt _____

b. sie / nie / telefoniert / abends _____

c. immer / schläft / Mittag / sie / nach _____

d. gerne / Schokolade / isst / er _____

e. studiert / intensiv / sie _____

f. meistens / Auto / fährt / er / mit _____

g. Bücher / selten / liest / er   _____

h. essen / wir / draußen / oft   _____

i. schwimmt / regelmäßig / er   _____

j. singt / sie / wunderschön   _____

Ü 19.5) Fill in the blanks with an appropriate adverb from the box.

immer, selten, schnell, leider, besonders, direkt, vorsichtig, wirklich, endlich, gut

a. Er fährt _____ mit dem Fahrrad.

b. Sie kommt _____ zu spät.

c. _____ habe ich mein Handy verloren.

d. Dieser Film war _____ interessant.

e. Sprichst du _____ Deutsch?

f. Sie lebt _____ neben dem Supermarkt.

g. Es ist _____ Sommer.

h. Sei _____ auf der rutschigen Straße.

i. Ich verstehe das _____ nicht.

j. Ich sehe ihn _____.

CHAPTER 20
COMPARATIVES

⊘ CHECKBOX – WHAT IS THE COMPARATIVE?

The comparative is a linguistic tool used to **compare two or more entities**, expressing a higher or lower degree of a particular quality. It allows for the **comparison of adjectives and adverbs** to indicate whether one thing is more or less of something than another.

The comparative is formed in different ways depending on the length of the adjective or adverb. For shorter adjectives and adverbs, the comparative is created by adding "*-er*" to the base form. For longer adjectives and adverbs, the comparative is formed by using "*mehr*" (more) before the adjective or adverb.

Examples of comparatives with short adjectives:

schnell (fast)	becomes	schneller (faster)
hoch (high/tall)	becomes	*höher* (higher/taller)

○ **DIALOGUE – URLAUBSVERGLEICH**

(Mia and Tom, friends discussing their recent vacations, compare their experiences and preferences.)

Mia: *Tom, wie war dein Urlaub in den Bergen?*

Tom: *Es war gut, aber der Strandurlaub letztes Jahr war **besser**.*

Mia: *Wirklich? Ich finde Berge **interessanter** als Strände.*

Tom: *Die Berge sind **ruhiger**, das stimmt. Aber ich **sonne** mich **lieber**.*

Mia: *Ich verstehe. Mein Hotel in Berlin war **das beste**, in dem ich je war.*

Tom: ***Besser** als das in Paris?*

Mia: *Ja, das Pariser Hotel war **luxuriöser**, aber das Berliner war **gemütlicher**.*

Tom: *Das Essen in Italien ist doch am **leckersten**, oder?*

Mia: *Da könntest du recht haben. Italienisches Essen ist oft **schmackhafter** als das Essen hier.*

Tom: *Trotzdem koche ich zu Hause **am schnellsten**!*

Mia: *Und ich backe den **leckersten** Kuchen!*

The dialogue showcases the use of the positive, comparative, and superlative forms of both adjectives and adverbs in a conversational context.

VOCABULARY LIST – URLAUBSVERGLEICH			
(der) Urlaub [*n.*] (-e)	vacation	luxuriös [*adj.*]	luxurious
(der) Berg [*n.*] (-e)	mountain	gemütlich [*adj.*]	cozy
(der) Strandurlaub [*n.*] (-e)	beach vacation	recht haben [*v.*]	(to be) right
interessant [*adj.*]	interesting	lecker [*adj.*]	delicious
sonnen [*v.*]	(to) tan	schmackhaft [*adj.*]	tasty
(das) Hotel [*n.*] (-s)	hotel	(das) Essen [*n.*] (-)	food
kochen [*v.*]	(to) cook	(der) Kuchen [*n.*] (-)	cake
backen [*v.*]	(to) bake	schnell [*adj.*]	quick

20.1 INTRODUCTION TO COMPARATIVES

TIERE IM VERGLEICH

groß — größer — am größten

In the realm of adjectives and adverbs, comparatives hold a special place. Their primary role is to **compare the qualities or attributes of two different entities**. In English, this usually involves adding "-er" to the adjective or adverb or using "more" or "less" in front. Similarly, in German, comparatives serve to express degrees of certain qualities.

For instance, consider the dialogue between Mia and Tom. They discuss their holidays, comparing them in various aspects. From their conversation, it's evident that they use comparatives to contrast their experiences: mountains vs beaches, different hotels, and even food in different locations.

Take the line: *"Tom, wie war dein Urlaub in den Bergen?"* (Tom, how was your vacation in the mountains?). Tom's response: *"Es war gut, aber der Strandurlaub letztes Jahr war **besser**."* reveals his preference by using the comparative form *"**besser**"* (better) to weigh the mountain vacation against the beach one.

Similarly, Mia's statement, *"Ich finde Berge **interessanter** als Strände"* uses the comparative *"**interessanter**"* (more interesting) to state her preference for mountains over beaches.

The use of comparatives, as we see in this dialogue, helps in articulating preferences, making assessments, and judging one thing against another. The depth of German comparatives goes beyond simple direct comparisons; they also help in layering meaning and subtlety in conversations.

20.2 FORMING COMPARATIVE ADJECTIVES

In German, comparative adjectives are formed by adding "-er" to the end of the adjective. This is quite similar to English, where we add "-er" to create the comparative form of most adjectives. The rule applies to both one-syllable and multi-syllable adjectives.

| *interessant* | becomes | *interessant**er*** |
| (interesting) | | (more interesting) |

| *schnell* | becomes | *schnell**er*** |
| (fast) | | (faster) |

When it comes to comparisons using adjectives, German language also uses "*als*" (than) to draw comparisons, just like "than" in English.

Dieses Auto ist schneller als das andere.   *Dein Kuchen ist leckerer als meiner.*
(This car is faster than the other one.)   (Your cake is tastier than mine.)

It's important to note that while the comparative form is used in attributive, predicative and adverbial uses, the adjective ending may change in attributive use depending on the case, gender, and number of the noun it's describing, due to the German declension system.

20.2.1 Using Comparative Adjectives in Sentences

Whenever we describe things and want to draw a comparison between their attributes, we employ comparative adjectives. In German sentences, the structure for such comparisons often involves the <u>conjunction "*als*</u>" (than). The **comparative adjective is placed directly before the noun it modifies**, and when it's used in a **predicative sense, it stands alone without a noun following it**.

*Der Elefant ist **<u>größer</u>** <u>als</u> das Pferd.*   *Dieser Kaffee schmeckt **<u>besser</u>** <u>als</u> der Tee.*
(The elephant is **bigger** than the horse.)   (This coffee tastes **better** than the tea.)

However, sometimes comparative adjectives can be used without a direct comparison. In such cases, they often indicate a change or difference over time or from a previous state.

Es wird **kälter**.
(It's getting **colder**.)

It's essential to remember that when comparative adjectives are used attributively (before a noun), they need to agree in case, gender, and number. Therefore, their endings might change, much like regular adjectives do in German.

ein **größeres** *Haus*
(a **bigger** house)

ein **schnellerer** *Zug*
(a **faster** train)

20.3 FORMING COMPARATIVE ADVERBS

While comparative adjectives compare the qualities of nouns, comparative adverbs serve to compare actions or states. The manner in which they are created from their positive forms mirrors the process for adjectives. For many adverbs, you simply **add the "-er" suffix** to form their comparative version.

schnell (fast)	becomes	*schneller* (faster)	as an adverb

Er rennt **schnell**.
(He runs fast.)

Er rennt **schneller** *als sein Bruder.*
(He runs **faster** than his brother.)

laut (loud)	becomes	*lauter* (louder)	as an adverb

Die Musik spielt **laut**.
(The music plays loud.)

Heute spielt die Musik **lauter** *als gestern.*
(Today, the music plays **louder** than yesterday.)

20.4 SUPERLATIVE FORMS OF ADJECTIVES AND ADVERBS

The superlative form in German is **utilized to describe the highest or lowest degree of a particular quality or action**. Whether we're declaring something as "the best" or "the most interesting" we're venturing into the realm of superlatives.

The superlative form for both adjectives and adverbs is crafted by **adding "-st" to the positive form and placing "am" before the adjective or adverb**.

Thus, the typical structure looks like this:

am + positive form + *-sten*

groß (big)	turns into	**am größten** (biggest)	for superlatives

*Das ist ein **großes** Haus.*
(That is a big house.)

*Das ist das **größte** Haus in der Stadt.*
(That is the biggest house in the city.)

schnell (fast)	transforms to	**am schnellsten** (fastest)	for superlatives

*Er rennt **schnell**.*
(He runs fast.)

*Er rennt **am schnellsten** von allen.*
(He runs the fastest of all.)

Yet again, we must be wary of irregularities. Some adjectives and adverbs have irregular superlative forms:

gut	becomes	**am besten**

*Sie macht ihre Arbeit **gut**.*
(She does her work well.)

*Sie macht ihre Arbeit **am besten**.*
(She does her work the best.)

viel (much)	turns into	**am meisten** (most)

*Er liest **viel**.*
(He reads a lot.)

*Er liest **am meisten** von uns allen.*
(He reads the most of all of us.)

The superlative forms often require context, since you're declaring something as the most or least of a particular quality or action. This often necessitates the use of determiners, like articles (e.g., "*das*", "*der*", "*die*") to provide clarity.

*Das ist **der interessanteste** Film.*
(That's the most interesting film.)

*Sie ist **die klügste** Person hier.*
(She's the smartest person here.)

✏️ EXERCISES

Ü 20.1) Read the sentences and identify which word is in the comparative form.

Example: Das Wetter heute ist wärmer als gestern.　　→　　Answer: wärmer

    a. Dieser Kuchen ist süßer als der andere.

    b. Mein Bruder ist älter als ich.

    c. Dieses Buch ist interessanter als jenes.

    d. Der Berg ist höher als der Hügel.

    e. Der Film war langweiliger als erwartet.

    f. Das Wasser im Fluss ist kälter als im See.

    g. Sein Auto ist neuer als meins.

    h. Ihre Blumen sind schöner als meine.

    i. Dieser Tee ist bitterer als der Kaffee.

    j. Dieses Kleid ist teurer als das andere.

Ü 20.2) Use the provided adjective to create the comparative form.

Example: schön　　→　　schöner

    a. gut　　→　　_____

    b. jung　　→　　_____

    c. alt　　→　　_____

    d. klein　　→　　_____

    e. groß　　→　　_____

    f. warm　　→　　_____

    g. kalt　　→　　_____

    h. billig　　→　　_____

i. lang   →   _____

j. kurz   →   _____

Ü 20.3) Complete the sentences using the comparative form of the adjective in brackets.

Example: Das Auto ist **schneller** (schnell) als das Fahrrad.

a. Der Tiger ist _____ (stark) als die Katze.

b. Der Ozean ist _____ (tief) als der See.

c. Die Suppe ist _____ (heiß) als das Wasser.

d. Der Bus ist _____ (langsam) als der Zug.

e. Das Haus ist _____ (groß) als die Wohnung.

f. Der Film ist _____ (spannend) als das Buch.

g. Die Torte ist _____ (süß) als der Keks.

h. Der Stuhl ist _____ (bequem) als der Sessel.

i. Das Glas ist _____ (voll) als die Flasche.

j. Das Hemd ist _____ (dreckig) als die Hose.

Ü 20.4) Identify if the adjective in the sentence is in the comparative or superlative form.

Example: Das ist der schönste Tag meines Lebens.

	Comparative	Superlative
a. Berlin ist größer als Hamburg.	☐	☐
b. Das ist das beste Eis, das ich je gegessen habe.	☐	☐
c. Mein Hund ist klüger als die Katze.	☐	☐
d. Heute ist der kälteste Tag des Winters.	☐	☐
e. Dieser Apfel ist saurer als jener.	☐	☐

f. Das ist das höchste Gebäude in der Stadt. □ □

g. Deine Idee ist besser als meine. □ □

h. Er ist der älteste Mann im Dorf. □ □

i. Das Wasser ist kälter als gestern. □ □

j. Sie ist die jüngste Person in der Klasse. □ □

Ü 20.5) Fill in the blanks using the comparative form of the adjective to complete the dialogue.

Example: A: Ist das Eis kalt?

B: Nein, die Limonade ist _____ (kalt).

a. A: Ist der Kaffee süß?

B: Nein, der Tee ist _____ (süß).

a. A: Ist der Film interessant?

B: Das Buch war _____ (interessant).

a. A: Ist das Restaurant teuer?

B: Das Café nebenan ist _____ (teuer).

a. A: Ist das Hemd sauber?

B: Die Jacke ist noch _____ (sauber).

a. A: Ist der Tisch groß?

B: Der Tisch draußen ist _____ (groß).

CHAPTER 21
PREPOSITIONS

⊘ CHECKBOX – WHAT ARE PREPOSITIONS?

Prepositions are essential elements that **establish relationships between sentence components**. These connecting words indicate various aspects such as **time**, **place**, **direction**, and **manner**. Prepositions are typically **followed by nouns**, **pronouns**, or **noun phrases**, forming prepositional phrases that offer additional information about the main parts of a sentence.

Common examples of prepositions in German include "*in*" (in), "*auf*" (on), "*unter*" (under), "*neben*" (beside), "*mit*" (with), "*für*" (for), "*an*" (at/on), "*durch*" (through), "*gegenüber*" (opposite), and many others.

*Das Buch liegt **auf** dem Tisch.*
(The book is on the table.)

*Ich gehe **in** die Schule.*
(I am going to school.)

*Er fährt **mit** dem Auto.*
(He is traveling by car.)

*Sie wohnt **neben** dem Park.*
(She lives next to the park.)

⭕ **DIALOGUE – IM BÜRO**

(Clara and Moritz, colleagues working in the office, have a brief conversation about office items and a colleague's business trip.)

Clara: Moritz, weißt du, wo die Akten sind?

Moritz: Ja, sie liegen **auf** dem Tisch.

Clara: Und wo ist der neue Drucker?

Moritz: Er steht **neben** dem Schrank. Aber sei vorsichtig, er funktioniert **mit** einer neuen Software.

Clara: Hast du den Bericht **für** Herrn Schmidt?

Moritz: Ich habe ihn **an** Herrn Müller gegeben, aber er sollte jetzt **in** seinem Büro sein.

Clara: Gut. Hast du gehört, dass Sandra **nach** Berlin gereist ist?

Moritz: Ja, sie fährt immer **mit** dem Zug **durch** Deutschland.

Clara: War sie **während** des Meetings schon zurück?

Moritz: Nein, sie kam **nach** dem Meeting zurück.

Clara: Verstehe. Und wie lange bleibt sie **in** Berlin?

Moritz: Sie bleibt **bis** zum Ende des Monats.

Clara: Das ist lange. Hoffentlich hat sie **vor** ihrer Rückkehr alles erledigt.

Moritz: Ich hoffe es auch. Und bevor du gehst, könntest du das Fenster **hinter** dir schließen?

Clara: Natürlich, kein Problem!

VOCABULARY LIST – IM BÜRO			
(der) Tisch [*n.*] (-e)	table	(das) Büro [*n.*] (-s)	office
(der) Drucker [*n.*] (-)	printer	geben [*v.*]	(to) give
(der) Schrank [*n.*] (Schränke)	cabinet	hören [*v.*]	(to) hear
funktionieren [*v.*]	(to) work	reisen [*v.*]	(to) travel
(der) Bericht [*n.*] (-e)	report	durch [*prep.*]	by
(die) Software [*n.*] (-s)	software	(der) Monat [*n.*] (-e)	month
neben [*prep.*]	next to	(die) Rückkehr [*n.*] (-)	return
vorsichtig [*adj.*]	careful	(das) Fenster [*n.*] (-)	window
hinter [*prep.*]	behind	schließen [*v.*]	(to) close

21.1 INTRODUCTION TO PREPOSITIONS

Prepositions in German, much like in other languages, play a vital role in creating connections between different elements within a sentence. These tiny words, although often overlooked, are pillars in giving depth and direction to a sentence. Prepositions help determine relationships between objects, actions, and time frames, making them indispensable for effective communication.

In German, prepositions are **essential** not just for meaning but also for grammatical correctness. They can **influence the case of the noun or pronoun they relate to**, thereby **changing the article or ending of that noun or pronoun**. Let's consider a simple sentence from the dialogue: *"Ja, sie liegen auf dem Tisch."* Here, *"auf"* is a preposition indicating the location of the files, and *"dem"* is the dative masculine article for "the", which is influenced by the preposition.

Another basic example is the phrase *"in seinem Büro"*. Here, *"in"* signifies the location of the report, with *"seinem"* (his) being in the dative case due to the influence of the preposition.

21.2 TYPES OF PREPOSITIONS

Prepositions can be categorized based on various aspects like time, place, direction, and manner.

- **Time-related prepositions** help to locate an event or action within the continuum of time. For instance, in the dialogue, *"während des Meetings"* (during the meeting) and *"bis zum Ende des Monats"* (until the end of the month) provide specific time frames.

- **Place-related prepositions** pinpoint the location of an object or individual. As seen in *"auf dem Tisch"* (on the table) or *"neben dem Schrank"* (next to the cupboard), they offer clear spatial contexts.

- **Directional prepositions** illuminate the path or trajectory of an object or person, such as *"nach Berlin"* (to Berlin) from the conversation, indicating the destination:

- **Manner-related prepositions**, though not explicitly seen in the dialogue, focus on the method or way something is done, like *"mit Freude"* (with joy).

Prepositions with Dative Case

↳ German dative prepositions always **require the noun or pronoun after them to be in the dative case**. Common dative prepositions include *"mit"* (with), *"zu"* (to), *"aus"* (from), *"bei"* (at), and *"von"* (of/from). For example, in the dialogue, the phrase *"mit dem Zug"* uses *"mit"*, a dative preposition. Thus, *"Zug"* (train) is in the dative case, indicated by *"dem"*.

Prepositions with Accusative Case

↳ Accusative prepositions, such as *"für"* (for), *"um"* (around), *"durch"* (through), and *"ohne"* (without), **influence the subsequent noun or pronoun to take the accusative case**. For instance, the phrase *"durch Deutschland"* from the dialogue employs *"durch"*, resulting in *"Deutschland"* staying in its natural accusative form.

Mixed Prepositions with Dative and Accusative

↳ Some prepositions can govern both dative and accusative cases, with the meaning often differing slightly based on the case. Examples are *"in"* (in/into), *"auf"* (on/onto), *"an"* (on/onto), and *"über"* (over/above). The **case** used typically **depends on whether there's movement or static positioning involved**. In our dialogue, *"in seinem Büro"* uses *"in"* with dative because it signifies a static location, whereas *"nach Berlin"* employs accusative to denote movement towards Berlin.

Prepositions with Noun Endings and Pronouns

↳ Prepositions in German can **influence the endings of nouns**, especially with cases. In *"während des Meetings"*, *"während"* governs the genitive case, changing *"das Meeting"* to *"des Meetings"*. Similarly, prepositions **can affect pronoun forms**, such as *"mit ihm"* (with him) where *"ihm"* is the dative form of *"er"* (he) due to the preposition *"mit"*.

TYPE OF PREPOSITION	CASE	EXAMPLES	USAGE IN A SENTENCE
Time Prepositions	Depends on Preposition	*während* (during), *nach* (after), *vor* (before), *bis* (until)	*Wir kommen* **gegen** *5 Uhr an.* (Accusative)
Place and Direction Prepositions	Depends on Preposition	*auf* (on), *unter* (under), *neben* (next to), *zwischen* (between)	*Er steht* **neben** *dem Schrank.* (Dative)
Manner Prepositions	Depends on Preposition	*mit* (with), *ohne* (without), *durch* (by/through)	*Sie fährt immer* **mit** *dem Zug.* (Dative)
Prepositions with Dative	Dative	*bei* (at/near), *mit* (with), *von* (from), *zu* (to)	*Die Akten liegen* **auf** *dem Tisch.* (Dative)
Prepositions with Accusative	Accusative	*durch* (through), *für* (for), *gegen* (against), *ohne* (without)	*Ich habe ihn* **an** *Herrn Müller gegeben.* (Accusative)
Mixed Prepositions	Dative or Accusative	*an* (on), *auf* (on), *hinter* (behind), *in* (in)	*Sie fährt* **mit** *dem Zug* **durch** *Deutschland.* (Dative, then Accusative)
Prepositions with Verbs	Depends on Verb/ Preposition Combo	*denken an* (think of), *warten auf* (wait for), *hören von* (hear from)	*Clara hat* **von** *der Reise gehört.* (Dative)

 **EXERCISES**

Ü 21.1) Fill in the blanks with the correct preposition from the options given.

Example: Er arbeitet _____ (an/auf/in) einem Projekt.

⤷ Er arbeitet **an** einem Projekt.

a. Sie wohnt _____ (auf/an/in) der Straße.

b. Er setzt sich _____ (über/neben/unter) mich.

c. Ich habe das Buch _____ (unter/zwischen/auf) den Tisch gelegt.

d. Sie denkt oft _____ (über/an/auf) ihren Urlaub.

e. Die Blumen stehen _____ (neben/zwischen/vor) dem Fenster.

f. Wir treffen uns _____ (auf/an/in) der Ecke.

g. Er hat Angst _____ (vor/über/unter) Spinnen.

h. Der Hund liegt _____ (auf/unter/neben) dem Sofa.

i. Ich bin _____ (an/auf/in) der Universität.

j. Der Stift ist _____ (zwischen/unter/in) den Büchern.

Ü 21.2) Fill in the blanks with the correct form of the noun after the preposition.

Example: Sie ist in _____ (die Stadt).

⤷ Sie ist in **der Stadt**.

a. Ich wohne bei _____ (der Freund).

b. Er geht in _____ (das Kino).

c. Sie schaut auf _____ (die Uhr).

d. Er stellt sich zwischen _____ (der Baum und das Haus).

e. Sie sitzt neben _____ (der Lehrer).

f. Das Buch liegt auf _____ (der Tisch).

g. Er hat Angst vor _____ (der Hund).

h. Sie geht zu _____ (die Schule).

i. Er legt es unter _____ (das Bett).

j. Sie ist über _____ (die Brücke) gegangen.

Ü 21.3) Match the verb with the correct preposition that often accompanies it.

Example: denken _____ (an/über/auf)   →   an

a. sich freuen _____ (an/auf/unter)

b. warten _____ (an/auf/in)

c. sprechen _____ (an/über/unter)

d. träumen _____ (von/auf/über)

e. sich interessieren _____ (für/neben/zwischen)

f. sich konzentrieren _____ (auf/in/zwischen)

g. hoffen _____ (an/auf/in)

h. sich beschweren _____ (an/über/von)

i. fragen _____ (nach/an/auf)

j. sich erinnern _____ (an/auf/in)

Unit 6

OTHER FEATURES

While the primary building blocks of a language like nouns, verbs, and adjectives often take center stage, it's the nuanced features that truly enable a speaker to navigate the complexities and subtleties of conversation. German is a language rich in such features, and this unit focuses on four fundamental elements that offer versatility to your expressions: modal verbs, auxiliary verbs, prefixes (both separable and inseparable), and negations.

Modal verbs, for instance, play a key role in indicating a speaker's attitude towards an action, be it necessity, possibility, or wish. Auxiliary verbs, on the other hand, give structure to many tenses and moods, serving as essential supporting elements in the architecture of a sentence. Dive deeper into prefixes, and you'll uncover the intriguing way in which separable and inseparable prefixes can change the meaning of a verb, allowing for a myriad of expressions using a single base. Lastly, mastering negations is pivotal to expressing contrast, denial, or the absence of something.

This unit seeks to shed light on these integral, yet often overlooked features of the German language. By understanding and employing these elements, you'll be able to craft sentences that are not only grammatically accurate but also rich in depth and meaning.

CHAPTER 22
MODAL VERBS

⊘ CHECKBOX – WHAT ARE MODAL VERBS?

In German grammar, modal verbs **hold a significant role in expressing attitudes**, **abilities**, **permissions**, and **necessity**. Understanding these versatile verbs is essential for grasping the subtleties of language and effectively communicating various ideas and intentions.

Modal verbs, also known as "*Modalverben*" in German, are a specific group of auxiliary verbs that modify the meaning of the main verb in a sentence. They **convey the speaker's perspective on the action or indicate the likelihood of an event occurring**.

The most common modal verbs in German include:

können	*müssen*	*wollen*
(can, to be able to)	(must, to have to)	(want, to want to)
dürfen	*sollen*	*mögen*
(may, to be allowed to)	(should, to should)	(like, to like to)

🎧 💬 DIALOGUE – REISEPLANUNG IM CAFÉ

(Markus and Johanna, friends meeting at a café, discuss their travel plans for an upcoming trip.)

Markus: Johanna, **kannst** du den Zugfahrplan für Samstag überprüfen?

Johanna: Sicher, ich **wollte** ohnehin die Abfahrtszeiten herausfinden.

Markus: Perfekt! Ich **muss** wissen, wann wir losfahren.

Johanna: Glaubst du, dass wir früh aufbrechen **sollten**?

Markus: Ja, am besten so früh wie möglich. Wann **möchtest** du zurück sein?

Johanna: Ich **möchte** spätestens um 20 Uhr wieder zu Hause sein.

Markus: Das **kann** ich verstehen. **Dürfen** wir deinen Wagen für die Fahrt zum Bahnhof nutzen?

Johanna: Klar, ihr **dürft** meinen Wagen nehmen. **Soll** ich dir die Schlüssel geben?

Markus: Das wäre super, danke! Mit deinem Auto **wird** die Reise viel einfacher.

Johanna: Kein Problem! Ohne Teamarbeit **wäre** so eine Planung immer komplizierter.

VOCABULARY LIST – REISEPLANUNG IM CAFÉ			
(der) Zugfahrplan [*n.*] (Zugfahrpläne)	train timetable	überprüfen [*v.*]	(to) check
(die) Abfahrtszeit [*n.*] (-en)	train/bus departure times	losfahren [*v.*]	(to) set off
		früh [*adj. / adv.*]	early
(der) Wagen [*n.*] (Wagen)	carriage		
(die) Fahrt [*n.*] (-en)	journey	spätestens [*adv.*]	latest
(der) Schlüssel [*n.*] (-)	key	kompliziert [*adj.*]	complicated
(die) Teamarbeit [*n.*] (-en)	teamwork	aufbrechen [*v.*]	(to) start
(die) Planung [*n.*] (-en)	planning	(das) Problem [*n.*] (-e)	(the) problem

22.1 COMMON MODAL VERBS

Modal verbs are a special category of verbs in German. They don't just convey actions, but the speaker's attitude towards that action. Instead of indicating what happens, they often tell us about a possibility, necessity, or other attitudes towards the action.

The six most common modal verbs are **können** (can, to be able to), **müssen** (must, have to), **dürfen** (may, to be allowed to), **sollen** (should, to be supposed to), **mögen** (like, to like to).

MODAL VERB	ENGLISH EQUIVALENT	MEANING/USAGE	EXAMPLE (GERMAN)	EXAMPLE (ENGLISH)
können [ˈkœnən]	can, to be able to	Ability or possibility	*Ich kann Deutsch sprechen.*	I can speak German.
wollen [ˈvɔlən]	want, to want to	Wish or desire	*Ich will ein Eis.*	I want an ice cream.
müssen [ˈmʏsn]	must, have to	Obligation or necessity	*Ich muss arbeiten.*	I have to work.
dürfen [ˈdʏʁfən]	may, to be allowed to	Permission	*Darf ich gehen?*	May I leave?
sollen [ˈzɔlən]	should, to be supposed to	Advice or expectation	*Du sollst nicht lügen.*	You shouldn't lie.
mögen [ˈmøːgən]	like, to like to	Liking something or someone	*Ich mag Kaffee.*	I like coffee.

In the dialogue, Johanna's line "*ich **wollte** ohnehin die Abfahrtszeiten herausfinden*" uses the modal verb "**wollen**" to express an intention or desire.

22.2 FORMATION AND USAGE OF MODAL VERBS

Modal verbs in German, as in many languages, differ somewhat from regular verbs in their conjugation. Their unique patterns need special attention when learning German grammar.

Understanding the Conjugation and Usage of Modal Verbs:

- **Third Person Singular**

  One key characteristic of German modal verbs is that the third person singular form doesn't take the typical '-*t*' ending. For instance, with the modal verb "*können*" the third person singular is "*kann*" and not "*könnt*".

"können" (can, to be able to):

	PERSON	CONJUGATION
1st person (sing.)	ich	kann
2nd person (sing.)	du	kannst
3rd person (sing.)	er/sie/es	**kann**
1st person (pl.)	wir	können
2nd person (pl.)	ihr	könnt
3rd person (pl.)	sie	können
Formal (sing. & pl.)	Sie	können

"wollen" (want, to want to):

	PERSON	CONJUGATION
1st person (sing.)	ich	will
2nd person (sing.)	du	willst
3rd person (sing.)	er/sie/es	**will**
1st person (pl.)	wir	wollen
2nd person (pl.)	ihr	wollt
3rd person (pl.)	sie	wollen
Formal (sing. & pl.)	Sie	wollen

"müssen" (must, have to):

	PERSON	CONJUGATION
1st person (sing.)	ich	muss
2nd person (sing.)	du	musst
3rd person (sing.)	er/sie/es	**muss**
1st person (pl.)	wir	müssen
2nd person (pl.)	ihr	müsst
3rd person (pl.)	sie	müssen
Formal (sing. & pl.)	Sie	müssen

→ The same pattern of conjugation (with slight variations) applies to other modal verbs.

- **Conjugation with Different Subjects and Tenses**

  While the present tense conjugation for modal verbs is irregular, in the simple past (Präteritum), their conjugation is more regular. For instance, the simple past form of "können" is "konnte".

Modal verbs take the second position in the sentence. The **main verb** appears in **infinitive form** at the end.

Ich **kann** *Tennis* **spielen**.
(I can play tennis.)

Markus uses the modal verb "*können*" when he says, "*Johanna,* **kannst** *du den Zugfahrplan für Samstag überprüfen?*" Here, the verb "*können*" is used to ask for the ability or possibility of doing something. Notice how the main verb "*überprüfen*" comes at the end of the sentence.

In subordinate clauses, the modal verb moves to the end, right before the **infinitive**:

Ich bin froh, dass ich Tennis **spielen** kann.
(I'm glad that I can play tennis.)

When used in a negative structure, the modal verb typically precedes the **negation word** "*nicht*".

Er darf **nicht** *gehen*.
(He's not allowed to go.)

In questions, the modal verb comes before the **subject**.

Kannst **du** *mir helfen?*
(Can you help me?)

✏️ EXERCISES

Ü 22.1) Underline the modal verb in each sentence.

Note: in some cases, when modal verbs such as 'wollen' or 'möchten' are used, the other infinitive verb may be omitted. This is a common feature of spoken colloquial German.

Example: Sie <u>kann</u> Deutsch sprechen.

    a. Er muss zum Arzt gehen.

    b. Sie wollen ins Kino.

    c. Du solltest mehr Wasser trinken.

    d. Ich darf das nicht essen.

    e. Wir würden gerne bezahlen.

Ü 22.2) Fill in the blank with the appropriate modal verb.

Example: Sie _____ Deutsch sprechen. (können)   →   Sie <u>kann</u> Deutsch sprechen.

    a. Er _____ nach Hause gehen. (wollen)

    b. Du _____ das Buch lesen. (sollen)

    c. Wir _____ hier parken. (dürfen)

    d. Sie _____ gut singen. (können)

    e. Ich _____ nicht lügen. (mögen)

    f. Er _____ den Kuchen essen. (dürfen)

    g. Du _____ deine Hausaufgaben machen. (müssen)

    h. Sie _____ uns besuchen. (wollen)

    i. Ich _____ den Film sehen. (möchten)

    j. Er _____ besser Tennis spielen. (können)

Ü 22.3) Rewrite the sentence, making the modal verb negative.

Example: Sie **kann** das tun.　　→　　Sie **kann** das **nicht** tun.

　　a. Er **muss** die Hausaufgaben machen.

　　_____

　　b. Sie **dürfen** hier rauchen.

　　_____

　　c. Wir **wollen** nach Berlin fahren.

　　_____

　　d. Du **solltest** das wissen.

　　_____

　　e. Ich **könnte** das Buch lesen.

　　_____

　　f. Sie **möchte** einen Kaffee.

　　_____

　　g. Er **würde** das kaufen.

　　_____

　　h. Ihr **sollt** das lernen.

　　_____

　　i. Du **darfst** das Fenster öffnen.

　　_____

　　j. Ich **muss** ins Büro gehen.

　　_____

Ü 22.4) Match the modal verb with its meaning.

Example: können   →   be able to/can

a. müssen   should/ought to

b. dürfen   would like to

c. wollen   be allowed to/may

d. sollen   would

e. mögen   must/have to

f. möchten   should

g. würden   be able to/could

h. könnten   want to

i. solltet   like

j. dürfte   be permitted to

Ü 22.5) Complete the sentence using a modal verb that makes sense.

Example: Bei Regen ___ du einen Regenschirm mitnehmen.

         ↳   Bei Regen <u>solltest</u> du einen Regenschirm mitnehmen.

a. Er _____ immer so laut sprechen.

b. Ich _____ leider nicht kommen.

c. Sie _____ ihre Schlüssel finden.

d. Du _____ das Auto fahren, wenn du möchtest.

e. Wir _____ diesen Film sehen.

f. Ihr _____ nicht so viele Süßigkeiten essen.

g. Er _____ schon schlafen, es ist spät.

h. Sie _____ Deutsch in der Schule lernen.

i. Du _____ das Buch zurückgeben.

j. Sie _____ gerne ins Theater gehen.

CHAPTER 23
AUXILIARY VERBS

⊘ CHECKBOX – WHAT ARE AUXILIARY VERBS?

Auxiliary verbs, also known as "*Hilfsverben*" in German, are u**sed in conjunction with the main verb to create different tenses, voices, and moods**. The two most common auxiliary verbs in German are "*haben*" (to have) and "*sein*" (to be).

<u>"*Haben*" as an Auxiliary Verb:</u>

"*Haben*" is used to form the perfect tenses, such as the present perfect and past perfect. It is combined with the past participle of the main verb to indicate actions that have been completed in the past.

Ich habe das Buch gelesen.	Wir hatten schon gegessen.
(I have read the book.)	(We had already eaten.)

<u>"*Sein*" as an Auxiliary Verb:</u>

"*Sein*" is used to form the compound tenses of certain verbs, mainly intransitive verbs of motion or change. It is also used to form the passive voice in combination with the past participle.

Er ist gestern nach Hause gegangen.	Das Buch ist geschrieben worden.
(He went home yesterday.)	(The book has been written.)

⏻ **DIALOGUE – KOCHEXPERIMENTE**

(Robert and Marina, friends with a shared love for cooking, discuss their recent culinary experiments.)

Robert: Marina, **hast** du in letzter Zeit etwas Neues gekocht?

Marina: Ja, ich **habe** versucht, eine spanische Paella zu machen. Es war eine Herausforderung! Und du?

Robert: Ich **bin** gerade dabei, Brotbacken zu lernen. Mein erstes Brot **war** leider ein bisschen hart.

Marina: Das klingt spannend! **Hast** du ein spezielles Rezept verwendet?

Robert: Ich **habe** ein Rezept aus einem alten Kochbuch meiner Großmutter genommen. Ich **glaube**, ich **muss** noch ein bisschen üben.

Marina: Das **wird** schon! Übung macht den Meister. Vielleicht **könnten** wir bald mal zusammen kochen?

Robert: Das **wäre** eine tolle Idee! Ich **würde** gerne einige deiner Rezepte lernen.

VOCABULARY LIST – KOCHEXPERIMENTE			
Übung macht den Meister = Practice makes perfect			
(das) Neue [*n.*]	new	(das) Rezept [*n.*] (-e)	recipe
kochen [*v.*]	cooking	(das) Kochbuch [*n.*] (Kochbücher)	cookbook
spanisch [*adj.*]	Spanish	einiges [*pron.*]	some
(die) Herausforderung [*n.*] (-en)	challenge	toll [*adj.*]	great
(das) Brot [*n.*] (-e)	bread	zusammen [*adv.*]	together
ein bisschen [*adv.*]	a little		

23.1 FORMATION AND USAGE OF AUXILIARY VERBS

In German, the primary auxiliary verbs are *"haben"* (to have) and *"sein"* (to be). They are fundamental in forming compound tenses.

- **"haben"**

  Typically used with verbs that describe an action or a condition.

  *Ich **habe** gelesen.*
  (I have read.)

  Present Perfect:

  *Sie **hat** ein Buch gelesen.*
  (She has read a book.)

  Past Perfect:

  *Sie **hatte** ein Buch gelesen.*
  (She had read a book.)

- **"sein"**

  Used with verbs that indicate movement or change of state.

  *Ich **bin** gegangen.*
  (I have gone.)

  Present Perfect:

  *Er **ist** nach Hause gegangen.*
  (He has gone home.)

  Past Perfect:

  *Er **war** nach Hause gegangen.*
  (He had gone home.)

23.2 POSITIONING OF AUXILIARY VERBS

The position of the auxiliary verb often depends on the type of sentence (main clause, subordinate clause) and the tense/mood being used.

In **main clauses**, the <u>auxiliary verb</u> usually occupies the second position, pushing the main verb to the end, especially in compound tenses.

> *Ich* **habe** *ein Buch* **gelesen**.
> (I have read a book.)

In **subordinate clauses**, both the <u>auxiliary</u> and the main verb move to the end of the sentence, with the auxiliary verb coming last.

> *Ich weiß, dass du das Buch* **gelesen** <u>**hast**</u>.
> (I know that you have read the book.)

Differences between main verbs and auxiliary verbs:

Main verbs carry the primary meaning of the sentence, while auxiliary verbs help in defining the tense, mood, or voice of the main verb. In sentences with modal auxiliary verbs, the main verb appears at the end in its infinitive form.

> *Ich* **möchte** *Kaffee* <u>**trinken**</u>.
> (I would like to drink coffee.)

<u>From the dialogue:</u>

<u>*Robert*</u>: "*Ich* **bin** *gerade dabei, Brotbacken zu* <u>**lernen**</u>." (I am currently learning to bake bread.) Here, "*bin*" is the auxiliary verb and "*lernen*" is the main verb. Notice the placement of both verbs.

Auxiliary Verbs in Questions and Negations:

In German, when forming questions using auxiliary verbs, there's typically an inversion of the subject and the auxiliary verb.

Du **hast** *ein Buch* **gelesen**. (You have read a book.)	becomes	*Hast du ein Buch gelesen?* (Have you read a book?)
Er **will** *ins Kino gehen.* (He wants to go to the cinema.)	becomes	*Will er ins Kino gehen?* (Does he want to go to the cinema?)

From the dialogue:

Robert: "Marina, **hast** du in letzter Zeit etwas Neues **gekocht**?"
(Marina, have you cooked something new recently?)

    ↳   The auxiliary verb "*hast*" precedes the subject "*du*", showcasing the subject-auxiliary inversion in a question.

The word "*nicht*" (not) is typically used to negate sentences in German. It's often placed before the main verb in simple tenses or at the end before the auxiliary in compound tenses.

*Er **kann** tanzen.*   becomes   *Er **kann nicht** tanzen.*
(He can dance.)   (He cannot dance.)

23.3 SPECIAL CASES WITH AUXILIARY VERBS

Auxiliary verbs in passive voice constructions:

    ↳   In passive constructions, the main verb appears in its past participle form, and the auxiliary verb "*werden*" is used to indicate the tense (📎 Ch. 12).

Present Passive:

*Der Brief **wird** geschrieben.*
(The letter is being written.)

Past Passive:

*Der Brief **wurde** geschrieben.*
(The letter was written.)

Using modal verbs in the subjunctive mood:

    ↳   The subjunctive (*Konjunktiv*) mood in German is used to express wishes, hypothetical situations, or polite requests. Auxiliary modal verbs play a crucial role here (📎 Ch. 14).

       For instance, the verb "*möchten*" is a form of "*mögen*" in the subjunctive mood and is often used to express a polite desire or wish.

       *Ich **möchte** einen Kaffee.*
       (I would like a coffee.)

       When using modal verbs in the subjunctive, the main verb remains at the end in the infinitive form.

       *Ich **würde** gern schwimmen **gehen**.*
       (I would like to go swimming.)

✏️ EXERCISES

Ü 23.1) Mark the auxiliary verb in each sentence.

Example: Sie **hat** das Buch gelesen.

a. Wir können Deutsch sprechen.

b. Er wird nach Berlin fliegen.

c. Sie hatte viel gegessen.

d. Ihr solltet zu Hause bleiben.

e. Es hat geregnet.

f. Sie haben im Park gespielt.

g. Ich werde dir helfen.

h. Du kannst das Fenster öffnen.

i. Er müsste früh aufstehen.

j. Sie hatten einen Film gesehen.

Ü 23.2) Complete each sentence with *"haben"*, *"sein"*, **or** *"werden"*.

Example: Er **ist** nach Hause gegangen.

a. Sie _____ morgen zu uns kommen.

b. Wir _____ einen Kuchen gebacken.

c. Er _____ im Garten gearbeitet.

d. Das Wetter _____ schön gewesen.

e. Du _____ das Buch gelesen.

f. Sie _____ in Berlin geboren.

g. Ich _____ ein neues Auto gekauft.

h. Er _____ Arzt werden.

i. Die Kinder _____ im Park gespielt.

j. Sie _____ letztes Jahr verreist.

Ü 23.3) Change the following present tense sentences to future tense.

Example: Sie spielt Klavier. → Sie wird Klavier spielen.

a. Ich lese ein Buch. _____

b. Er geht ins Kino. _____

c. Du lernst Deutsch. _____

d. Wir essen Pizza. _____

e. Sie schreibt einen Brief. _____

f. Ihr seht einen Film. _____

g. Es regnet. _____

Ü 23.4) Insert the auxiliary verb in the appropriate form.

Example: Er _____ schwimmen. (können) → kann

a. Ich _____ gern einen Kaffee trinken. (möchten)

b. Sie _____ nicht so laut sprechen. (sollen)

c. Du _____ die Antwort wissen. (müssen)

d. Er _____ den Text übersetzen. (können)

e. Wir _____ später kommen. (dürfen)

f. Ihr _____ eure Hausaufgaben machen. (sollen)

g. Sie _____ so viel essen. (mögen)

h. Du _____ nicht so spät ins Bett gehen. (sollen)

i. Er _____ nach Berlin fahren. (wollen)

j. Sie _____ das nicht tun. (müssen)

CHAPTER 24
SEPARABLE AND INSEPARABLE PREFIXES

⊘ CHECKBOX – WHAT ARE SEPARABLE AND INSEPARABLE PREFIXES?

A prefix is a **group of letters added to the beginning of a base verb, altering its meaning or creating a new verb altogether**.

<u>Separable Prefixes</u>

Separable prefixes are prefixes that **can be detached from the base verb** and placed at the end of the sentence in certain verb tenses. When used in present tense or imperative mood, separable prefixes are separated from the verb stem, allowing for flexibility in sentence structure.

"anrufen" (to call)–The prefix *"an-"* can be separated: *"Ich rufe meine Freundin an."* (I am calling my friend.)

<u>Inseparable Prefixes</u>

Inseparable prefixes, as the name suggests, are prefixes that **remain attached to the verb stem** at all times and **cannot be separated**. These prefixes do not change position in the sentence and are an integral part of the verb.

"verstehen" (to understand)–The prefix *"ver-"* cannot be separated: *"Ich verstehe die Frage."* (I understand the question.)

⌕ DIALOGUE – TAGESPLÄNE

(Karin and Sandra, friends catching up in a relaxed setting, discuss their daily plans and activities.)

Karin: *Sandra, du siehst müde aus.* **Bist** *du gestern spät* **auf***gestanden?*

Sandra: *Nein, ich* **bin** *früh* **auf***gewacht, aber ich habe gestern Abend einen Film* **an***geschaut und bin spät* **ein***geschlafen.*

Karin: *Oh, welchen Film hast du* **an***gesehen?*

Sandra: *Einen Dokumentarfilm. Es war so interessant, dass ich ihn nicht* **aus***schalten konnte.*

Karin: *Ich verstehe. Hast du heute etwas vor?*

Sandra: *Ja, ich muss meine Arbeit* **be***enden und dann möchte ich* **ein***kaufen gehen.*

Karin: *Ich denke darüber nach, einen Kuchen zu backen. Kannst du Sahne* **mit***bringen?*

Sandra: *Natürlich, ich werde sie nicht* **ver***gessen.*

Karin: *Super! Und wenn du Zeit hast, können wir später zusammen joggen gehen.*

Sandra: *Das klingt gut. Ich werde versuchen, früher* **zu***rückzukommen.*

VOCABULARY LIST – TAGESPLÄNE			
müde [*adj.*]	tired	verstehen [*v.*]	(to) understand
aufstehen [*v.*]	(to) get up	vorhaben [*v.*]	(to) intend
aufwachen [*v.*]	(to) wake up	(der) Kuchen [*n.*] (-)	cake
gestern [*adv.*]	yesterday	(die) Sahne [*n.*] (-)	cream
einschlafen [*v.*]	(to) fall asleep	vergessen [*v.*]	(to) forget
ansehen [*v.*]	(to) watch	super [*adj.*]	super
(der) Dokumentarfilm [*n.*] (-e)	documentary	joggen [*v.*]	(to) jog
ausschalten [*v.*]	(to) turn off	zurückkommen [*v.*]	(to) come back
mitbringen [*v.*]	(to) bring	versuchen [*v.*]	(to) try

24.1 SEPARABLE PREFIXES

Separable prefixes are verb prefixes that, as the name suggests, **can be separated from the base verb** in certain grammatical structures. For instance, in the present tense, the prefix often moves to the end of the clause. The verb "*anrufen*" (to call) becomes "*Ich **rufe** dich **an***" in the present.

There's a list of common separable prefixes, such as "*an-*", "*auf-*", "*ein-*", "*aus-*", "*mit-*", and "*zu-*", among others. They often give the verb a specific directional or qualitative nuance.

From the dialogue:

"**auf**gestanden"	–	from "**auf**stehen"	(to stand up/get up)
"**auf**gewacht"	–	from "**auf**wachen"	(to wake up)
"**an**geschaut"	–	from "**an**schauen"	(to watch/look at)
"**ein**geschlafen"	–	from "**ein**schlafen"	(to fall asleep)

BASE VERB	SEPARABLE PREFIX	COMBINED VERB	ENGLISH MEANING	EXAMPLE SENTENCE (GERMAN)	EXAMPLE SENTENCE (ENGLISH)
gehen	*aus-*	*ausgehen*	to go out	*Wir gehen heute Abend aus.*	We are going out tonight.
fahren	*an-*	*anfahren*	to start driving	*Er fährt das Auto an.*	He starts the car.
machen	*mit-*	*mitmachen*	to participate	*Willst du bei uns mitmachen?*	Do you want to join us?
hören	*zu-*	*zuhören*	to listen to	*Du solltest mir besser zuhören.*	You should listen to me more closely.
schreiben	*auf-*	*aufschreiben*	to write down	*Kannst du das bitte aufschreiben?*	Can you write that down, please?
sehen	*an-*	*ansehen*	to look at/ watch	*Sie sieht sich den Film an.*	She is watching the movie.
stehen	*auf-*	*aufstehen*	to stand up/ get up	*Er steht jeden Morgen um 6 Uhr auf.*	He gets up every morning at 6.
nehmen	*mit-*	*mitnehmen*	to take with	*Ich nehme meinen Hund mit.*	I'm taking my dog with me.

24.2 WORD ORDER WITH SEPARABLE PREFIXES

When a verb with a separable prefix is used in a main clause in the **present tense**, the **prefix is separated from the base verb and placed at the end of the sentence**. In the **past tense** (especially with the perfect tense), the **prefix remains attached to the verb in its past participle form**. For example, "*aufstehen*" becomes "*ist aufgestanden*" in the past.

In the infinitive form, the verb and its prefix stay together (e.g., "*einschlafen*"). But when conjugated in present tense, it gets separated (e.g., "*Ich schlafe heute früh ein*").

Example from the dialogue:

"*du siehst müde aus*" – the verb "*aussehen*" (to look/appear) is used here in the present tense.
"*ich habe ... angeschaut*" – the verb "*anschauen*" (to watch) is used here in the perfect tense.

24.3 INSEPARABLE PREFIXES

Inseparable prefixes are prefixes that always remain attached to their base verb, regardless of the tense or mood. Common inseparable prefixes in German include: *be-*, *ver-*, *ent-*, and *er-*. Verbs with these prefixes do not split, even when conjugated.

It's essential to memorize the most common inseparable prefixes and recognize them in verbs. Unlike separable prefixes, the stress in verbs with inseparable prefixes is often on the base verb and not on the prefix.

Examples:

verstehen (to understand)   *entdecken* (to discover)
erklären (to explain)   *bekommen* (to receive)

24.4 DISTINGUISHING BETWEEN SEPARABLE AND INSEPARABLE PREFIXES

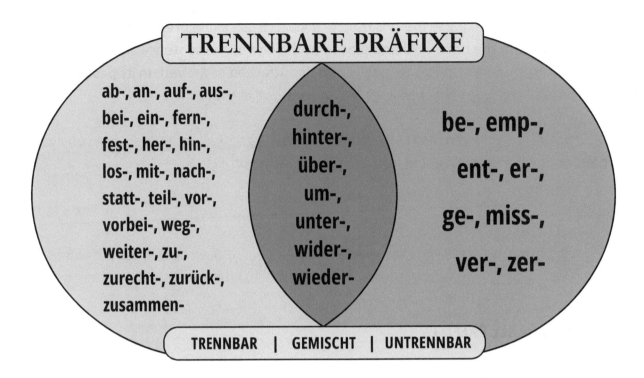

The main **distinction** between separable and inseparable prefixes is **the way they behave in a sentence**. While separable prefixes detach from their base verb in main clauses, inseparable prefixes always remain attached, no matter the tense or sentence structure.

Prefixes can significantly alter a verb's meaning. For instance, the verb "*stellen*" means "to place", but with the prefix "*vor-*" (separable) it becomes "*vorstellen*", meaning "to introduce" or "to imagine". With the prefix "*ver-*" (inseparable), it becomes "*verstellen*", meaning "to adjust" or "to block".

For prefixes that can be both separable and inseparable, such as "*-um*", caution should be taken when considering the meaning of verbs that have such präfixes. For instance, "*umfahren*" can mean both "to run over" or "to drive around", depending on the context.

 **EXERCISES**

Ü 24.1) Identify whether the following verbs have separable prefixes.

Example: aufstehen → separable

		separable	inseparable
a.	begegnen	☐	☐
b.	umfahren	☐	☐
c.	entdecken	☐	☐
d.	durchlaufen	☐	☐
e.	verstehen	☐	☐
f.	ankommen	☐	☐
g.	zerbrechen	☐	☐
h.	besuchen	☐	☐
i.	aufwachen	☐	☐
j.	durchlesen	☐	☐

Ü 24.2) Write the main verb and the prefix for the following verbs.

Example: einkaufen → kaufen, ein

a. anrufen _____

b. zubereiten _____

c. aufmachen _____

d. herkommen _____

e. vorlesen _____

f. abholen _____

g. mitnehmen _____

h. zusehen _____

i. durchgehen   _____

j. umdrehen   _____

Ü 24.3) Select the correct prefix from the box to complete the verb. Some may be used more than once.

Example: _____ stellen → **auf**stellen

durch-, um-, be-, zer-, auf-, ab-, an-

a. _____gehen

b. _____fahren

c. _____schreiben

d. _____brechen

e. _____nehmen

f. _____laufen

g. _____kommen

h. _____machen

i. _____setzen

j. _____sagen

CHAPTER 25
NEGATION

⊘ CHECKBOX – WHAT IS NEGATION?

Negation is a fundamental concept used to express the **negation or denial of statements, actions**, or **ideas**. By adding negation to sentences, individuals can express the absence, non-existence, or contradiction of certain elements, thereby expanding the range of meanings and nuances in their communication.

Negation can be applied to various elements within a sentence, including nouns, pronouns, adverbs, and entire sentences. Each type of negation utilizes specific words or structures to convey the negative meaning.

Negation of Nouns

Ich habe kein Buch.
(I don't have a book.)

Das ist keine Katze.
(That is not a cat.)

Negation of Pronouns and Adverbs

Er kommt nicht.
(He is not coming.)

Das ist nicht richtig.
(That is not correct.)

Negation of Verbs

Ich arbeite heute nicht.
(I am not working today.)

Er hat das Buch nicht gelesen.
(He did not read the book.)

○ **DIALOGUE – KLEINE PROBLEME**

(Michael and Emily, coworkers sharing an office space, have a brief conversation about some minor issues they're experiencing.)

Emily: *Nein, ich **habe hier keinen** Kugelschreiber gesehen. Und ich **benutze** auch **nicht** deinen.*

Michael: *Es ist **nicht** so wichtig. Vielleicht finde ich ihn später. **Hast du nicht** auch Probleme mit dem Internet hier?*

Emily: ***Überhaupt nicht**. Bei mir funktioniert das Internet perfekt. Bist du sicher, dass du **nicht** das Passwort falsch **eingegeben** hast?*

Michael: *Ich **glaube nicht**. Vielleicht sollte ich es **noch mal überprüfen**. Kannst du mir **nicht** helfen?*

Emily: *Klar, aber **nicht** jetzt. Ich habe gerade **keine** Zeit. Vielleicht später?*

Michael: *Kein Problem. Wir **müssen** ja **nicht** alles sofort erledigen.*

Emily: *Richtig. Manchmal muss man einfach mal **nichts** tun und eine Pause machen.*

VOCABULARY LIST – KLEINE PROBLEME

(der) Kugelschreiber [*n.*] (-)	ballpoint pen	erledigen [*v.*]	(to) do
wichtig [*adj.*]	important	tun [*v.*]	(to) do
(das) Internet [*n.*] (-)	Internet	(die) Pause [*n.*] (-n)	break
(das) Passwort [*n.*] (Passwörter)	password	sofort [*adv.*]	immediately
eingeben [*v.*]	(to) enter	überhaupt [*adv.*]	at all
überprüfen [*v.*]	(to) check	helfen [*v.*]	(to) help

25.1 NEGATION OF NOUNS

When it comes to negating nouns in German, we predominantly use two main negation words: "*kein*" and "*nicht*". However, their application differs:

Applying negation to nouns using "kein" and "nicht":

- **Kein**

    This is used for negating nouns that have an indefinite article or no article. The term "*kein*" is effectively a fusion of "*nicht*" and "*ein*" (not + a/an). Remember, "*kein*" will change its form depending on the gender (masculine, feminine, neuter) and the case (nominative, accusative, dative, genitive) of the noun it precedes. This declension is similar to the indefinite article.

    For example

    *Ich habe **keinen** Kugelschreiber.*
    (I don't have a pen.–masculine, accusative)
    *Das ist **keine** Lampe.*
    (This is not a lamp.–feminine, nominative)

- **Nicht**

    Unlike "*kein*", "*nicht*" is generally used to negate nouns with a definite article or possessive pronouns.

    For example

    *Ich sehe den Hund **nicht**.*
    (I don't see the dog.)
    *Ich mag deinen Kuchen **nicht**.*
    (I don't like your cake.)

Differences between "kein" and "nicht" in negating nouns:

While both "*kein*" and "*nicht*" serve to negate nouns, they're used in different contexts. As mentioned, "*kein*" is for negating nouns that have an indefinite article or no article. If you are denying the existence or absence of a particular object or suggesting you don't possess an undefined quantity of something, "*kein*" is your go-to. "*Nicht*", on the other hand, is when you're negating something specific, often denoted by a definite article or a possessive pronoun.

In the dialogue, we notice both usages:

> ↳ *Ich habe hier **keinen** Kugelschreiber gesehen.*
>   Emily is suggesting that she hasn't seen any pen in particular.

> ↳ *Ich benutze auch **nicht** deinen.*
>   Here, Emily clarifies that she isn't using Michael's specific pen.

25.2 NEGATION OF PRONOUNS AND ADVERBS

Pronouns and adverbs in German can also be negated, and once again, "*kein*" and "*nicht*" play pivotal roles in this process.

Negating pronouns using "kein" and "nicht":

Similar to nouns, pronouns can be negated using both "*kein*" and "*nicht*". However, "*kein*" is particularly prevalent when we negate indefinite pronouns.

For example,

- **Kein**

  Einer: _Einige Leute mögen Pizza._
  (Some people like pizza.)

  Keiner: _Einige Leute mögen keine Pizza._
  Some don't like pizza.)

- **Nicht**

  Das: _Das ist mein Buch._
  (That is my book.)

  Nicht das: _Das ist nicht mein Buch._
  (That is not my book.)

Negating adverbs using _"kein"_ and _"nicht"_:
These are primarily negated using _"nicht"_.

For example,

- **Oft**

  Oft: _Ich gehe oft ins Kino._
  (I often go to the cinema.)

  Nicht oft: _Ich gehe nicht oft ins Kino._
  (I don't often go to the cinema.)

Positioning of negated pronouns and adverbs in sentences:

Position is crucial in the German language, especially when negating pronouns and adverbs. The placement can affect the emphasis and clarity of the negation.

- **Nicht**

  The adverb "nicht" typically comes before the pronoun or adverb it negates.

  Ich habe das nicht gemacht.
  (I didn't do that.)

Er kommt nicht oft hierher.
(He doesn't come here often.)

- ## *Kein*

  Since "*kein*" is an article, it directly precedes the noun it's linked with, which may be represented by a pronoun.

  Ich habe keinen Stift.
  (I do not have a pen.)

  Hast du keins?
  (Don't you have one?–referring to a neuter noun)

In our dialogue, Emily employs "*nicht*" with a pronoun to clarify a specific point: "*Ich benutze auch nicht deinen.*" Here, she emphasizes the pronoun "*deinen*" (yours) to stress that she hasn't been using Michael's specific pen.

25.3 NEGATION OF VERBS

When it comes to verbs, the primary tool for negation in German is "*nicht*". The positioning of "*nicht*" is vital because it determines which part of the sentence is being negated.

In main clauses, "*nicht*" typically stands before the part of the sentence you want to negate.

Basic verb negation:

Ich esse.
(I eat.)

*Ich esse **nicht**.*
(I do not eat.)

Negating verb with an object:

Ich mag Schokolade.
(I like chocolate.)

*Ich mag Schokolade **nicht**.*
(I do not like chocolate.)

However, things get a bit trickier with separable verbs and compound verb tenses.

- ## *Separable verbs*

  When working with separable verbs, the "*nicht*" usually stands between the prefix and the main verb.

Sie steht auf.	*Sie steht **nicht** auf.*
(She gets up.)	(She doesn't get up.)

- **Compound tenses**

  With tenses like the *Perfekt* (the conversational past), the negation surrounds the auxiliary verb.

Er hat den Film gesehen.	Er hat den Film nicht gesehen.
(He saw the movie.)	(He didn't see the movie.)

- **Modal verbs**

  With modal verbs, the negation "nicht" is placed before the infinitive verb at the end of the sentence.

Ich kann singen.	*Ich kann **nicht** singen.*
(I can sing.)	(I can't sing.)

The position of "*nicht*" in a sentence can alter its meaning and emphasis.

- **Negating only the verb**

  The "nicht" directly follows the conjugated verb.

Sie schreibt.	*Sie schreibt **nicht**.*
(She writes.)	(She doesn't write.)

- **Negating an adverb**

  The "*nicht*" is placed in front of the adverb.

Er läuft schnell.	*Er läuft **nicht** schnell.*
(He runs fast.)	(He doesn't run fast.)

From the dialogue, we see a clear example in the sentence, "*Ich habe gerade keine Zeit.*" Here, the verb "*habe*" is negated in relation to the noun "*Zeit*" (time), indicating the lack of time.

✏️ EXERCISES

Ü 25.1) Read each sentence and underline the negative word or phrase.

Example: Ich habe das Buch <u>nicht</u> gelesen.

    a. Sie spricht kein Deutsch.

    b. Ich habe nie Kaffee getrunken.

    c. Er geht nirgendwo hin.

    d. Es ist niemand zu Hause.

    e. Wir haben keinen Hunger.

    f. Sie hat das Buch nicht gelesen.

    g. Ich möchte nirgends bleiben.

    h. Es gibt keine Äpfel.

    i. Er hat nie gelogen.

    j. Sie fährt nicht Auto.

Ü 25.2) Fill in the blanks with the appropriate negative word: *nicht, kein*

Example: Ich habe _____ Zeit.   →   Ich habe <u>keine</u> Zeit.

    a. Er isst _____ Fleisch.

    b. Ich bin _____ müde.

    c. Sie hat _____ Bruder.

    d. Das ist _____ gute Idee.

    e. Sie trinkt _____ Milch.

    f. Ich gehe _____ ins Kino.

    g. Sie möchte _____ Kaffee.

    h. Das ist _____ mein Stift.

i. Ich sehe _____ Fernsehen.

j. Er hat _____ Fehler gemacht.

Ü 25.3) Write the opposite of the given sentence by adding the appropriate negation.

Example: Er liest ein Buch.　　　→　　　Er liest **kein** Buch.

a. Sie spielt Klavier.　　　_____

b. Ich esse Schokolade.　　_____

c. Er geht zur Schule.　　　_____

d. Das ist meine Tasche.　　_____

e. Sie schreiben einen Brief.　_____

f. Wir fahren nach Berlin.　　_____

g. Er hört Musik.　　　　　_____

h. Ich trage einen Hut.　　　_____

i. Sie liebt Tiere.　　　　　_____

j. Das ist interessant.　　　_____

Ü 25.4) Decide whether the statement is true or false and negate it to form its opposite.

		True	False
Example:	Der Himmel ist blau.	☑	☐
	<u>Der Himmel ist nicht blau.</u>		

		True	False
a.	Wasser ist trocken.	☐	☐

_____

| **b.** | Katzen sind Vögel. | ☐ | ☐ |

_____

CONCLUSION

Congratulations! You have reached the end of our comprehensive German Grammar Made Easy workbook. This guide led you through the vast expanse of German grammar, allowing you to dive into its intricacies and peculiarities. By following this journey, you've laid a solid groundwork for German grammar, preparing you for your continued pursuit of fluency.

It's no secret that German grammar, with its rich tapestry of rules and their exceptions, can appear overwhelming initially. But by segmenting it into digestible pieces and consistently practicing, you've made commendable progress towards conquering this splendid language. It's worth noting that the journey of language acquisition is unending. Your insights into the language will only deepen with more practice and immersion.

In this guide, we started with foundational concepts, including pronunciation and syllabification, and ventured into the language's pillars like nouns, articles, and pronouns. You've also familiarized yourself with verb conjugation across various tenses. The complexities of sentence construction, the roles of different types of clauses, conjunctions, prepositions, adjectives, and adverbs were all unpacked in detail.

As you've navigated through this workbook, numerous examples, exercises, and practice sentences helped cement your understanding. Continuous practice remains paramount to internalizing these grammar rules and wielding them confidently. We encourage you to consistently revisit the exercises in this workbook and consider other resources like the German language book series by Lingo Mastery.

Yet, grammar is just one facet of language mastery. True proficiency arises when you immerse yourself in the culture and broader contexts of the German language. To supplement your journey, consider the following:

- Learning a language from a textbook is certainly great for starting out and for gaining a basic understanding of its underlying rules. However, fluency comes through engaging with native speakers and through picking up and assimilating the way they use the language (after all, this is how you became fluent in your first language as a child). Try finding a German tandem language partner (in-person or online) who will teach you their language from a native speaker's angle!

- Broaden your exposure to German through diverse media. Enjoy German books, movies, or shows that pique your interest. Using subtitles can aid comprehension initially, but as you advance, challenge yourself by reducing your reliance on them.

- The digital age offers a plethora of online resources. Several German broadcasting platforms provide news and other content in simplified German, both in written and audio formats. These can be invaluable in enhancing comprehension.

- Institutions like the Goethe Institut are valuable troves of resources on German culture and language. Although primarily based in Germany, they have centers worldwide and can be a great source for materials and courses.

With these parting words, we bid you *Auf Wiedersehen* and wish you *viel Erfolg und alles Gute* on your German learning journey!

ANSWER KEY

PRONUNCIATION GUIDE

Ü P1)

(rasch, tot, ihm, Stock, mehr, Nacht, gut, Stadt, Mund, Depp, knapp, mit, rot, Wurst, Lohn, Rahm, Fuß, Tag, Test, Tick, Los, Mist, Band, Lehm)

VOWEL	SHORT	LONG
a	rasch, Nacht, Stadt, knapp, Band	Rahm, Tag
e	Depp, Test	mehr, Lehm
i	mit, Tick, Mist	ihm
o	Stock	tot, rot, Lohn, Los
u	Mund, Wurst	gut, Fuß

Ü P2)

> Hallo Herr **Müller**,
>
> Ich habe mich sehr **über** unser Treffen letzte Woche gefreut. Ihre Ideen **für** die anstehende Handelsmesse haben unserem **Geschäftsführer** gefallen. Wir **würden** allerdings vorschlagen, dass Sie auch Ihren Vorstand zur Messe mitbringen. Dann **können** wir die Optionen gemeinsam besprechen. Ich hoffe, Sie hatten noch ein paar **schöne** Tage in Berlin. Wir sehen uns also **nächste** Woche!
>
> Mit freundlichen **Grüßen**
> Peter Scholz

Ü P3)

*Gestern Na**ch**t wa**ch**te <u>Ch</u>ristian plötz<u>l</u>i**ch** auf. Er su**ch**te na**ch** dem Li**ch**tschalter der*

d   d   k   l   d   d   l

*Na**ch**ttischlampe, die re**ch**ts neben ihm stand. Es war eine teure Lampe aus **ch**inesis**ch**em*

d   l   l

*Porzellan. Als er den Schalter zunä**ch**st ni**ch**t fand, hörte er etwas durch den Raum schlei**ch**en.*

                        l   l   l

*Er hor**ch**te in die Dunkelheit hinein. Do**ch** es war still. Er da**ch**te si**ch**, dass er wohl wieder*

     l   d   d   l

*schlafen sollte. Er schlief glei**ch** wieder ein. Als er am nä**ch**sten Morgen die Augen öffnete,*

                      l   l

*wurde ihm sofort klar, wer für die nä**ch**tliche Störung verantwortli**ch** gewesen war:*

                            l   l

*Sein Kater **Ch**amillo schnurrte behagli**ch** neben ihm.*

         k   l

Ü P4)

a) <u>A</u>bend	**g)** <u>Su</u>ppe	**m)** Phy<u>s</u>ik	**s)** Maler<u>ei</u>
b) <u>Leu</u>te	**h)** Universit<u>ä</u>t	**n)** wider<u>l</u>egen	**t)** Majest<u>ä</u>t
c) Mu<u>s</u>ik	**i)** be<u>d</u>auern	**o)** Gele<u>hr</u>ter	
d) <u>s</u>agen	**j)** stud<u>ie</u>ren	**p)** termin<u>ie</u>ren	
e) Bäcker<u>ei</u>	**k)** ver<u>sp</u>rechen	**q)** <u>A</u>bfall	
f) Fanta<u>sie</u>	**l)** Kuriosit<u>ä</u>t	**r)** Comp<u>u</u>ter	

UNIT 1
NOUNS AND PRONOUNS

CHAPTER 1

Ü 1.1)

a) Jupiter	PN		**a)** Hitze	CNA
b) Hunger	CNA		**b)** Matterhorn	PN
c) Oktoberfest	PN		**c)** Bleistift	CNC
d) Stuhl	CNC		**d)** Hamburg	PN
e) Konrad Adenauer	PN		**e)** Petersdom	PN
f) Hass	CNA		**f)** Familie	CNA
g) Europäische Zentralbank	PN		**g)** Donau	PN
h) Ferien	CNA		**h)** Frank Sinatra	PN
i) Königsstraße	PN		**i)** Taj Mahal	PN
j) Lassie	PN		**j)** Wasser	CNC

Ü 1.2)

a) <u>Der</u> Lehrer kommt.

b) <u>Die</u> Rose ist schön.

c) <u>Die</u> Universität ist groß.

d) <u>Der</u> Honig ist süß.

e) <u>Die</u> Wohnung ist sauber.

f) <u>Die</u> Köchin kocht das Essen.

g) <u>Der</u> Pianist spielt Klavier.

h) <u>Das</u> Instrument ist teuer.

i) <u>Das</u> Datum steht hier.

j) <u>Der</u> Regen hört nicht auf.

k) <u>Das</u> Judentum ist eine Religion.

l) <u>Die</u> Krankheit ist tödlich.

m) <u>Der</u> Rektor leitet die Schule.

n) <u>Die</u> Flagge flattert im Wind.

o) <u>Das</u> Auge ist gerötet.

p) <u>Die</u> Familie ist zu Hause.

q) <u>Der</u> Morgen graut.

r) <u>Das</u> Vöglein singt.

s) <u>Der</u> Zucker ist weiß.

t) <u>Der</u> Käse kommt aus Frankreich.

Ü 1.3)

a) der Verkäufer	**die Verkäuferin**		**e)** der Bauer	**die Bäuerin**
b) der Astronaut	**die Astronautin**		**f)** der Bischof	**die Bischöfin**
c) der Bär	**die Bärin**		**g)** der Kollege	**die Kollegin**
d) der Dirigent	**die Dirigentin**		**h)** der Ehemann (!)	**die Ehefrau**

Ü 1.4)

GROUP I (Plural:–/ ¨)	GROUP II (Plural: -e / ¨e)	GROUP III (Plural: -er / ¨er)	GROUP IV (Plural: -n / -en / -nen)	GROUP V (Plural: -s)
die Mädchen die Spiegel	die Berufe die Füße die Bälle die Tage die Hände die Schuhe die Töne die Telefone die Städte die Regale	die Bäder die Wälder die Bilder die Dörfer	die Kulturen die Friseurinnen die Blumen die Taschen die Bäckereien	die Hotels die PCs die Radios die Handys

CHAPTER 2

Ü 2.1)

a) Die <u>Frau</u> gibt dem <u>Mann</u> den <u>Autoschlüssel</u>.
       N   D   A

b) Die <u>Lehrer</u> erzählen <u>Geschichten</u> für die <u>Kinder</u>.
       N   A   A

c) Die <u>Frau</u> des <u>Bürgermeisters</u> hat ein <u>Auto</u> gekauft.
       N   G   A

d) Hier ist ein <u>Foto</u> unseres <u>Hauses</u>.
         N   G

e) Zum <u>Geburtstag</u> bekam er ein <u>Buch</u>.
        D   A

f) <u>Karl</u> versprach seiner <u>Tochter</u> ein <u>Eis</u>.

   N   D   A

g) Der <u>Koch</u> bereitet die <u>Speisen</u> vor.

     N   A

h) Der <u>Lehrer</u> gibt der <u>Schülerin</u> eine gute <u>Note</u>.

    N   D   A

i) Das <u>Messer</u> des <u>Kochs</u> muss scharf sein.

    N   G

j) Der <u>Vater</u> trägt seinen <u>Sohn</u> auf der <u>Schulter</u>.

    N   A   D

Ü 2.2)

NOUN	DER BERG (-E)		DIE STUNDE (-N)		DAS FENSTER (-)	
	Singular					
	article	noun	article	noun	article	noun
Nominative	der	Berg	die	Stunde	das	Fenster
Genitive	des	Berges	der	Stunde	des	Fensters
Dative	dem	Berg	der	Stunde	dem	Fenster
Accusative	den	Berg	die	Stunde	das	Fenster
	Plural					
Nominative	die	Berge	die	Stunden	die	Fenster
Genitive	der	Berge	der	Stunden	der	Fenster
Dative	den	Bergen	den	Stunden	den	Fenstern
Accusative	die	Berge	die	Stunden	die	Fenster

Ü 2.3)

Familie(**-**) Müller macht heute einen Ausflug(**-**) in den Zoo(**-**). Die Kinder(**-**) wollen die exotischen Tier(**e**) sehen. Gleich am Eingang(**-**) sehen sie zwei Papagei(**en**). Sie geben den bunten Vögel(**n**) einen Keks(**-**). Als Nächstes sehen sie sich die Affe(**n**) an. Die lustigen Schrei(**e**) der Primat(**en**) gefallen den Kinder(**n**). Am Löwengehege(**-**) staunen sie über die Mähne(**-**) des Löwe(**n**). Auch die Elefant(**en**) gefallen den Kinder(**n**). Am liebsten würden sie den Elefant(**en**) Erdnüss(**e**) in den Rüssel(**-**) stecken. Am Ende(**-**) des Ausflug(**s**) bekommen die Kinder(**-**) noch ein Eis(**-**). Am Ausgang(**-**) winkt Familie(**-**) Müller den Papagei(**en**) wieder zu.

CHAPTER 3

Ü 3.1)

a) **Die** Universität ist alt.

b) **Der** Mann schreibt.

c) Ist **das** Mädchen krank?

d) **Der** Junge studiert.

e) **Die** Wohnung ist kalt.

f) **Das** Wetter ist schön.

g) Warum schreit **das** Kind?

h) **Die** Frau ist hübsch.

i) **Der** Lehrer ist jung

j) **Der** Vogel singt.

Ü 3.2)

a) Ich gehe in **die** Schule.

b) Ich fahre zu **dem** Arzt.

c) Das ist das Spielzeug **des** Kindes.

d) Ich bin in **dem** Büro.

e) Ich gehe zu **der** Apotheke.

f) Ich gehe in **das** Büro.

g) Der Chef dankte **den** Mitarbeitern.

h) Ich muss **die** E-Mails beantworten.

i) Welcher Polizist untersucht **den** Fall?

Ü 3.3)

a) Dort ist **ein** Junge.

b) **Eine** Gabel ist aus Silber.

c) Das ist **ein** Käfer.

d) **Ein** Mädchen kommt.

e) Dort steht **ein** Museum.

f) Ist das **eine** Lilie?

g) Dort liegt **eine** Pille.

h) **Eine** Wohnung ist teuer.

i) Das ist **ein** Cent.

j) Dort hängt **ein** Apfel.

a) Ist das ein Museum?   **Nein, das ist kein Museum.**

b) Ist das eine Bushaltestelle?   **Nein, das ist keine Bushaltestelle.**

c) Hat Dieter ein Auto?   **Nein, Dieter hat kein Auto.**

d) Möchtest du einen Kaffee?   **Nein, ich möchte keinen Kaffee.**

e) Hat Peter einen Bruder?   **Nein, Peter hat keinen Bruder.**

f) Hat Mareike ein neues Haustier?   **Nein, Mareike hat kein neues Haustier.**

g) Hat das Hotel eine Bar?   **Nein, das Hotel hat keine Bar.**

h) Brauchst du eine neue Kamera?   **Nein, ich brauche keine neue Kamera.**

i) Hat Augsburg eine U-Bahn?   **Nein, Augsburg hat keine U-Bahn.**

Ü 3.5)

a) Frau Bäcker ist **X** Bankkauffrau und wohnt in **der** Ottomannstraße.

b) Ich finde **das** Leben als **X** Journalist ziemlich gut.

c) Er ist **X** Österreicher, aber sie ist **eine** gebürtige Französin.

d) Karin ist in **der** Schweiz geboren und ist **X** Ärztin.

e) Nach **dem** Abendessen werden sie **X** Gitarre spielen.

f) In **der** Schule lernen wir viel über **X** Großbritannien.

g) Obwohl **das** Christentum hier weit verbreitet ist, ist er **X** Buddhist.

CHAPTER 4

Ü 4.1)

a) Unser Auto ist nicht hier, weil **es** in der Garage steht.

b) Du hast doch einen Garten. Ist **er** groß?

c) Wir möchten bitte diese Suppe, aber **sie** muss heiß sein!

d) Ich mag mein Haus, nur ist **es** leider zu klein.

e) Die Schuhe passen gut und außerdem waren **sie** billig.

f) Wie viel hat der Laptop gekostet und wird **er** noch verkauft?

Ü 4.2)

Ein Junge fand im Garten eine Rose. **Sie** duftete wunderbar. Das gefiel **ihm** sehr. **Er** meinte: „Aus **ihr** kommt ein so herrlicher Duft, sicher kann man **sie** auch essen. **Sie** schmeckt sicher so köstlich, wie **sie** duftet." Neugierig nahm **er** einige Blütenblätter in den Mund. Ihr bitterer Geschmack überraschte **ihn**. **Er** verzog das Gesicht. „Betrügerin!", schrie **er** und warf **sie** auf die

Erde. „Mit deinem Duft hast du mich getäuscht!" Die Rose erwiderte *ihm*: „Wer mehr als Duft von mir erwartet, täuscht sich selbst."

Ü 4.3)

a) **Unser** Postbote (m, Nom.) ist schon seit vielen Jahren in **unserem** Stadtviertel (n, Dat.) tätig.

b) **Sein** Lächeln (n, Akk.), **seine** Freundlichkeit (f, Akk.) und **seine** Fröhlichkeit (f, Akk.) mögen wir sehr.

c) **Seinen** Job (m, Akk.) erledigt er immer sehr pünktlich.

d) Jeden Morgen um 10 Uhr wirft er die Post in **unsere** Briefkästen (Pl., Akk.).

e) Aber manchmal finde ich Briefe für **unsere** neuen Nachbarn (Pl., Akk.) in **unserem** Postkasten (m, Dat.).

f) Sie dagegen finden in **ihrem** (m, Dat.) Kasten Briefe an **unsere** Adresse (f, Akk.).

g) Das ist nicht schlimm, wir geben ihnen einfach **ihre** Postsendungen (Pl, Akk.) und bekommen **unsere** Briefe (Pl., Akk.) von ihnen.

h) Auf diese Weise haben wir **unsere** neuen Nachbarn (Pl., Akk.) kennengelernt.

i) Jetzt laden wir sie gern zum Grillen in **unseren** Garten (m, Akk.) ein, und sie bitten uns zu Partys in **ihr** Haus (n, Akk.).

j) Wir freuen uns über **unsere/ihre** neue Freundschaft (f, Akk) und lieben deshalb **unseren** Postboten (m, Akk.) noch mehr.

Ü 4.4)

a) Wir nehmen das Auto von mir.	→	Wir nehmen **meins**.
b) Ist das Bettinas Tasche?	→	Ja, das ist **ihre**.
c) Ist das Arnolds Mantel?	→	Ja, das ist **seiner**.
d) Das ist der Computer von Steffi.	→	Das ist **ihrer**.
e) Sind das die Bücher von dir?	→	Ja, das sind **meine**.
f) Das sind Susis und Margrets Bücher.	→	Das sind **ihre**.

CHAPTER 5

Ü 5.1)

a) Hast du von Klaus gehört? <u>Den</u> habe ich schon lang nicht mehr gesehen.

b) Ich finde <u>diesen</u> Hut nicht schön, aber <u>jener</u> Hut gefällt mir gut.

c) Sie ist <u>diejenige</u>, die gestern einen Autounfall hatte.

d) Schön, dass du hier bist. <u>Das</u> ist eine <u>solche</u> Überraschung!

e) <u>Dasselbe</u> habe ich dir gestern schon am Telefon gesagt.

f) <u>Dieses</u> Foto habe ich gemacht, aber <u>jenes</u> Foto hat meine Frau gemacht.

g) Karin trifft ihre Schwester und <u>deren</u> Mann.

h) <u>Das</u> sind alles Laptops <u>derselben</u> Marke.

i) Kennst du <u>diesen</u> Mann? <u>Der</u> kommt mir bekannt vor.

j) Tanja und Anke? Mit <u>denen</u> habe ich erst gestern Kaffee getrunken.

Ü 5.2)

a) Dies**er** Pullover gefällt mir nicht, aber jen**er** sieht schön aus.

b) Ich habe dies**e** Frau hier schon einmal gesehen, aber jen**e** noch nicht.

c) Dies**e** Gläser sind sauber, aber jen**e** müssen in die Spülmaschine.

d) Ich bin mit dies**er** Fluggesellschaft schon oft geflogen, aber von jen**er** habe ich noch nie gehört.

e) Mit dies**en** Dingen kenne ich mich nicht aus, aber ich bin ein Experte für jen**e** Dinge.

Ü 5.3)

a) Das ist **derselbe** Mann, den ich gestern im Supermarkt getroffen habe.

b) Das sind alles Produkte **desselben** Unternehmens.

c) **Diejenigen**, die mit der Arbeit fertig sind, dürfen in die Pause gehen.

d) Ich habe **denselben** Fehler zwei Mal gemacht.

e) Ich werde in **demjenigen** Hotel übernachten, das am günstigsten ist.

f) Sie geht mit **demselben** Jürgen aus, der mit dir in die Schule gegangen ist.

Ü 5.4)

1) Seit wann kennst du Klaus?
2) Welches Kind hat sich verletzt?
3) Welches ist dein Auto?
4) Wem gehört der Laptop?
5) Sollen wir uns einen Horrorfilm ansehen?
6) Das Lied kommt mir bekannt vor.
7) Wer bekommt einen Preis?
8) Fährst du mit Karin nach Berlin?
9) In jenem Winter vor 10 Jahren hat es viel geschneit.
10) Mein Chef hat mich gefeuert.

a) **Jenes** dort drüben, auf dem Parkplatz.
b) Ja, es ist **dasselbe** Lied, das auf der Party gespielt wurde.
c) Nein, mit **der** fahre ich nirgends mehr hin.
d) **So** eine Frechheit!
e) Ja, aber in **diesem** Winter hat es noch kaum geschneit.
f) **Den** kenne ich seit einem Monat.
g) **Dasjenige**, das mit dem Ball gespielt hat.
h) Nein, **solche** Filme mag ich nicht.
i) Er gehört **demjenigen**, der vorher nach dem Wifi-Passwort gefragt hat.
j) Einen Preis bekommen **diejenigen**, die alle Fragen richtig beantworten.

1)	2)	3)	4)	5)	6)	7)	8)	9)	10)
f	g	a	i	h	b	j	c	e	d

UNIT 2
VERBS AND VERB TENSES

CHAPTER 6

ACTION	PROCESS	STATE OF BEING
gehen, schreiben, essen, fragen, drücken, kehren, bauen	einschlafen, verhungern, erfrieren, altern, sterben, wachsen, aufwachen	leben, schlafen, bevorzugen, sitzen, staunen, glauben, lieben

Ü 6.2)

    a) Er <u>sieht</u> am Abend oft fern.   **3**rd **person singular**

    b) Am Wochenende <u>besuche</u> ich meinen Freund.   **1**st **person singular**

    c) Bei schönem Wetter <u>gehen</u> wir heute Abend noch joggen. **1**st **person plural**

    d) Danke, dass du mir <u>hilfst</u>.   **2**nd **person singular**

    e) Kurt und Alex <u>spielen</u> gern gemeinsam Tennis.   **3**rd **person plural**

    f) Warum <u>sagt</u> ihr eurem Chef nichts davon? **2**nd **person plural**

Ü 6.3)

INFINITIVE	PRESENT PARTICIPLE	PAST PARTICIPLE
warten, hören, lügen, schreiben, zunehmen, grüßen	sprechend, winkend, essend, lachend, schlafend	gesungen, gesagt, gelebt, gefüllt, gebracht, gesucht, gekommen

CHAPTER 7

Ü 7.1)

a) Hallo, wie **heißt** du?

b) Alexander **wohnt** in Berlin.

c) Er **geht** jeden Tag joggen.

d) Carmen **spricht** Spanisch, Chinesisch und Deutsch.

e) Worauf **wartest** du?

f) Wir **essen** gern beim Italiener.

g) Ich **verstehe** sechs Sprachen.

h) Was **sind** Sie von Beruf?

i) **Habt** ihr auch Hunger?

j) Die Kinder **besuchen** am Wochenende ihre Großeltern.

Ü 7.2)

	MACHEN	**WOLLEN**	**SEHEN**	**LESEN**	**WERDEN**	**SEIN**
ich	mache	will	sehe	lese	werde	bin
du	machst	willst	siehst	liest	wirst	bist
er/sie/es	macht	will	sieht	liest	wird	ist
wir	machen	wollen	sehen	lesen	werden	sind
ihr	macht	wollt	seht	lest	werdet	seid
sie/Sie	machen	wollen	sehen	lesen	werden	sind

Ü 7.3)

(er geht, er lädt, er gilt, er singt, er stirbt, er schwimmt, er tritt, er betritt, er läuft, er stiehlt)

gehen, laden, gelten, singen, sterben, schwimmen, treten, betreten, laufen, stehlen

CHAPTER 8

Ü 8.1)

a) Ich **lernte** Deutsch in der Schule.

b) Sie **tanze** gestern Abend auf der Party.

c) Wir **arbeiteten** letztes Jahr in Berlin.

d) Er **spielte** Tennis jeden Samstag.

e) Du **kauftest** ein neues Auto.

f) Sie **wohnten** in einem großen Haus.

g) Wir **hörten** das Radio.

h) Er **ging** ins Kino.

i) Die Kinder **sahen** den Film nicht.

j) Du **schliefst** lange am Wochenende.

k) Sie **las** das Buch.

l) Ich **trank** Kaffee.

m) Wir **fanden** den Schlüssel nicht.

n) Du **kamst** spät nach Hause.

Ü 8.2)

a) Ich **habe** meine Hausaufgaben **gemacht**.

b) Sie **ist** nach Paris **gefahren**.

c) Das Buch **ist** auf den Boden **gefallen**.

d) Er **ist** im Park **gelaufen**.

e) Wir **haben** Pizza **gegessen**.

f) Du **bist** im Meer **geschwommen**.

g) Sie **hat** ein neues Kleid **getragen**.

Ü 8.3)

a) Sie **war** in Berlin **gewesen**, bevor sie nach München umzog.

b) Ich **hatte** das Essen **gegessen**, bevor es kalt wurde.

c) Die Kinder **hatten** draußen **gespielt**, bevor es regnete.

d) Er **hatte** den Tee **getrunken**, bevor er zu süß wurde.

e) Wir **hatten** den Ball **verloren**, bevor wir nach Hause gingen.

f) Du **hattest** das Buch **gelesen**, bevor der Film startete.

g) Sie **hatte** den Brief **geschrieben**, bevor der Postbote kam.

Ü 8.4)

a) Sie **lernte** Deutsch letztes Jahr.

⮡ The simple past tense should be used for a specific event in the past.

b) Er **hat** gestern Fußball **gespielt**.

⮡ Incorrect conjugation of the auxiliary verb *"haben"* and wrong word order.

c) Das Buch **ist** auf den Boden **gefallen**.

⮡ The word order is incorrect. The verb "fallen" in the present perfect tense requires *"sein"* as the auxiliary verb and *"gefallen"* as its past participle.

d) Wir **sind** im Meer **geschwommen**.

⮡ The word order is incorrect. The verb *"schwimmen"* requires the auxiliary verb *"sein"* in the perfect tenses, and *"hatte"* is singular while *"wir"* is plural.

e) Sie **ist** nach Berlin **gefahren**.

⮡ The word order is incorrect. Incorrect conjugation of the auxiliary verb *"sein"* for the third person singular.

f) Er **hat** auf der Party **getanzt**.

⮡ Incorrect conjugation of the auxiliary verb *"haben"* for the third person singular and word order.

CHAPTER 9

Ü 9.1)

a) Morgen **werde** ich zum Arzt **gehen**.
b) Sie **wird** bald Urlaub **haben**.
c) Nächstes Jahr **werden** wir nach Deutschland **reisen**.
d) Meine Schwester **wird** das Buch später **lesen**.
e) Die Kinder **werden** draußen **spielen**, wenn es warm wird.
f) Ich **werde** nächste Woche ein neues Auto **kaufen**.
g) Er **wird** einen Brief an seine Freundin **schreiben**.

a) Er denkt, dass es morgen **regnen wird**.

b) Ich hoffe, dass du mir **helfen wirst**.

c) Vielleicht **wird** sie zur Party **kommen**.

d) Er **wird** es sicherlich nicht **vergessen**.

e) Ich bin sicher, dass du **gewinnen wirst**.

f) Meine Eltern **werden** mich nächsten Monat **besuchen**.

g) Sie **wird** das Essen bald **bestellen**.

Ü 9.3)

a) Bis morgen **wird** sie alles **gelernt haben**.

b) Ich denke, dass er den Schlüssel **gefunden haben wird**.

c) Nächstes Jahr **werden** wir schon **gereist sein**.

d) Er wird sein Auto verkauft haben.

e) Sie wird bis 10 Uhr geschlafen haben.

f) Ich **werde gekocht haben**, bis du zurückkommst.

g) Wenn er ankommt, **wird** sie schon **gegessen haben**.

Ü 9.4)

a) Er wird das Buch gelesen haben.	**Future II**
b) Wir werden nach Italien fahren.	**Future I**
c) Sie wird gekocht haben.	**Future II**
d) Du wirst tanzen.	**Future I**
e) Ich werde den Brief geschrieben haben.	**Future II**
f) Wir werden morgen studieren.	**Future I**
g) Sie wird das Essen gemacht haben.	**Future II**

Ü 9.5)

a) Wenn ich ankomme, wird sie schon gegangen sein.

b) Bis du zurückkommst, werde ich meine Arbeit beendet haben.

c) Er hofft, dass, wenn er älter **wird**, er viel **gereist sein wird**.

d) Wenn das Wetter gut ist, **werde** ich **spazieren gehen**.

e) Sie hofft, dass sie bis dahin genug **gelernt haben wird**.

f) Ich denke, wenn du ihn siehst, **wird** er dir die Wahrheit **sagen**.

g) Bis sie ankommt, **werden** wir schon **gegessen haben**.

CHAPTER 10

Ü 10.1)

a) Ich **freue mich** auf den Urlaub.

b) Du **wäschst dir** die Hände.

c) Sie **erinnert sich** an ihre Kindheit.

d) Wir **treffen uns** im Café.

e) Ihr **langweilt euch** ohne Fernsehen.

f) Es **lohnt sich** nicht.

g) **Setzen Sie** sich bitte!

Ü 10.2)

a) Er hat **sich** beim Sport verletzt.

b) Sie interessiert **sich** für Kunst.

c) Sie freuen **sich** auf die Party.

d) Ich putze **mir** jeden Morgen die Zähne.

e) Es hat **sich** schnell verkauft.

f) Ihr zieht **euch** warm an.

g) Wir beeilen **uns**, damit wir pünktlich sind.

h) Er rasiert **sich** jeden Tag.

i) Du solltest **dich** mehr entspannen.

j) Sie können **sich** hier ausruhen.

k) Das Kind wäscht **sich** alleine.

l) Ihr habt **euch** für das Konzert angezogen.

m) Die Katze putzt **sich** nach dem Essen.

Ü 10.3)

sich erholen - to recover

sich beschweren - to complain

sich entscheiden - to decide

sich vorstellen - to introduce oneself

sich anziehen - to get dressed

sich verspäten - to be late

sich bemühen - to make an effort

sich verlieben - to fall in love

Ü 10.4)

a) Jeden Morgen **duscht sich** Martin und dann **zieht er sich an**.

b) Bevor sie zur Arbeit geht, **schminkt sich** Sandra.

c) Nach der Arbeit **entspanne** ich **mich** gerne mit einem Buch.

d) In der Mittagspause **treffen sich** die Kollegen immer im Park.

e) Am Wochenende **schlafen sich** Petra und Tom immer lange **aus**.

f) Abends vor dem Schlafen **putzen sich** die Kinder die Zähne.

g) Bei Stress **erholt sich** Herr Müller oft in der Sauna.

Ü 10.5)

a) A: Warum kommt Lisa zu spät zur Party?

B: Sie hat **sich verlaufen** und findet den Weg nicht.

b) A: Wie fühlst du dich heute?

B: Ich **fühle mich** ein bisschen müde.

c) A: Wo trefft ihr euch vor dem Konzert?

B: Wir **treffen uns** am Haupteingang.

d) A: Willst du nicht tanzen?

B: Nein, ich **schäme mich** für meine Tanzfähigkeiten.

e) A: Warum schaut ihr den Film nicht?

B: Wir **interessieren uns** nicht für Horrorfilme.

f) A: Warum hat Paul diesen Job angenommen?

B: Er **freut sich** auf die Herausforderungen und Möglichkeiten.

g) A: Hast du Sarah gesehen?

B: Ja, sie **sonnt sich** drüben im Garten.

h) A: Warum rennst du so?

B: Ich **beeile mich,** weil mein Zug in 10 Minuten fährt.

Ü 10.6)

a) Meine Schwester hat **sich** heute Morgen sehr lange im Bad aufgehalten.

b) Peter und Maria wollen **sich** in Berlin treffen.

c) In der Pause habe ich **mir** ein Sandwich gemacht.

d) Die Kinder ziehen **sich** schnell an, wenn es kalt ist.

e) Thomas freut **sich** über das schöne Geschenk.

f) Wir setzen **uns** neben die Großeltern im Theater.

g) Lisa, beeil **dich**! Der Bus kommt gleich.

h) Bei der Meditation versuchen viele, **sich** zu entspannen.

CHAPTER 11

Ü 11.1)

a) Die Blumen blühen im Garten.   I

b) Der Junge liest ein Buch.   T

c) Der Vogel singt.   I

d) Sie trinkt einen Tee.   T

e) Das Baby schläft.   I

f) Er öffnet die Tür.   T

g) Die Kinder spielen im Park.   I

h) Sie kauft ein neues Kleid.   T

i) Der Kater schnurrt.   I

j) Der Mann baut ein Haus.   T

Ü 11.2)

a) Die Lehrerin korrigiert die Hausaufgaben.

b) Maria bestellt eine Pizza.

c) Der Vater liest seinem Sohn eine Geschichte vor.

d) Die Schüler schreiben den Test.

e) Wir beobachten die Sterne in der Nacht.

f) Der Kellner serviert das Essen.

g) Sie versteht die Frage nicht.

h) Der Mechaniker repariert das Auto.

i) Mein Bruder spielt die Gitarre jeden Abend.

j) Der Direktor präsentiert den neuen Plan.

Ü 11.3)

Sample Responses:

    a) <u>Transitive</u>: Er isst einen Apfel.

       <u>Intransitive</u>: Er isst schnell.

    b) <u>Transitive</u>: Sie fährt das Auto.

       <u>Intransitive</u>: Sie fährt nach Berlin.

    c) <u>Transitive</u>: Er beginnt den Vortrag um 10 Uhr.

       <u>Intransitive</u>: Das Meeting beginnt.

    d) <u>Transitive</u>: Die Schülerin schreibt einen Brief.

       <u>Intransitive</u>: Sie schreibt gut.

    e) <u>Transitive</u>: Die Band spielt ein Lied.

       <u>Intransitive</u>: Die Kinder spielen im Garten.

Ü 11.4)

    a) Der Lehrer gibt <u>dem Schüler</u> ein <u>Buch</u>.
    b) Meine Mutter kocht <u>mir</u> ein <u>leckeres Abendessen</u>.
    c) Der Chef zeigt <u>der Assistentin</u> den <u>Bericht</u>.
    d) Er erzählt <u>seinem Freund</u> eine <u>interessante Geschichte</u>.
    e) Das Mädchen kauft <u>ihrer Mutter</u> einen <u>Blumenstrauß</u>.
    f) Der Verkäufer bietet <u>dem Kunden</u> einen <u>Rabatt</u> an.
    g) Sie schickt <u>ihrem Bruder</u> eine <u>Postkarte</u>.
    h) Der Kellner serviert <u>dem Gast</u> ein <u>Glas Wasser</u>.
    i) Die Großmutter strickt <u>ihrem Enkel</u> einen <u>Pullover</u>.
    j) Der Direktor erklärt <u>den Angestellten</u> das <u>neue Projekt</u>.

Ü 11.5)

    a) Der Stoff **wird** von der Lehrerin **erklärt**.
    b) Das Brot **wird** vom Bäcker **gebacken**.
    c) Das Fahrrad **wird** vom Mechaniker **repariert**.
    d) Die Hauptrolle **wird** von der Schauspielerin **gespielt**.
    e) Das Bild **wird** vom Künstler **gemalt**.

f) Der Artikel **wird** von der Autorin **geschrieben**.

g) Die Blumen **werden** vom Gärtner **gepflanzt**.

h) Das Essen **wird** von der Köchin **zubereitet**.

i) Das Foto **wird** vom Fotografen **aufgenommen**.

j) Der neue Mitarbeiter **wird** vom Direktor **eingestellt**.

UNIT 3
MOOD AND VOICE

CHAPTER 12

Ü 12.1)

a) Das Buch wird von ihr gelesen.	P
b) Er spielt Fußball.	A
c) Die Türen wurden geschlossen.	P
d) Ich schreibe den Brief.	A
e) Das Fenster wird geöffnet.	P
f) Sie kauft ein Kleid.	A
g) Das Haus wurde von ihm gebaut.	P
h) Wir besuchen den Zoo.	A
i) Die Suppe wird serviert.	P
j) Er wird von dem Hund gejagt.	P

Ü 12.2)

a) Die Hausaufgaben werden von ihr gemacht.

b) Das Essen wird vom Koch zubereitet.

c) Die Tests werden von der Lehrerin korrigiert.

d) Der Hund wird von dem Jungen gefüttert.

e) Das Lied wird von der Mutter gesungen.

f) Das Fenster wird von ihm geöffnet.

g) Das Auto wird von ihr gekauft.

h) Die Regel wird vom Lehrer erklärt.

i) Der Saft wird von uns getrunken.

j) Das Spiel wird von den Kindern gespielt.

Ü 12.3)

a) Die Tür **wird** von ihm **geschlossen**.

b) Das Essen **wird** von der Köchin **zubereitet**.

c) Das Fahrrad **wird** in der Werkstatt **repariert**.

d) Der Vertrag **wird** vom Chef **unterschrieben**.

e) Die Bücher **werden** in der Buchhandlung **verkauft**.

f) Der Garten **wird** von der Gärtnerin **gepflegt**.

g) Die Musik **wird** von den Nachbarn **gehört**.

h) Die Kleidung **wird** im Waschsalon **gewaschen**.

i) Die Worte **werden** von den Schülern **aufgeschrieben**.

j) Das Wasser **wird** von den Tieren **getrunken**.

Ü 12.4)

a) Das Lied wird von **Lara** gesungen.

b) Das Auto wird von **meinem Vater** gefahren.

c) Die Geschichte wird von **einem alten Mann** erzählt.

d) Die Suppe wird von **der Köchin** gekocht.

e) Die Aufgabe wird vom **Schüler** gelöst.

f) Der Ball wird von **den Spielern** geworfen.

g) Der Artikel wird von **der Journalistin** geschrieben.

h) Das Theaterstück wird von **einer bekannten Gruppe** aufgeführt.

i) Die Schokolade wird von **dem Kind** gegessen.

j) Die Bilder werden von **einem talentierten Künstler** gemalt.

Ü 12.5) Sample Answer

Die Straßen werden von Autos befahren.

Die Bürgersteige werden von Fußgängern benutzt.

Die Geschäfte werden von Kunden besucht.

Die Musik wird aus einem nahe gelegenen Café gehört.

Die Blumen werden von der Sonne beschienen.

Die Zeitungen werden von Verkäufern verkauft.

Die Vögel werden am Himmel gesehen.

Die Lampen werden eingeschaltet, da es dunkel wird.

Das Essen wird in den Restaurants serviert.

Ü 12.6)

a) Das Haus wird gekauft.

b) Das Lied wird gesungen.

c) Die Türen werden geschlossen.

d) Der Film wird gedreht.

e) Das Buch wird geschrieben.

f) Das Essen wird zubereitet.

g) Die Bilder werden aufgenommen.

h) Die Kleidung wird entworfen.

Ü 12.7)

a) muss, werden

b) sollte, werden

c) könnte, werden

d) müsste, werden

e) soll, werden

f) könnte, werden

g) dürfen, werden

h) sollten, werden

i) müssten, werden

j) kann, werden

Ü 12.8)

a) Das Essen wird - von ihr gekocht.

b) Der Bericht wurde - von dem Reporter geschrieben.

c) Die Hausaufgaben müssen - von den Kindern gemacht werden.

d) Die Fenster sollten - regelmäßig geöffnet werden.

e) Die Show wurde - von vielen gesehen.

f) Das Buch kann - von uns gelesen werden.

g) Die Nachrichten werden - täglich aktualisiert.

h) Die Lieder wurden - jeden Abend gehört.

i) Das Gemälde wird - von einem Künstler gemalt.

j) Der Kuchen wird - von allen geliebt.

CHAPTER 13

Ü 13.1)

Informal imperative	Formal imperative
a) Geh! (informal)	Gehen Sie! (formal)
b) Iss!	Essen Sie!
c) Trink!	Trinken Sie!
d) Hör!	Hören Sie!
e) Schreib!	Schreiben Sie!
f) Lies!	Lesen Sie!

g) Spiel!   <u>Spielen Sie!</u>

h) Nimm!   <u>Nehmen Sie!</u>

i) Sprich!   <u>Sprechen Sie!</u>

j) Fahr!   <u>Fahren Sie!</u>

Ü 13.2)

a) Gib

b) Sprich

c) Öffne

d) Mach

e) Gib

f) Bleib

g) Lauf

h) Parke

i) Bleib

j) Mach

Ü 13.3)

a) Informal

b) Formal

c) Formal

d) Informal

e) Formal

f) Informal

g) Formal

Ü 13.4)

a) Sieh den Film!

b) Probieren Sie die Suppe!

c) Nimm den Schirm!

d) Fragen Sie den Lehrer!

e) Schließ die Tür!

f) Buchen Sie das Hotelzimmer!

g) Hör die Musik!

h) Überprüfen Sie die E-Mails!

i) Triff deine Freunde!

j) Füllen Sie das Formular aus!

Ü 13.5)

a) Geh nicht!

b) Essen Sie nicht!

c) Schreib nicht!

d) Hören Sie nicht!

e) Spiel nicht!

f) Lesen Sie nicht!

g) Nimm nicht!

Ü 13.6)

a) Mach das Licht an!

b) Sei leise!

c) Gib mir einen Stift!

d) Schließe das Fenster!

e) Ich will bestellen!

Ü 13.7)

a) Trink

b) Schließe

c) Geh

d) Lies

e) Mach

Ü 13.8)

→ This exercise doesn't have a set answer key due to its interactive nature.

CHAPTER 14

Ü 14.1)

a) Konjunktiv II

b) Konjunktiv I

c) Konjunktiv II

d) Konjunktiv I

e) Konjunktiv II

f) Konjunktiv II

g) Konjunktiv I

h) Konjunktiv II

i) Konjunktiv I

j) Konjunktiv II

Ü 14.2)

a) Er sagt, er **gehe** ins Kino.

b) Maria behauptet, das **sei** ihr Buch.

c) Peter meint, sie **kämen** später.

d) Sie erzählt, sie **habe** einen Hund.

e) Er sagt, sie **seien** im Park.

f) Sie sagt, sie **werde** bald reisen.

g) Thomas meint, das **sei** sein Fehler.

h) Er sagt, er **könne** das tun.

i) Maria sagt, sie **möge** Schokolade.

j) Er behauptet, das **ergäbe** keinen Sinn.

Ü 14.3)

a) Wenn ich zur Party **ginge** …

b) Wenn sie den Weg **kennen würden** …

c) Wenn wir ein Auto **hätten** …

d) Wenn du hier **wärest** …

e) Wenn er das Haus **kaufte** …

f) Wenn sie im Büro **arbeitete** …

g) Wenn ich den Kuchen **äße** …

Ü 14.4)

a) habe

b) wäre

c) komme

d) gesagt hättest

e) bleibe

f) könnte

g) wüsste

h) sei

i) hätte

Ü 14.5)

a) könnte

b) mache

c) hätte

d) lese

e) wäre

f) sei

g) hätte

h) wohne

i) fragte

j) wolle

Ü 14.6)

a) Er glaubt, dass sie die Antwort kennt.

b) Wenn ich ein Auto hätte, würde ich zur Arbeit fahren.

c) Sie meint, dass sie das tun kann.

d) Wenn er hier wäre, würde er ein Eis kaufen.

e) Sie sagt, dass sie Hunde mag.

f) Er hofft, dass er morgen in der Schule ist.

g) Wenn ich mehr Geld hätte, würde ich ein neues Haus kaufen.

h) Sie denkt, dass er seine Hausaufgaben macht.

UNIT 4
CASES, CLAUSES AND WORD ORDER

CHAPTER 15

Ü 15.1)

a) <u>Die Sonne</u> scheint hell.

b) <u>Der Hund</u> bellt laut.

c) <u>Der Lehrer</u> erklärt den Stoff.

d) <u>Die Vögel</u> singen im Wald.

e) <u>Meine Schwester</u> kocht Pasta.

f) <u>Der Computer</u> funktioniert nicht.

g) <u>Die Katzen</u> schlafen.

h) <u>Der Apfel</u> fällt vom Baum.

i) <u>Sie</u> lernen Deutsch.

Ü 15.2)

a) Anna <u>liest</u> ein Buch.

b) Der Baum <u>wächst</u> schnell.

c) Der Zug <u>kommt an</u>.

d) Die Blumen <u>blühen</u>.

e) Peter und Maria <u>tanzen</u>.

f) Das Auto <u>fährt</u>.

g) Sie <u>schreibt</u> einen Brief.

h) Die Kinder <u>lachen</u>.

i) Die Vögel <u>fliegen</u>.

j) Der Regen <u>fällt</u>.

Ü 15.3)

a) Sie trinkt <u>Tee</u>.

b) Ich liebe meine Familie.

c) Der Lehrer unterrichtet <u>Mathematik</u>.

d) Meine Mutter kauft <u>das Kleid</u>.

e) Er sieht <u>den Film</u>.

f) Das Mädchen gibt dem Hund einen Knochen.

g) Der Bäcker verkauft Brot.

h) Er liest das Magazin.

i) Sie hört Musik.

j) Die Kinder essen Kuchen.

Ü 15.4)

a) Die Blume duftet süß.

b) Der Mann trägt einen Hut.

c) Die Studenten lernen Geschichte.

d) Das Auto hat eine Panne.

e) Die Vögel suchen Futter.

f) Das Mädchen mag Eis.

g) Der Opa erzählt eine Geschichte.

h) Der Lehrer korrigiert die Tests.

i) Die Katze jagt die Maus.

j) Der Tourist fotografiert die Sehenswürdigkeiten.

Ü 15.5)

a) Der Apfel fällt vom Baum.

b) Die Katze schläft im Korb.

c) Die Kinder essen Schokolade.

d) Der Vogel fliegt im Himmel.

e) Anna liest das Buch.

f) Es regnet in der Stadt.

g) Der Mann hört Radio.

h) Die Fische schwimmen im Teich.

i) Die Frau kauft rote Schuhe.

j) Das Mädchen singt im Chor.

Ü 15.6)

a) (A) einen Apfel

b) (C) das Auto

c) (B) die Musik

d) (A) die Maus

e) (C) das Brot

f) (B) den Tee

g) (B) die Aufsätze

h) (A) die Bilder

i) (A) die Patienten

a) Meine <u>Tante</u> feiert Geburtstag.

b) Die Blumen <u>wachsen</u> im Garten.

c) Der Bäcker <u>backt</u> Kuchen.

d) Sie <u>schenkt</u> ihrem Neffen ein Geschenk.

e) Die <u>Rosen</u> blühen schön.

f) Er <u>kauft</u> Brot beim Bäcker.

g) Der Schneider <u>näht</u> täglich.

h) Sie pflegt ihre <u>Großmutter</u>.

i) Meine Mutter <u>wünscht</u> sich Kuchen zum Geburtstag.

j) Der <u>Lehrer</u> bringt den Schülern neuen Stoff bei.

a) Das Kindern spielen im Garten.   <u>Die Kinder spielen im Garten.</u>

b) Er lieben Pizza.   <u>Er liebt Pizza.</u>

c) Die Lehrerin erklär die Regel.   <u>Die Lehrerin erklärt die Regel.</u>

d) Der Hunde bellt laut.   <u>Der Hund bellt laut.</u>

e) Sie haben ein rotes Kleider.   <u>Sie hat ein rotes Kleid.</u>

f) Das Bücher ist spannend.   <u>Das Buch ist spannend.</u>

g) Der Mädchen singt ein Lied.   <u>Das Mädchen singt ein Lied.</u>

h) Die Blume duftet guter.   <u>Die Blume duftet gut.</u>

i) Der Autos fahren schnell.   <u>Das Auto fährt schnell.</u>

j) Ich mag Eiscremes.   <u>Ich mag Eiscreme.</u>

a) Die Vögel fliegen hoch.

b) Das Kind lernt im Klassenzimmer.

c) Die Autos sind schnell.

d) Der Apfel ist saftig.

e) Die Frauen kaufen Gemüse.

f) Die Pferde galoppieren auf der Wiese.

g) Das Buch ist auf dem Tisch.

h) Die Stühle sind alt.

i) Das Fenster ist offen.

j) Die Lehrer korrigieren die Tests.

CHAPTER 16

Ü 16.1)

a. Oft er spielt Fußball. _____
b. Er spielt oft Fußball. __✓__
c. Er oft spielt Fußball. _____

a. Sie liebt Musik hören. _____
b. Musik liebt sie hören. _____
c. Sie liebt es, Musik zu hören. __✓__

a. Schokolade sie mag sehr. _____
b. Sie mag Schokolade sehr. __✓__
c. Sie Schokolade mag sehr. _____

a. Er hat einen Apfel gegessen. __✓__
b. Gegessen einen Apfel hat er. _____
c. Er einen Apfel hat gegessen. _____

a. Immer ins Kino sie geht. _____
b. Sie geht immer ins Kino. __✓__
c. Sie immer geht ins Kino. _____

a. Er liest das Buch. __✓__
b. Das Buch er liest. _____
c. Er das Buch liest. _____

a. Der Hund schläft im Haus. __✓__
b. Im Haus der Hund schläft. _____
c. Schläft im Haus der Hund. _____

a. In einem Büro sie arbeiten. _____
b. Einem Büro sie arbeiten in. _____
c. Sie arbeiten in einem Büro. __✓__

Ü 16.2)

a) Die Blumen sind schön.
b) Wir haben heute zu Hause gegrillt.
c) Ich trinke morgens immer Kaffee.
d) Sie hat ein großes Haus.
e) Er wohnt nicht in Berlin.
f) Ich weiß nicht, wo er arbeitet.
g) Sie isst Pizza gerne.
h) Ich lese Bücher gerne im Bett.
i) Er fährt oft nach Berlin.
j) Die Kinder spielen im Garten.

a) Besucht sie das Museum?

b) Lernt er Deutsch?

c) Haben sie ein neues Auto?

d) Singen die Vögel?

e) Regnet es heute?

f) Essen sie Pizza?

g) Schlafen die Kinder?

h) Schreibt er einen Brief?

i) Landet das Flugzeug?

j) Tanzt sie im Club?

a) **Was** möchtest du trinken?

b) Sie **ist** nach Paris geflogen.

c) **Warum** gehen sie ins Kino?

d) **Abends** trinkt sie immer Tee.

e) **Täglich** spielt er Klavier.

f) Wann **gehst** du ins Bett?

g) Warum **kommt** sie so spät?

h) Wie **hat** sie das gemacht?

i) **Warum** lernen sie Deutsch?

j) **Woher** hat er so viel Geld?

a) Das Mädchen - hat ein neues Kleid.

b) Die Katze - isst den Fisch.

c) Die Eltern - lesen die Zeitung.

d) Der Mann - kauft ein Buch.

e) Der Zug - fährt um fünf Uhr ab.

f) Die Jungs - spielen Fußball.

g) Die Oma - kocht Suppe.

h) Der Vogel - singt ein Lied.

i) Die Lehrerin - erklärt die Aufgabe.

j) Die Schüler - schlafen schon.

Ü 16.6)

a) <u>Im Winter</u> fahre ich Ski.

b) <u>Letzten Sommer</u> waren wir in Italien.

c) Sie besucht uns <u>jeden Sonntag</u>.

d) <u>Morgen</u> wird es regnen.

e) <u>Nächstes Jahr</u> werde ich studieren.

f) Er ruft mich <u>jeden Abend</u> an.

g) <u>Im April</u> blühen die Blumen.

h) Sie haben <u>vor zwei Wochen</u> geheiratet.

i) Ich sehe sie <u>einmal im Monat</u>.

j) <u>Am Wochenende</u> gehen wir wandern.

Ü 16.7)

a) haben

b) sind

c) hat

d) sind

e) sind

f) habe

g) ist

h) ist

i) ist

j) ist

Ü 16.8)

a) Er <u>darf</u> nicht ins Kino gehen.

b) Sie <u>können</u> gut singen.

c) Ich <u>möchte</u> ein Eis.

d) Wir <u>müssen</u> jetzt gehen.

e) Sie <u>will</u> ins Theater.

f) Er <u>mag</u> keinen Käse.

g) Du <u>darfst</u> das nicht tun.

h) Ich <u>kann</u> das Fenster öffnen.

i) Sie <u>müssen</u> das Formular ausfüllen.

CHAPTER 17

Ü 17.1)

a) Er sagte, dass er morgen kommen würde.

b) Ich gehe schwimmen, <u>obwohl es kalt ist</u>.

c) <u>Wenn es regnet</u>, bleibe ich zu Hause.

d) Sie fragte, ob ich Kaffee möchte.

e) <u>Bevor du gehst</u>, ruf mich an.

f) Er kann nicht kommen, <u>weil er krank ist</u>.

g) Sie hat geübt, damit sie den Test besteht.

h) Ich schlafe, wenn du fernsiehst.

i) <u>Obwohl er müde war</u>, hat er weitergearbeitet.

j) Das ist der Mann, den sie geheiratet hat.

Ü 17.2)

(These are suggestions; there could be other suitable subclauses.)

a) Sie geht spazieren,	… obwohl es regnet.
b) Obwohl er Geld hat,	… kauft er das Auto nicht.
c) Wenn sie Zeit hat,	… liest sie ein Buch.
d) Er hat gelacht,	… weil es so lustig war.
e) Ich werde es tun,	… wenn du mir hilfst.
f) Bevor du einschläfst,	… denke an mich.
g) Sie hat geweint,	… weil sie traurig war.
h) Wenn es schneit,	… gehen wir Schlittenfahren.
i) Nachdem sie gegessen hatte,	… ging sie spazieren.
j) Sie schreibt ihm,	… damit er sich erinnert.

Ü 17.3)

a) Weil	g) Wenn
b) weil	h) Wenn
c) Wenn	i) Nachdem
d) dass	j) Wenn
e) damit	
f) Während	

Ü 17.4)

a) weil es spät ist, ist er gegangen

b) weil ich besorgt war, habe ich sie angerufen

c) wenn wir hungrig sind, bestellen wir Pizza

d) wenn ich Zeit habe, werde ich es tun

e) wenn ich schlafen gehe, wird sie Fernsehen

f) sie fragte, ob du kommen würdest

g) obwohl er Geld hat, will er es nicht kaufen

h) ich hoffe, dass ich dich sehen werde

Ü 17.5)

a) Weil er Hunger hat, isst er einen Apfel.

b) Weil es regnet, nimmt sie einen Schirm.

c) Weil sie Tee möchte, kocht sie Wasser.

d) Ich träume, dass ich fliege.

e) Weil du müde bist, gehst du ins Bett.

f) Weil sie Angst hat, schreit sie.

g) Weil es spät ist, geht er nach Hause.

h) Obwohl er Geld hat, gibt er mir keins.

i) Während ich einen Film sehe, schläfst du.

j) Indem sie ein Buch liest, lernt sie viel.

Ü 17.6)

a) Ich komme, wenn du mich einlädst.

b) Obwohl er müde ist, arbeitet er noch.

c) Nachdem sie ihr Essen beendet hatte, ging sie.

d) Ich verstehe nicht, warum sie verärgert ist.

e) Er fragte, ob ich den Film gesehen habe.

Ü 17.7)

a) <u>Weil es regnet</u>, gehe ich nicht aus.

b) <u>Während sie schläft</u>, liest er ein Buch.

c) <u>Obwohl sie müde ist</u>, spielt sie Klavier.

d) <u>Wenn es warm ist</u>, geht er schwimmen.

e) <u>Weil sie Hunger</u> hat, kocht sie.

f) <u>Nachdem ich Hausaufgaben gemacht habe</u>, werde ich fernsehen.

a) Ich habe gehört, <u>dass es regnet</u>.

b) Ich habe gesehen, <u>dass sie ein neues Auto hat</u>.

c) Es ist beeindruckend, <u>dass er Deutsch sprechen kann</u>.

d) Es ist schade, <u>dass das Museum geschlossen ist</u>.

e) Ich bin stolz, <u>dass sie ihre Hausaufgaben gemacht hat</u>.

f) Ich rieche, <u>dass das Essen fertig ist</u>.

g) Es ist gut, <u>dass du die Aufgabe verstehst</u>.

h) Sie hat gesagt, <u>dass der Film spannend war</u>.

i) Ich habe bemerkt, <u>dass das Wetter kälter wird</u>.

j) Es ist traurig, <u>dass er sein Buch verloren hat</u>.

UNIT 5
MODIFIERS

CHAPTER 18

Ü 18.1)

a) Das <u>blaue</u> Meer ist <u>wunderschön</u>.

b) Sie hat <u>langes</u>, <u>lockiges</u> Haar.

c) Der <u>alte</u> Mann sitzt auf einer Bank.

d) Er kauft ein <u>neues</u> Auto.

e) Die <u>kleinen</u> Kinder lachen <u>laut</u>.

f) Der Film war wirklich <u>interessant</u>.

g) Die <u>kalte</u> Limonade ist <u>erfrischend</u>.

h) Ich habe <u>großen</u> Hunger.

i) Ihr Zimmer ist immer <u>ordentlich</u>.

j) Das ist ein <u>schwieriges</u> Rätsel.

Ü 18.2)

a) schnell - langsam

b) hell - dunkel

c) schwer - leicht

d) glücklich - unglücklich

e) warm - kalt

f) sauber - schmutzig

g) voll - leer

h) laut - leise

i) hoch - tief

j) weich - hart

Ü 18.3)

a) roten

b) schöne

c) teures

d) kaltes

e) großen

f) neuen

g) spannende

h) langer

i) kurze

j) leckerer

Ü 18.4)

comparative	superlative
a) kleiner	am kleinsten
b) länger	am längsten
c) schneller	am schnellsten
d) kälter	am kältesten
e) jünger	am jüngsten
f) größer	am größten
g) höher	am höchsten
h) schwerer	am schwersten
i) kürzer	am kürzesten
j) teurer	am teuersten

Ü 18.5)

a) klaren

b) laute

c) hungrig

d) sauer

e) voll

f) faul

g) traurig

h) schmal

i) grüne

j) starken

Ü 18.6)

a) False

b) False

c) True

d) False

e) False

f) True

g) False

h) True

i) False

j) False

CHAPTER 19

Ü 19.1)

a) Er läuft <u>schnell</u>.

b) Sie singt <u>wunderschön</u>.

c) Der Hund bellt <u>laut</u>.

d) Sie schreibt <u>oft</u> Briefe.

e) Er liest <u>selten</u> Bücher.

f) Wir arbeiten <u>hart</u> für das Projekt.

g) Sie denkt <u>immer</u> an ihre Familie.

h) Er kommt <u>nie</u> zu spät.

i) Sie spricht <u>deutlich</u>.

j) Er isst <u>gerne</u> Schokolade.

Ü 19.2)

	Adverb	Adjective
a) Er ist ein **schneller** Läufer.	☐	☑
b) Sie singt **klar**.	☑	☐
c) Das ist ein **hartes** Brot.	☐	☑
d) Er spricht **laut**.	☑	☐
e) Das **alte** Haus ist schön.	☐	☑
f) Sie arbeitet **effizient**.	☑	☐
g) Die **kalte** Suppe schmeckt nicht.	☐	☑
h) Er hört **aufmerksam** zu.	☑	☐
i) Das **schöne** Lied berührt mich.	☐	☑
j) Sie lachen **lautlos**.	☑	☐

Ü 19.3)

a) selten → Wir gehen <u>selten</u> ins Kino.

b) leise → Er spielt <u>leise</u> Musik, wenn das Baby schläft.

c) manchmal → <u>Manchmal</u> trinke ich Tee anstatt Kaffee.

d) besonders → Dieses Dessert ist <u>besonders</u> lecker.

e) schlecht → Er fühlt sich <u>schlecht</u> nach dem Essen.

f) klar → Sie hat <u>klar</u> und deutlich gesprochen.

g) direkt → Er ging <u>direkt</u> nach Hause nach der Arbeit.

h) tatsächlich   →   Ich habe <u>tatsächlich</u> das ganze Buch an einem Tag gelesen.

i) genauso   →   Das neue Modell sieht <u>genauso</u> aus wie das alte.

j) zufällig   →   Ich habe sie <u>zufällig</u> im Supermarkt getroffen.

Ü 19.4)

a) Er kommt vielleicht morgen.

b) Sie telefoniert nie abends.

c) Sie schläft immer nach Mittag.

d) Er isst gerne Schokolade.

e) Sie studiert intensiv.

f) Er fährt meistens mit dem Auto.

g) Er liest selten Bücher.

h) Wir essen oft draußen.

i) Er schwimmt regelmäßig.

j) Sie singt wunderschön.

Ü 19.5)

a) schnell

b) immer

c) leider

d) besonders

e) gut

f) direkt

g) endlich

h) vorsichtig

i) wirklich

j) selten

CHAPTER 20

Ü 20.1)

a) süßer

b) älter

c) interessanter

d) höher

e) langweiliger

f) kälter

g) neuer

h) schöner

i) bitterer

j) teurer

Ü 20.2)

a) besser

b) jünger

c) älter

d) kleiner

e) größer

f) wärmer

g) kälter

h) billiger

i) länger

j) kürzer

Ü 20.3)

a) stärker

b) tiefer

c) heißer

d) langsamer

e) größer

f) spannender

g) süßer

h) bequemer

i) voller

j) dreckiger

Ü 20.4)

	Comparative	Superlative
a) Berlin ist größer als Hamburg.	☑	☐
b) Das ist das beste Eis, das ich je gegessen habe.	☐	☑
c) Mein Hund ist klüger als die Katze.	☑	☐
d) Heute ist der kälteste Tag des Winters.	☐	☑
e) Dieser Apfel ist saurer als jener.	☑	☐
f) Das ist das höchste Gebäude in der Stadt.	☐	☑
g) Deine Idee ist besser als meine.	☑	☐
h) Er ist der älteste Mann im Dorf.	☐	☑
i) Das Wasser ist kälter als gestern.	☑	☐
j) Sie ist die jüngste Person in der Klasse.	☐	☑

Ü 20.5)

a) A: Ist der Kaffee süß?

B: Nein, der Tee ist **süßer**.

b) A: Ist der Film interessant?

B: Das Buch war **interessanter**.

c) A: Ist das Restaurant teuer?

B: Das Café nebenan ist **teurer**.

d) A: Ist das Hemd sauber?

B: Die Jacke ist noch **sauberer**.

e) A: Ist der Tisch groß?

B: Der Tisch draußen ist **größer**.

CHAPTER 21

Ü 21.1)

Note: More than one answer can be correct.

a) Sie wohnt **auf** der Straße.
b) Er setzt sich **neben** mich.
c) Ich habe das Buch **auf** den Tisch gelegt.
d) Sie denkt oft **an** ihren Urlaub.
e) Die Blumen stehen **vor** dem Fenster.
f) Wir treffen uns **an** der Ecke.
g) Er hat Angst **vor** Spinnen.
h) Der Hund liegt **unter** dem Sofa.
i) Ich bin **an** der Universität.
j) Der Stift ist **unter** den Büchern.

Ü 21.2)

a) dem Freund
b) das Kino
c) die Uhr
d) den Baum und das Haus
e) dem Lehrer
f) dem Tisch
g) dem Hund
h) der Schule
i) das Bett
j) die Brücke

Ü 21.3)

a) auf
b) auf
c) über
d) von
e) für
f) auf
g) auf
h) über
i) nach
j) an

UNIT 6
OTHER FEATURES

CHAPTER 22

Ü 22.1)

a) Er <u>muss</u> zum Arzt gehen.

b) Sie <u>wollen</u> ins Kino.

c) Du <u>solltest</u> mehr Wasser trinken.

d) Ich <u>darf</u> das nicht essen.

e) Wir <u>würden</u> gerne bezahlen.

Ü 22.2)

a) will

b) sollst

c) dürfen

d) kann

e) mag

f) darf

g) musst

h) will

i) möchte

j) kann

Ü 22.3)

a) Er **muss** die Hausaufgaben **nicht** machen.

b) Sie **dürfen** hier **nicht** rauchen.

c) Wir **wollen nicht** nach Berlin fahren.

d) Du solltest das nicht wissen.

e) Ich **könnte** das Buch **nicht** lesen.

f) Sie möchte keinen Kaffee.

g) Er **würde** das **nicht** kaufen.

h) Ihr **sollt** das **nicht** lernen.

i) Du **darfst** das Fenster **nicht** öffnen.

j) Ich **muss nicht** ins Büro gehen.

Ü 22.4)

a) müssen		should/ought to
b) dürfen		would like to
c) wollen		be allowed to/may
d) sollen		would
e) mögen		must/have to
f) möchten		should
g) würden		be able to/could
h) könnten		want to
i) solltet		like
j) dürfte		be permitted to

Ü 22.5)

a) muss	**f)** solltet
b) kann	**g)** sollte
c) muss	**h)** muss
d) darfst	**i)** sollst
e) wollen	**j)** möchte

CHAPTER 23

Ü 23.1)

a) Wir **können** Deutsch sprechen.

b) Er **wird** nach Berlin fliegen.

c) Sie **hatte** viel gegessen.

d) Ihr **solltet** zu Hause bleiben.

e) Es **hat** geregnet.

f) Sie **haben** im Park gespielt.

g) Ich **werde** dir helfen.

h) Du **kannst** das Fenster öffnen.

i) Er **müsste** früh aufstehen.

j) Sie **hatten** einen Film gesehen.

Ü 23.2)

a) wird	**g)** habe
b) haben	**h)** wird
c) hat	**i)** haben
d) ist	**j)** sind
e) hast	
f) sind	

Ü 23.3)

a) Ich werde ein Buch lesen.

b) Er wird ins Kino gehen.

c) Du wirst Deutsch lernen.

d) Wir werden Pizza essen.

e) Sie wird einen Brief schreiben.

f) Ihr werdet einen Film sehen.

g) Es wird regnen.

Ü 23.4)

a) möchte

b) sollte

c) musst

d) kann

e) dürfen

f) sollt

g) mag

h) solltest

i) will

j) muss

CHAPTER 24

Ü 24.1)

	separable	inseparable
a) begegnen	☐	☑
b) umfahren	☑	☑
c) entdecken	☐	☑
d) durchlaufen	☑	☑
e) verstehen	☐	☑
f) ankommen	☑	☐
g) zerbrechen	☐	☑
h) besuchen	☐	☑
i) aufwachen	☑	☐
j) durchlesen	☑	☐

Ü 24.2)

a) rufen, an

b) bereiten, zu

c) machen, auf

d) kommen, her

e) lesen, vor

f) holen, ab

g) nehmen, mit

h) sehen, zu

i) gehen, durch

j) drehen, um

Ü 24.3)

a) durch-

b) um-

c) be-

d) zer-

e) auf-

f) um-

g) an-

h) auf-

i) auf-

j) ab-

CHAPTER 25

Ü 25.1)

a) Sie spricht <u>kein</u> Deutsch.

b) Ich habe <u>nie</u> Kaffee getrunken.

c) Er geht <u>nirgendwo</u> hin.

d) Es ist <u>niemand</u> zu Hause.

e) Wir haben <u>keinen</u> Hunger.

f) Sie hat das Buch <u>nicht</u> gelesen.

g) Ich möchte <u>nirgends</u> bleiben.

h) Es gibt <u>keine</u> Äpfel.

i) Er hat <u>nie</u> gelogen.

j) Sie fährt <u>nicht</u> Auto.

Ü 25.2)

a) kein

b) nicht

c) keinen

d) keine

e) keine

f) nicht

g) keinen

h) nicht

i) kein

j) keinen

Ü 25.3)

a) Sie spielt <u>kein</u> Klavier.

b) Ich esse <u>keine</u> Schokolade.

c) Er geht <u>nicht</u> zur Schule.

d) Das ist <u>nicht</u> meine Tasche.

e) Sie schreiben <u>keinen</u> Brief.

f) Wir fahren <u>nicht</u> nach Berlin.

g) Er hört <u>keine</u> Musik.

h) Ich trage <u>keinen</u> Hut.

i) Sie liebt <u>keine</u> Tiere.

j) Das ist <u>nicht</u> interessant.

Ü 25.4)

a) False	→		Wasser ist nicht trocken.
b) False	→		Katzen sind keine Vögel.
c) True	→		Berlin ist nicht in Frankreich.
d) False	→		Zwei plus zwei ist nicht fünf.
e) True	→		Sonntag ist kein Arbeitstag.
f) False	→		Fische fliegen nicht.
g) True	→		Äpfel sind nicht blau.
h) True	→		Ein Jahr hat nicht dreizehn Monate.
i) False	→		Mäuse sind nicht groß.
j) False	→		Milch ist nicht schwarz.

MORE BOOKS BY LINGO MASTERY

We are not done teaching you German until you're fluent!

Here are some other titles you might find useful in your journey of mastering German:

✓ German Short Stories for Beginners

✓ Intermediate German Short Stories

✓ 2000 Most Common German Words in Context

✓ Conversational German Dialogues

But we have many more!

Check out all of our titles at **www.LingoMastery.com/german**

Made in United States
Troutdale, OR
03/25/2025